THE GOTHAM LIBRARY
OF THE NEW YORK UNIVERSITY PRESS

The Gotham Library is a series of original works and critical studies. Devoted to significant works and major authors and to literary topics of enduring importance, Gotham Library texts offer the best in literature and criticism.

Comparative and Foreign Language Literature:
Robert J. Clements, Editor

Comparative and English Language Literature:
James W. Tuttleton, Editor

Portrait of Chekhov painted by I. E. Braz in 1898.
Tret'yakov Gallery, Moscow

CHEKHOV'S GREAT PLAYS

A CRITICAL ANTHOLOGY

EDITED AND WITH AN INTRODUCTION BY
JEAN-PIERRE BARRICELLI

NEW YORK UNIVERSITY PRESS
NEW YORK & LONDON

Permissions

*The Cherry Orchard: A Theater Poem of the Suffering of Change** by Francis Fergusson
* "The Plot of The Cherry Orchard" / "Chekhov's Histrionic Art: An End and a Beginning," in Francis Fergusson, *The Idea of a Theater: A Study of Ten Plays. The Art of Drama in Changing Perspective* (copyright 1949 © 1977 by Princeton University Press; Princeton Paperback 1972), pp. 161–177. Reprinted by kind permission of the Princeton University Press.

"Counterpoint Of The Snapping String: Chekhov's The Cherry Orchard"* by Jean-Pierre Barricelli
* Reprinted from *California Slavic Studies*, Vol. X (1977), 121–136, with the kind permission of the University of California Press.

"Uncle Vanya's Predicament"*
by Ieva Vitins
* Reprinted from *Slavic and East European Journal*, Vol. 22, No. 4 (1978), 454–463, with the kind permission of the editor.

List of Illustrations

Portrait of Chekhov painted by I. E. Braz in 1898.
Tret'yakov Gallery, Moscow

The photograph of the logo of the MAT was made from Nikolay Efros, *Moskovskiy khudozhestvennyy teatr* (1898–1923) (Moscow-Petersburg: Gosizdat, 1924).

The Nemirovich-Danchenko quotation may be found in Ivanova, Ye., ed., *P'yesy A. P. Chekhova v Moskovskom Khudozhestvennom Teatre* (Moscow: Iskusstvo, 1961), p. 13.

Library of Congress Cataloging in Publication Data
Main entry under title:

Chekhov's great plays.

(The Gotham library of the New York University Press)
Includes bibliographical references.
Contents: Chekhov's Seagull / by Robert Louis Jackson—Chekhov's The seagull and Maupassant's Sur l'eau / by Jerome H. Katsell—Uncle Vanya's predicament / by Ieva Vitins—[etc.]
1. Chekhov, Anton Pavlovich, 1860–1904—Dramatic works—Addresses, essays, lectures. I. Barricelli, Jean-Pierre.
PG3458.Z9D723   891.72'3   81-3968
ISBN 0-8147-1036-0   AACR2

Manufactured in the United States of America
10 9 8 7 6 5 4 3

TO MY
MOTHER

THAT MELANCHOLY REALIST
WITH POETRY IN HER HEART

CONTENTS

———————

PART II

A POETIC PRESENCE

Chekhov: the pertinent heading might well be "Poetic Naturalism." If, as has been said, every theater generation has its Chekhov, we might argue that, though close to eighty years after his death, he is the dramatist of our generation. The wittiness of Shaw, the pathology of O'Neill, the paradoxes of Pirandello, the ideological biases of Brecht, the pat absurdities of Ionesco, and the existential quivers of Beckett may respond to certain aspects of contemporary sensibility and stimulate any number of thought centers, but Chekhov, while doing all these things, imbues his great plays constantly with a tremolo of poetry that others do not have, or, like Pirandello and Beckett, reflect occasionally.

We note how much earlier than these he appeared on the scene; a contemporary of such figures outside Russia as Ibsen and Strindberg, Zola and Verga, Hardy and Galdós, Dreiser and Fontane, he is shoved in literary histories into chapters on realism and naturalism. Yet something about him transcends his period, leaves naturalism behind, and engages firmly the times of those generations that succeeded him. And perhaps—who knows?—he bypasses them, too. In eluding every context—impressionism, symbolism, realism, naturalism, expressionism, existentialism—he keeps suggesting a beyond, in the spirit of his characters Vershinin, Anya, Trofimov, and Sonya. Hence his poetry. But more about this later.

Chekhov crossed into our century, born Anton Pavlovich in 1860, to live to be only forty-four. A medical degree from Moscow in 1884 gave him easy access to the pseudoscientific attitudes and practices of literary naturalism. But medicine colored only the background of his life (although he worked diligently during epidemics); the foreground was shaped by a new vocation, embraced at age nineteen: literature. "Medicine is my legal spouse, while literature is my mistress." The grocer's son, grandson of a freed serf, from that dreary little Azov seaport of Taganrog, steadily imposed his presence on the Russian capital with his writing. Surely, at first, the young man who had assumed the responsibilities as head of the family—of his artistically talented but financially unproductive salesman father Pavel, of his warmhearted, sacrificing, and harassed (by Pavel) mother Yevgeniya, and of his four brothers (Aleksandr, Nikolay, Ivan, and Mikhail) and one sister, Marya, none of whom, through dissipation, inadequacy, or submissiveness, could benefit the household—wrote quickly and for money. "I've scratched off a mangy little sketch." In 1883 alone he "spun off" 120 short stories, mostly for the humorous weekly *The Splinters*, and in 1885 he produced 129 "slapdash" pieces. But as the literati of St. Petersburg began to notice him, he became more serious, more scrupulous of his craft, and while he spent even more hours writing, in 1886 his literary production had dwindled to a bare 12 items. During this year, he wrote his first successful play, *Ivanov*. Chekhov had entered the theater; he wrote all his better plays during the last fifteen years of his life.

Whatever he did for the stage—one-act plays and the *Wood Demon* date from 1888–89—he insisted, must "show life and men as they are," not just their habit and table, but indeed their inner anguish and the contrast between this and outer events. But dramatic manner in the more exclamatory sense, for him, was a poor conductor of inner reality. The drama must be subdued, an undertone with potent resonances. For this reason, we might surmise, he eschewed participation in the raucous political activities of 1880–1900, the revolutionary fermentation at the university owing to the failure of Aleksandr II's reforms and the proletarization of wretched peasants as they were driven from farm to factory. Rather than by dramatic political demonstration, Chekhov "protested" by social observation and by reproducing what he saw, with all the hidden vibrations. So on the stage did life become "as it is," and to this extent Chekhov was a naturalist writer.

To this extent he was a man of his day. For by this time, naturalism had knocked sharply on the theater door of Europe. Taine had declared that a sense of the real must govern the dramatist; no subjective imagination, had enjoined Arno Holz. Everywhere the majority mused about a "useful theater" serving the purpose of social renewal. The Rostands and their romantic Cyranos to come were minority. One had heard an announcement in Italy, where Bracco and Verga continued the work of Martini or Giacosa or Rovetta, as in Spain Galdós took over for Echegaray. Zola's *Le Naturalisme au théâtre*, of 1881, had denounced traditional declamation and ridiculous drawing room lies *à la* Augier, Dumas *fils*, and Sardou. Better it was to reveal, with the positivistic and clinical methods of scientific research, the minute and sordid details of ordinary existence, the injured lives of the destitute and the sick, the ravenous society that feeds on the hungry, the animal nature to which humans revert when deprived of all hope and dignity. Antoine's Théâtre Libre in Paris had sought these subjects when it began in 1887, as had Brahm's Freie Bühne in Berlin two years later. Zola, the Goncourt brothers, Becque, Ibsen, Strindberg, Tolstoy, Turgenev, Bjørnson, Heijermans, Hauptmann—these were "the reproducers of life," its social photographers. And, ultraphotographically, the stage had hung not conventional sets but natural trees, real plaster, genuine ceilings, even raw meat, for the milieu serves as the determining factor to explain anyone's behavior. Truth translated into literalness. In England, Grein followed suit in 1891 with the Independent Theatre Society of London, where Ibsen furnished the impetus as he had also done in Paris and Berlin, and where Shaw insisted on the importance of psychological and conventional conflicts for realistic (i.e., naturalistic) drama.

Drawing encouragement on the inside from Pisemskiy, Gogol', Ostrovskiy, Tolstoy . . . , now Russia had its turn. In 1898 the actor-producer K. S. Stanislavskiy and the writer—later partner—V. I. Nemirovich-Danchenko founded the Moscow Art Theater, the M.A.T.; and as it grew to become known as "Chekhov's house" it thereby also became the "theater of moods" and of "underground streams of emotion." There the much-sought-after author met Ol'ga Knipper (1898), the actress whom he married in 1901. There *The Seagull*, whose première had failed at the Aleksandrinskiy Theater in 1896, was turned into a success. Still today, the play's logogram adorns the M.A.T. curtain. Then followed *Uncle Vanya* (also 1896), *The Three Sisters* (1900), and *The Cherry Orchard* (1903, produced 1904, the year of the playwright's death in the German health resort of Badenweiler). These were the Great Plays.

Symbolic and impressionistic qualities, at times in our terms even expressionistic and surrealistic, expressed the current discontent of life, the impersonality of the world, and the insignificance of the individual. This Chekhov was not far from Marinetti's manifesto of 1915, *Proclama sul teatro futurista*, and its cynical indication of machine dynamics, mechanized living, automation, acoustically conditioned verbal montages, and marionettish movements of characters on stage. Nor was this Chekhov too far from all those utterances of existential anguish that followed World War II.

Chekhov kept transcending even himself, as it were. Invariably gay, humorous, and attracted to practical jokes, all cynicism or contagiously tragic seriousness had to be transformed, transfigured. For some of us, the plays have remained fundamentally tragic, but a certain halo encircles them, never leaves them prey to irreducible morbidity. Stanislavskiy saw this at the outset, when after reading Chekhov's plays he meditated: nothing special, but . . . ; truthful though disappointing from a production standpoint, but . . . ; acting parts good, but not striking enough to stimulate an actor's ambition . . . ; yet, as you recollect phrases and scenes, you want to think about them longer . . . , you go over and over them . . . , you want to reread the play . . . , you realize the hidden depth under the surface. We could say that as in Dante's *Purgatorio* the action is totally internal: the outer reality—the "naturalism" of life as it is—conceals a deep well of inner, dark swirls.

So we come to the Chekhov we admire today, the naturalistic poet, about whom (and Ibsen) T. S. Eliot could say that he did things of which he, Eliot, would not otherwise have supposed prose to be capable. This prose, these dialogues, of the Great Plays—minutely realistic, in choppy episodes, meticulously unmoralistic on the surface—reveal the fragmented simplicity of whole lives of uncomprehended suffering, of lives that pace daily on the floor of silence. Insignificance creates "moods," and the underground emotions stem from the very awareness of banality, of the inalienable fact that in the banality lies the tragedy. So the characters move around, swirling (remember that supposedly incongruous dance in the last play), not like individuals—there are no heroes, no protagonists—but like tonalities that brush past each other as their words drift past each other, simple colors on a rather dull canvas, but a canvas that in its own magic way vibrates deeply and darkly with life. As Tolstoy remarked, Chekhov daubs his colors at random, yet his portrayals remain precise. His characters live, however, in days that flow within a calendar of existence that seems to wane, slowly, silently, constantly. The "naturalist" and physician Chekhov saw nature as the ally of life and the rhythm of days as ultimately useless. Each of the Great Plays suggests this covert and static "movement," unsentimental with the Greeks long before him as with Pirandello shortly after him, in which silence, the mouthpiece of destiny, talks as eloquently as words speak meaninglessly. Listen to all the pauses. The poetry is powerful. Chekhov needs a director who makes dialogues secondary to all the hidden vibrations of moods and the insecure motivations behind them, to those confusions that bespeak an inability to make any sense out of life. Even a pistol shot, which sounds conclusive, must be made to sound inconclusive, an active absurdity.

Yet, absurdity aside, there is no denying the illusion that sorrow, which shapes the world, also gives it a momentum. The powerful poetry grows more complex. This is not a matter of redemption, for Chekhov never discoursed with God. Reminiscence, love, hope are other such illusions that keep the conversations earthbound. Those people in *The Seagull* seek love and happiness—though in vain, and are destined to delusion. Those in *Uncle Vanya*, diseased by life, unknowingly seek old values—but cannot apply them or develop new ones. Those in *The Three Sisters* spontaneously seek why they suffer, try for some answer—but never discover why defeat looms as the fatal law and why their dreams and hopes are smothered. And those in *The Cherry Orchard*, spiritually wilted, seek the nostalgic comfort of recollection—though they allow a passive destiny to take over. Seekers by instinct who are nonseekers by choice. But, too, nonheroes who are at least creatures who through suffering betray a form of heroism. Something heroically intangible, therefore—that of being a Chekhov character—draws us to feel for these existences, all the more poetic because they are enduringly human.

In order to reach as broad an audience as possible, I have endeavored, in preparing this volume, to include essays, not only by leading Slavists, as one might expect, but also by scholars of other literatures, comparatists, historians of drama, directors, and translators. The variety of sources invites an equal variety of methodologies and points of view, in the first section of the volume devoted to the individual plays as well as in the second devoted to topical subjects. But although variety has its virtues, so does consistency. For this reason, I have asked every contributor to abide by a single system of transliteration, one that makes the spelling of Russian words, on balance, more accessible to the English-speaking reader. Perhaps I shall be forgiven if, for the sake of uncompromising consistency, I have made Gorki look like Gor'kiy and Tchaikovsky look like Chaykovskiy.

Throughout the endeavor, I have been sustained by the encouragement of Professor Robert J. Clements who, as editor of this New York University Press series, first gave me the opportunity to undertake the project, and of my wife Norma, whose love of Chekhov has provided an important background for my own interest in the dramatist. I am indebted to the following publishers for permission to reprint the essays by Professors Philip Bordinat, Francis Fergusson, Robert L. Jackson, Ieva Vitins, and myself: Prentice-Hall, Inc., the Princeton University Press, the Slavic and East European Journal, and the University of California Press. It goes without saying that in the absence of the goodwill of cooperating agencies like these, the present collection would not have been assembled in as neatly and rounded a fashion as I trust it appears in its present form.

My very special thanks go to all those contributors who graciously agreed to write original essays (Professors Eugene Bristow, Michael Heim, Simon Karlinsky, Jerome Katsell, Sonia Kovitz, Karl Kramer, Nicholas Moravčevich, Nils Åke Nilsson, Louis Pedrotti, Richard Risso, Laurence Senelick, and Maurice Valency, as well as Robert Jackson who reworked his earlier essay), and *in no uncertain way* to my valued colleague and friend, Louis Pedrotti, who assisted me in the many technicalities, linguistic and otherwise, that give this book inner coherence. Finally, I owe much gratitude to Laurel Vermilyea Cortés, who, in conversations and from her own significant vantage point of simply the intelligent spectator, has helped to make this enigma, Chekhov, compellingly human for me.

Jean-Pierre Barricelli
University of California at Riverside

ABOUT THE CONTRIBUTORS

Jean-Pierre Barricelli (Ph.D., Harvard, 1953), Professor of Comparative Literature, University of California at Riverside. Author of works on Balzac, Dante, Calderón, Manzoni, Pound, Zweig, Leopardi, Wergeland, Liszt, Chausson, Botticelli, Rauschenberg, romantic irony, literature and music, literature and law, Machiavelli, Chekhov.

Philip Bordinat (Ph.D., U. of Birmingham, England, 1952), Professor of English, West Virginia University. Author of works on criticism, folk stories from Nigeria, William Davenant, Shakespeare, Tolstoy, Ibsen, Lawrence, Hemingway, Chekhov.

Eugene K. Bristow (Ph.D., U. of Iowa, 1956), Professor in the Department of Theater and Drama and the Russian and East European Institute, Indiana University at Bloomington. Author of works on Ostrovskiy, Chekhov, Blok, Meyerkhol'd, variety theater, play directing.

Francis L. Fergusson (B.A., Oxford, 1926; hon. D. Litt., U. of New Mexico, 1955), Professor of Comparative Literature, Princeton University. Author of works on Dante, the theater, dramatic literature, Chekhov, criticism, poetry, Greek plays in translation.

Michael Heim (Ph.D., Harvard, 1971), Associate Professor of Slavic Languages and Literatures, University of California at Los Angeles. Author of works on Russian drama, intellectual history, eighteenth century literature, Czech literature.

Robert Louis Jackson (Ph.D., U. of California at Berkeley, 1956), Professor of Russian Literature, Yale University. Author of works on Dostoyevskiy, Tolstoy, Chekhov, Pasternak, Solzhenitsyn, philosophy of art, Marxist criticism.

Simon Karlinsky (Ph.D., U. of California at Berkeley, 1964), Professor of Slavic Languages and Literatures, University of California at Berkeley. Author of works on Russian poetry, drama, and music, Gogol', Chekhov, Zinaida Gippius, Marina Tsvetayeva, Stravinskiy, and Nabokov.

Jerome H. Katsell (Ph.D., U. of California at Los Angeles, 1972), Assistant Professor of Russian and Comparative Literature, University of California at San Diego. Author of works on Chekhov, Yuriy Olesha, Turgenev.

Sonia Kovitz (Ph.D., Ohio State U., 1971), recently Assistant Professor of Russian Language and Literature, Lawrence University, now employed in the Ohio State University Library. Author of works on Chekhov, irony, structuralism.

Karl D. Kramer (Ph.D. [Comparative Literature], U. of Washington, 1964), Associate Professor of Slavic Languages and Literatures and Comparative Literature, University of Washington. Author of works on Chekhov, impressionism, Vsevolod Garshin, Saltykov-Shchedrin, Yuriy Kazakov.

Nicholas Moravčevich (Ph. D. [Comparative Literature], U. of Wisconsin at Madison, 1964), Professor of Slavic Languages and Literatures, University of Illinois at Chicago Circle. Author of works on Chekhov, drama, Russian literature, Yugoslav literature.

Nils Åke Nilsson (Ph.D., Uppsala University, Sweden, 1950), Professor of Russian Language and Literature, University of Stockholm. Author of works on Gogol', Chekhov, the Russian imaginists, Osip Mandel'shtam, Pasternak, Russian romanticism.

Louis Pedrotti (Ph.D., U. of California at Berkeley, 1959), Associate Professor of Russian, University of California at Riverside. Author of works on Józef-Julian Sękowski, Gogol', Bunin, Pirandello.

Richard D. Risso (Ph.D., Stanford, 1964), Professor of Theater, University of California at Riverside. Actor and Director at the Oregon Shakespeare Festival Theater, the Pacific Conservatory of the Performing Arts, the Milwaukee Repertory Theater, the Utah Shakespearian Festival.

Laurence Senelick (Ph.D. [Comparative Literature], Harvard, 1972), Associate Professor of Drama, Tufts University, and member of the Russian Research Institute, Harvard University. Author of works on Chekhov, the Russian theater, Russian dramatists, the history of popular entertainments, dramatic criticism.

Maurice Valency (Ph.D., Columbia, 1939; Litt. D., Long Island U., 1976), Professor Emeritus of Dramatic Literature, Columbia University, Director of Academic Studies, The Juilliard School. Author of works on Chekhov, Ibsen, Strindberg, Shaw, symbolism, medieval literature; playwright and librettist.

Ieva Vitins (Ph.D, U. of California at Berkeley, 1974), Assistant Professor of Russian, Dalhousie University, Nova Scotia. Author of works on Chekhov, Marina Tsvetayeva.

PART I

CHEKHOV'S *SEAGULL:*
THE EMPTY WELL, THE DRY LAKE,
AND THE COLD CAVE*

BY ROBERT LOUIS JACKSON

Art is at the center of *The Seagull.* Four characters in the play are actresses or writers. Everybody talks about art. Everybody embodies or lives out a concept of art. The problem of talent—what it takes and means to become an artist—is a fundamental theme of the play.[1] Illusion and reality, dream and fulfillment in art and life constitute the innermost concern of the author. Finally, art in its most basic form as myth gives expression to the underlying dramatic conflicts and realities in the play: the myth of creation, the oedipal syndrome, and the metaphor of the journey.

In his myth play in Act I of Chekhov's *The Seagull* the young writer Konstantin Gavrilovich Treplev pictures a bleak future for the world: thousands of centuries have passed and all life has vanished. The bodies of living beings have long ago crumbled into dust, and eternal matter has turned them into stone, water, and clouds; their souls have merged into one. A doleful moon vainly sheds light on this desolation. And desolation it is: "Cold, cold, cold. Empty, empty, empty. Terrible, terrible, terrible."

Konstantin's play itself, as commentators on *The Seagull* have observed, is also terrible. It is a concoction of melodramatic posturing and mannered symbolism. Yet—though bad art—it is, paradoxically, full of

* "Chekhov's *Seagull:* The Empty Well, the Dry Lake, and the Cold Cave," in *Chekhov: A Collection of Critical Essays,* edited by Robert Louis Jackson,©1967, pp. 99–111. Reprinted by permission of Prentice-Hall, Inc., Englewood Cliffs, New Jersey. Essay slightly revised for this printing.

Chekhov's art. The action, the character-symbols and portents—all the devices that fail so miserably in Konstantin's play taken by itself and that seem merely a Chekhovian parody of a "decadent" theatrical style—have a distinctly allegorical character in the context of the larger play, *The Seagull*. Just as in Shakespeare's *Hamlet*, so in *The Seagull*, the play within the play reaches out into the psychological drama.[2] But whereas the import of Hamlet's theatrical is immediately evident, both before and after the performance, the significance of Konstantin's play is fully apparent only by the end of *The Seagull*. Chekhov's use of Konstantin's play is crucial to his whole development of the character of Konstantin and to the expression of some of the central ideas of *The Seagull*. A discussion of Chekhov's play, then, may properly begin with an analysis of the play within the play.

"Cold, cold, cold. Empty, empty, empty. Terrible, terrible, terrible."

The state of Konstantin's world of tomorrow, unpromising as it appears at first glance, is not entirely without hope. On closer investigation, it becomes apparent that Konstantin is dramatizing in mythopoetic language a physical world that is delicately poised between death and life, between sterility and creation, between the negative force of the "father of eternal matter, the devil," and the beneficent, life-stimulating power of "spirit." We have here, essentially, a dramatization of unliberated life and creation; and, it is further apparent, this is also a crucial self-dramatization. The author Konstantin not only projects a vision of a universe in biological limbo; he, or his alter ego, also inhabits it. But what is not quite clear or established is the poet-narrator's exact status in this created legend.

At the end of the first half of his soliloquy—after referring to the merging of the souls into one—the poet identifies himself directly with the force of spirit and creation that continues to inhabit the universe.

> The universal world soul—that's me, me. In me there is the soul of Alexander the Great, and of Caesar, and of Shakespeare, and of Napoleon, and of the last worm. In me the consciousness of people is united with the instincts of animals, and I remember everything, everything, everything, and I experience anew every life in myself.

This is the high point of the soliloquy. His self-centered exaltation is not without a sort of naïve charm. The poet completely identifies himself with his muse. And this muse is ascendant.

But at this point—and we are now halfway through Konstantin's play—the "marsh fires" (will-o'-the-wisp) appear. (The reader will recall that Konstantin's mother, the actress Irina Nikolayevna Arkadina, exclaims at this juncture: "This is something decadent"—to which Konstantin replies with a pleading "Mama!") The marsh fires, it is evident, take on the character of some kind of robot creature—symbols that have depressing import to the poet. Indeed, their appearance signals the collapse of his poetic ego: the "universal soul" metamorphoses into a petty anthropomorphic soul. "I am alone. Once in a hundred years I open my lips to speak and my voice echoes gloomily in this emptiness, and nobody hears me." The pale fires, born from the rotten bog, wander mindlessly and without will or beat of life toward the dawn. Fearing that life will awaken in them, the poet tells us, the "father of eternal matter, the devil" keeps the atoms in these fires in constant flux. "Only spirit remains constant and unchangeable in the universe." But now spirit seems to be keeping very much to itself. The poet, plainly, is abandoned by his muse.

> Like a prisoner thrown into an empty, deep well, I do not know where I am or what awaits me. One thing, however, is not concealed from me: in stubborn, savage struggle with the devil, with the element of material forces, I am destined to conquer, and then matter and spirit will unite in a beautiful harmony and the kingdom of the world will is to arrive.

Konstantin's play gives expression to the *pro* and *contra* in his nature. It dramatizes his creative yearnings, the flight of his poetic muse, but in the final analysis it is paradigmatic of the downward spiral of a hopelessly crippled creative spirit. "There's something in it," Doctor Dorn observes after seeing Konstantin's play, something "fresh, naïve." The play, indeed, partakes of poetry, as the audience realizes in Act IV when the young actress Nina Mikhaylovna Zarechnaya recites again the opening lines from Konstantin's youthful work. But apart from revealing a propensity for abstractions and symbols ("not a single character that's alive," Trigorin later observes of Konstantin's writings in general), the play discloses Konstantin's tendency toward grandiose dreams and impetuous challenges, on the one hand, and passive retreats and sterile reconciliations on the other. The movement of the play—all appearances to the contrary—is precipitous from self-exaltation to a depressed posture of defeat. Here in his well the poet prophesies "stubborn, savage struggle with the devil" and eventual victory. But this is empty prophecy: the well is dry. The poet himself is inwardly aware of the emptiness of his prophecy, of the utopian character of his mythic dream of "beautiful harmony" and of a "kingdom of world will." He resolves the contradiction between the reality of his nature (his weakness of will, his impotence) and his fantastic dream in the manner of a familiar Chekhovian type.

> But all this will only take place when, little by little, through long, long series of millennia, both the moon, and the bright Sirius, and the earth will turn into dust. And until then, horror, horror.

The horror here is, in a sense, an intuition: the self's forereading of its own tragic emptiness.

It may be argued that our analysis of the inner direction of Konstantin's play—the view that it moves toward compromise and defeat—must be permanently flawed by the fact that we are analyzing an incomplete drama: the play within the play, as we know, is cut short by a flurry of argument between mother and son. There is no question that the outcome of the poet-narrator's struggle with the devil cannot be deduced with complete certainty from Konstantin's text alone, just as it is impossible at the outset of *The Seagull* clearly to anticipate the denouement of Konstantin's struggle to become a mature artist. Both destinies are to a large extent "open." But in the action that brings Konstantin's play to an end Chekhov subtly prefigures the sad fate of Konstantin and, at the same time, indicates the inner direction of Konstantin's play, that is, discloses that *conclusion* which is embryonic in the play's development. This action is so ordinary and so distracting as to conceal its profound meaning. We have in mind Konstantin's altercation with his mother.

This altercation is the momentary point of intersection of two lines: the line of the poet-narrator's struggle with the devil in the play within the play, and the line of Konstantin's permanent psychological duel with his mother. The duel—one marked throughout *The Seagull* by alternating acts of hostility, magnanimity, and submission—forms a real-life prologue to Konstantin's play; it bisects the play at its halfway point (the appearance of the marsh fires and the deflation of poetic ego—the painful exchange between mother and son); finally, it is the immediate cause of the play's ending. "My mighty opponent, the devil, is now approaching," the poet declares. "I see his fearful, crimson eyes. . . ." At this point, Konstantin's own mighty antagonist, his mother, once and for all shatters his magic lantern with some disruptive, sarcastic comments on the play. Put out by this cruel teasing, Konstantin declares: "The play is finished! Enough! Curtain!" And in a childish fit he retires from the scene. His retreat, of course, constitutes an ironic commentary upon the bold resolve of his fictional alter ego. In the context of Chekhov's subtle juxtaposition and interplay of real and fictional lines in the episode of the play within the play, we recognize that Konstantin's announcement, "the play is finished," anticipates the abortive ending of his life drama; it constitutes a dramatic rehearsal for the ending of *The Seagull*.

The negative attitude of Madame Arkadina toward her son—unfavorable circumstances, indeed, for the artistic as well as psychological development of Konstantin's personality—cannot be underestimated in any evaluation of his personal tragedy. But in the final analysis it is Konstantin himself who chooses to ring down the curtain on his own life, as he does on his own play. We may note in passing, here, that Konstantin's impulsive retreat before his mother's jibes contrast pointedly with Nina's efforts, in the midst of the quarrel, to continue the play. His behavior in this episode, then, reveals fundamental character weaknesses that will manifest themselves in his life at large. Konstantin's confrontation with his mother is of a very petty nature. Yet as Chekhov once observed: "Let everything on the stage be just as complex and at the same time just as simple as in life. People dine, merely dine, but at that moment their happiness is being made or their life is being smashed." So, also, here—in an ordinary quarrel, in a single moment, Chekhov discloses the compound character and fate of his hero.

Konstantin created for himself in his play a legend not too different in character from the typical fairy tale with its demons, its embattled and enchanted knights, and its golden kingdoms at the end of the trail. As in a fairy tale, so in Konstantin's legend we are in a world of magic, of the supernatural. The hero in this legend, plainly, finds himself imprisoned by some evil force (the devil). But how will he get out? In stubborn, savage struggle, he declares, "I am destined to conquer" (*mne suzhdeno pobedit'*). The passive structuring of this thought is revealing. Who has destined this victory? What fairy of fate, what magic is going to liberate the hero from his dry prison well? The appeal here on the part of the poet to a force, fate (*sud'ba*), outside self points to the tragic flaw in Konstantin, this modern pseudotragic hero of *The Seagull*: his refusal to recognize his essential freedom and to accept the responsibility that it implies.

Chekhov alludes to this refusal at the very outset of the play when Konstantin casually tries his fortune by an age-old means: "*Picking petals from a flower.* She loves me, loves me not, loves me, loves me not, loves me, loves me not. *Laughs.* You see, my mother doesn't love me. You can say that again!" A search for authority, for a decision maker outside oneself, of course, is characteristic of all immaturity. The young actress Nina also reveals a penchant for fortune-telling: "Even or odd," she asks Trigorin at the beginning of Act III. "No," Nina sighs, "I have only one pea in my hand. I was trying my fortune: Should I become an actress or not? I wish somebody would advise me." Trigorin's reply—and we have no difficulty recognizing Chekhov in these words—is that "in this sort of thing nobody can give advice." We are free. Nina must accept her freedom: the choice must be one's own. "No general ethics can show you what is to be done," Sartre wrote in *L'Existentialisme est un humanisme* in connection with another case of decision making. "There are no omens in the world." This is a painful lesson that many of Chekhov's heroes experience. It is of the essence of Chekhov's conception of Nina that she ultimately accepts a world without omens, that, in a very real sense, she takes her fate into her own hands. "Boris Alekseyevich," she exclaims to Trigorin at the end of Act III, "I have made an irrevocable decision; the die is cast; I am going on the stage. Tomorrow I will not be here any longer; I am leaving my father, abandoning everything; I am beginning a new life." Nothing is fated, nothing postponed here; a choice is arrived at lucidly. If anything, Nina's decision constitutes a challenge to fate, to the force of circumstances (her family life) that is so hostile to her choice of an artistic career.

Chekhov sees in the individual's attitude toward "fate"—whether expressed in discussion or in casual or unconscious acts—a measure of the individual's capacity to respond to the sum total of forces acting upon him, to necessity, to the *given* in life. Chekhov's focus in his brilliant story, "A Woman's Kingdom" (1894), is upon the interrelation of this factor of the given (background and environment) and individual will, character, and fate, in the life of the heroine. She was not to blame for the fact that she never married, the young factory owner Anna Akimovna muses one Christmas morning. Chekhov takes us into her inner consciousness. "Fate itself had flung her from a simple worker's setting where, if one can believe memories, she had felt so comfortable and at home, into these huge rooms where she was completely unable to imagine what to do with herself, and could not understand why so many people were darting in front of her." But it is her passive character, her lack of courage that seals Anna's destiny. Her daydream that, if her father had lived longer, he would "surely have married her to a simple man, for example, to Pimenov"—would have "ordered her to marry him—and that would be that"; her general belief that "love will define my obligations, my work, illuminate my world view"; her conviction that "nobody will take me"; the symbolic scene at the card table when she asks to be "matched" with Pimenov, and then jumbles the cards—all this is symptomatic of Anna Akimovna's deep malaise, her inner impotence. "A man's character is his fate." "A Woman's Kingdom" embodies the insight of this maxim of the ancient Heraclitus.[3]

Those characters in Chekhov who accept the notion of fate, of a force acting independently and capriciously outside human will, seem to bear within themselves the element of defeat. The fatalistic philosophy of Tuzenbach, so poignantly expressed in Act II of *The Three Sisters*, is an ingredient of his tragic fate. "The die is cast," he exclaims in connection with his decision to retire from the army. But his decision to take charge of his life comes too late. This amiable but weak man is the victim, quite ironically, of the meaningless universe that he posits as a philosopher. His would-be partner in life, Irina, also relates passively to life; like Konstantin Treplev in *The Seagull*, she reveals the character of her world view in her casual play with cards: "It's coming out right, the patience, I see. We shall be in Moscow." Fate, chance, luck, of course, is not going to bring the sisters to Moscow, any more than Sharlotta Ivanovna's tricks (in *The Cherry Orchard*) will save the orchard. Chance is never productive, creative in the world of Chekhov. On the contrary. When the owners of the cherry orchard renounce their option to decide upon the fate of the estate, when they renounce their freedom actively to participate in their own fate, the estate and their lives are ceded both literally and symbolically to the caprice of chance—the auction block. We discern in the magician Sharlotta Ivanovna a symbol of that haphazard universe for which Lyubov' Andreyevna Ranevskaya and her brother opt (the scattering of money, the game of billiards are symbolic). It is the merchant Lopakhin—no relier on chance or the help of others, but a man who lifts himself by his own bootstraps—who takes fate into his own hands and who triumphs. It is perfectly true, of course, that the freedom of the estate owners is, *historically*, severely limited. Chekhov plainly depicts the estate owners—in the context of their suffering humanity, to be sure—as representatives of a moribund class that is impotently being overcome by the movement of time and history; on the other hand, the ability to "decide" and to act is given to a representative of a historically new class—Lopakhin. But Anya and Trofimov also take advantage of the option to shape their own lives. Are we pawns of history and circumstance? Orlov, in Chekhov's "An Anonymous Story," suggests that "in nature, in man's environment nothing happens indifferently. Everything has reason and is necessary." But we are not thereby relieved of responsibility for, or participation in, our fate. For all Chekhov's undoubted pessimism over the human condition, he is not an adherent of a theory of implacable determinism. Lopakhin's constant reiterations to "decide," "think seriously about it," "definitely decide," "decide once and for all," "think about it" point to the constant potential for freedom in man's life. The sense of doom and of guilt that weighs upon Lyubov' Ranevskaya and Gayev is not alone in the force of circumstances, in ineluctable "history"; it is *in* them, in their passive nature, in their philosophy. They have become their own history and, no less than Oedipus, are the source of their own undoing. "I am continually waiting for something, as though our own house must collapse over us." Chekhov significantly juxtaposes this observation of Ranevskaya with her brother's random (in form and content) billiard talk. "Today my fate is being decided," she remarks in Act III. Her fate is indeed out of her hands at this moment, but it is she who has cast it to the winds, as surely as she has scattered her wealth.

The objective passiveness of the three sisters in fact leaves everything open to counterproductive chance: their weak brother *gambles* away their money; his wife, Natasha, and her lover, Protopopov, untroubled by any fate or a sense of the meaninglessness of life, reap the benefits of this play with the wheel of fortune. "It's all the same," mutters the defunct doctor Chebutykin throughout the tragic Act IV of *The Three Sisters.* But whatever meaninglessness, chaos, or nonsense exists in the world outside Chebutykin's will, he generously contributes to it through his own action or inaction. He himself, in his renunciation of knowledge, his philosophy of nonexistence, his bankruptcy as a doctor, and his indifference to the fate of Tuzenbach (and therefore, for all practical purposes, to the fate of Irina) is the agent of blind, accidental fate. The life of Tuzenbach and the half happiness of Irina are sacrificed to Solenyy's bullet of chance. "He was sentimental," Dostoyevskiy observed of Fedor Karamazov, "he was evil and sentimental." These words might have been applied by a sterner Chekhov to Chebutykin.

Chebutykin's refrain, "it's all the same," is juxtaposed at the end of the play with the theme of knowledge, of knowing. "If we only knew, if we only knew!" Ol'ga exclaims. "A man must be a believer or must seek some belief," Masha says in the same play, "otherwise life is empty, empty. . . . Either he knows what he's living for, or it's all nonsense." Whether or not Chekhov believed that absolute insight into the meaning and purpose of life was attainable, he did believe that a creative life had to be based upon a striving for that knowledge. Happiness or despair, truth or void lie not outside man, not in Moscow or in the falling snow, but in man, in his choices, and in his attitude toward the world about him. "I am destined to conquer," Konstantin's protagonist declares. We are not a priori destined for anything—is Chekhov's reply in *The Seagull*. Nor is the universe a priori a meaningful one. Man creates meaning; he gives embodiment to his "history," his destiny. His first step, everywhere, must be to recognize his fate in himself, his past in his present, and so come to grips with the only real *given* in history: man. This step Konstantin Gavrilovich Treplev is incapable of making.

"I love you just as tenderly and devotedly as in childhood," Konstantin tells his mother. "Except for you there's nobody left me now." The neurotic deadlock that constitutes his relation with his mother remains unbroken from the beginning to the end of *The Seagull*. "Can you imagine anything more hopeless than my position in her house?" he asks his uncle Sorin, in Act I. But, unlike Nina, who wrenches herself free from the stifling confines of her family, Konstantin chooses to remain with his dilemma. His last words, in Act IV, after Nina runs out of the house and out of his world once and for all, point to his peculiar oedipal paralysis. "It would be too bad if anybody met her in the garden and then told Mama. That might upset Mama."

Konstantin cannot leave the illusory "magic lake"; he cannot step out of the magic circle of his love-hate relationship with his mother; he cannot cease being a child. He finds himself surrounded by successful people whom he despises and who, so he believes, despise him as the son of a "burgher of Kiev." Certainly imagination, as much as reality, feeds his hypersensitivity. "*It seemed to me* that with their glances they measured my insignificance, *I guessed* their thoughts and suffered from humiliation" (italics mine). He has contempt for the stale, though glamorous theatrical world of his mother. He is convinced that "new forms are necessary"; yet it is characteristic of his frayed and offended ego that he is equally convinced that "if we don't get them then nothing is necessary." Maupassant, he observes, "ran away from the Eiffel Tower which oppressed him with its vulgarity." But Konstantin himself does not run away from the vulgarity of his world: he stays with it, sinks ever more deeply into it, with his rankling ambition and sniveling self-depreciation, his wounded pride and peevish vanity.

He clearly seeks a kind of surrogate mother in Nina. Yet the tragedy of his emotional quest is not that he seeks warmth and affection, love, but that this love becomes a kind of sine qua non for any sustained interest and progress in art. As he broods over the "failure" of his play (significantly this is his own judgment), he complains to Nina about her coldness. "Your coldness is terrible, unbelievable, it's as though I woke up and looked out and saw this lake suddenly dried up or sunk into the earth." And later, embracing his mother after his quarrel with her, he exclaims: "If you only knew! I have lost everything. She does not love me, I can no longer write, all my hopes have been smashed."

"Love," Chekhov jotted down in his notebook, "is either the remnant of something long past which is dying out but was once tremendous, or it is a part of something which in the future will develop into something tremendous; at the present time, however, it doesn't satisfy, offers far less than one expects." "If you fear loneliness, then don't marry," reads another note. In his well-known letter to his brother Nikolay in March 1886, in which he defines a cultured person, Chekhov remarks that if the cultured person possesses talent he respects it, he sacrifices "peace, women, wine, vanity to it." The creative personality does not passively subject itself to the love relationship. Love alone, Chekhov suggests in *The Seagull*, does not provide a firm foundation for a creative life. The tragedy of Masha in *The Seagull* is that, unlike Nina, she desires nothing but love.

Chekhov, however, does not adopt a monastic attitude toward the love relationship. Nina, in her final talk with Konstantin (Act IV), indicates her readiness to plunge back again into the maelstrom of life. She says of Trigorin at this point: "I love him. I love him even more than before. 'An idea for a short story.' I love, I love passionately, I love to desperation." This is active love: love that is combined with a readiness to face life; it may not carry Nina to Arcadia, but it is love without illusions, love that seeks to envelop and not to be enveloped in warm self-oblivion.

Konstantin, on the other hand, seeks to be enveloped in love. He is "cold" and desires warmth; he yearns for the waters of the womb. Psychologically, he finds himself trapped in the "oedipal situation." But if he is trapped, he has nonetheless, like Oedipus or Hamlet, the option of self-discovery in art or action. This option he rejects, for he lacks the courage to face himself, his talent. The self-knowledge that he attains in the end is too incomplete and too incidental to his real condition to grant him any tragic stature. Like so many Chekhovian heroes, his tragedy consists in his inability to rise to the level of tragedy. He is far from being a Hamlet. And for all the noise of his departure from this world, the real truth is that he leaves this life—to borrow the words from T. S. Eliot—"not with a bang but a whimper."

The real knowledge of self, the blinding vision, the tragic perception, on the other hand, is granted to Nina. Her drama in its painful dialectic is symbolized in the complex image of the seagull; in its living and dead incarnations this image enters her being as a *pro* and *contra*. "I'm a seagull. No, that's not it. I'm an actress." In her anguished outpouring to Konstantin in Act IV she speaks of her growing spiritual strength. "Now I know, I understand, Kostya, that in our work—it makes no difference whether we are on the stage or writing—the main thing is not fame, not glory, not what I dreamed of, but the ability to endure. Be able to bear your cross and have faith. I have faith and it doesn't hurt me so much, and when I think about my calling, I do not fear life."

Just before the performance of Konstantin's play, Medvedenko matter of factly observes that Nina "will do the acting, while the play is written by Konstantin Gavrilovich." It is, indeed, Nina who *acts* in Konstantin's

play and in the broader drama of life, who summons the will to confront
the devil in "stubborn, savage struggle," who emerges in *The Seagull* as
the embodiment of Konstantin's "world soul."

The myth of Plato's "cave" and its inhabitants may or may not have
been a conscious allegorical point of reference for Chekhov when he
wrote *The Seagull*, especially its last act. But the fundamental elements
of this myth nonetheless inform Chekhov's play (as they do Gor'kiy's later
play, *The Lower Depths*) on its deepest level of meaning—that level in
art where character and idea merge with archetypal pattern and source.
The central problem here is unquestionably that of illusion and reality
and man's necessary movement from the former to the latter; the relevant
metaphor, appearing in art and epic, is the *journey*. It is Nina, like
Plato's wanderer, who leaves the magic world of illusions to make the
difficult journey—the Platonic "steep and rugged ascent"[4] to reality, to
knowledge, to quintessential meaning; it is Konstantin who chooses to
remain forever secure in his world of shadows, illusions, and disembodied forms. "You have found your road," he declares to Nina in Act IV,
"you know where you are going, but I am still moving in a chaos of
dreams and images, not knowing for what or for whom this is necessary.
I do not have faith and do not know where my calling lies."

Two worlds are juxtaposed in the last act of *The Seagull* (as they are in
the first scenes of *Hamlet*): the inner, comfortable world of warmth and
the outer world of dark, threatening reality. *"Evening. A single lamp with
a shade is lighted. Semidarkness. The sound from the outside of trees and
rustling and the wind howling in the chimney. The night watchman is
knocking."* Outside, behind the glass door to the terrace which faces the
audience, the garden is dark. Nina, like the wanderer in Plato's myth
who revisits his den of old, returns to her native nest. She observes: "It's
warm, nice here," and again: "It's nice here, warm, comfortable. Do you
hear—the wind outside? Turgenev says somewhere: 'Happy is he who in
such a night sits under the roof of a house, who has a warm spot.' I'm a
seagull. No, that's not it. Where was I? Yes, Turgenev. 'And God help
all homeless wanderers.' " And Nina, in her tears of pain and anguish,
tears evoked by the contrast of past and present, recalls her "clear, warm,
joyful, pure life," her naïve dreams of fame, and her dreamlike love. But
Konstantin misunderstands Nina's feelings. He begins to speak—trying to
pick up the threads of the past, to reweave the old pattern; he reaffirms

his love for her. Nina is brought up with a start. "Why does he talk that way, why does he talk that way?" The question is a pertinent one. Konstantin answers the question. "I am alone, not warmed by anybody's affection, I am cold, as in a cave, and no matter what I write it's dry, harsh, and gloomy. Stay here, Nina, I beg you, or let me go away with you. *Nina quickly puts on her hat and cape.*"

Why is Nina in such haste to leave? Socrates, discussing the return of the wanderer to the cave, observes that the wanderer would find it easier "to endure anything, rather than think as they do [in the cave] and live after their manner." Men in the cave would say of the wanderer, according to Socrates, that "up he went and down he came without his eyes; and that it was better not even to think of ascending." But for the wanderer—"he would rather suffer anything than entertain these false notions and live in this miserable manner." It is in these terms that we can understand Konstantin's view of Nina as a failure (his story of Nina's two years away from home) and Nina's attitude toward his appeal to remain with him. There can be no return to the innocence and illusions of the past. Nina's reply to Konstantin's plea is replete with real and symbolic meaning. "My horses are standing at the gate. Don't see me off. I'll make it by myself. *Through her tears.* Give me some water." Nina dashes into the play on a horse—"A red sky, the moon is already rising, and I raced the horse, I raced it." Nina's horse—Pegasus, winged horse of inspiration—stands ready to carry her away. Brutal reality ("we have both been drawn into the maelstrom") is preferable to Konstantin's sterile cave. "Give me some water." Nina's request for water—over and above its perfectly ordinary meaning—takes on special poetic significance in the context of the rich water imagery in *The Seagull* (Nina's name, Zarechnaya—"beyond or across the river," the "magic lake"). Water is creation, life. Konstantin offers Nina some water to drink. Yet in the arid world that he still inhabits there is none of the water for which Nina craves and upon which art and life flourish. The "magic lake" toward which Nina once had been drawn "like a seagull" has vanished. All that is left is a cold cave, a dry lake, an empty well.

"The main thing is to turn life upside down; all the rest is not important [*glavnoe—perevernut' zhizn', a vse ostal'noe ne vazhno*]," the young Sasha tells the heroine Nadya in Chekhov's last brilliant story, "The Betrothed." Like Nina after her meeting with Trigorin, Nadya turns her life upside down: "gay and full of spirits" she leaves her provincial town, unaware, however, that "all the rest"—the endless struggle with the conservatism of life—is really very important, indeed, the "main thing"; she leaves—Chekhov writes in the concluding line of the story—"as she supposed, forever." But there is no "forever" or finality in Chekhov's conception of life (though there is much of it in the lives of his heroes and heroines). Life is not a lineal movement toward a finite goal, but a process of endless striving, suffering, fall, and recovery. The mature idea of the "return" (*vernut'sya*) in "The Betrothed—the idea of the periodicity or lunar character of all experience and striving—is buried in Sasha's youthful hopes of giving a new turn to life (*perevernut'*) and in the heroine's belief in an "unfolding" (*razvernut'sya*) "spring life" "not here, but somewhere." The new, pure life, as Chekhov views it, is a permanent dream to which one returns again and again, but it is also one that makes one "want to cry" because of its inaccessibility. The idea of the "return" that informs "The Betrothed" on its deepest level (the theme of the prodigal son) is dramatized in Nina's return to the estate of her first dreams and strivings. Nina had turned her life upside down, but unlike the blithe Nadya she had already come to discover "all the rest." She returns poignantly to relive the tender dreams and hopes of her past. But return here does not involve a blind elevation of self (as in the case of Nadya) above those whom she had left behind and now once again leaves behind; nor does it signal retreat or defeat. Return here involves the humble and passionate inclusion of her past in her life and, therefore, its inclusion in her future; it involves above all recognition of suffering ("bear your cross") and knowledge ("now I know, I understand") that the meaning of life lies in the journey itself—one that is a series of endless returns and restartings.

The personal tragedy of Konstantin is that he chose not to make the journey of his life; overwhelmed by his character, he remains forever in the shadow of his fear of life. The triumph of Nina is her free choice of the journey, her willingness, finally, to *endure*. One may say, of course, that this is a very narrow, precarious triumph. But Chekhov, like Dostoyevskiy, was a realist where man is concerned. He knew that the only triumph that counts is the precarious one, the one, in short, that organically is fused with tragic knowledge and experience.

The painful relinquishment of golden childhood and the dream of innocence before the bitter necessity of knowing reality—this is the poignant and tragic side of Nina's journey into life. Art or, at least, "pure art" with its efflorescence of beauty, is somehow permanently linked with that dream of innocence. In this sense Nina's awakening in real life reenacts the tragedy of the fall. Yet it is clear that Chekhov does not envisage the renunciation of art or illusion (in the deepest creative sense) in the journey to reality. In the lucid confrontation with reality—the "paradox of the fortunate fall"—lies all realistic hope, the hope once again of reappropriating the dream.

NOTES

1. For a wide-ranging analysis of *The Seagull*—one that posits the central importance of the problems of art and talent in the play—see V. Yermilov's discussion in his *Dramaturgiya Chekhova* (Moscow: Sovetskiy pisatel', 1948), pp. 3–54.

2. For an interesting discussion of allusions to *Hamlet* in *The Seagull*, see Thomas G. Winner's "Chekhov's *Seagull* and Shakespeare's *Hamlet*: A Study of a Dramatic Device," in *American Slavic and East European Review*, 15 (February 1956), pp. 103–11.

3. The theme of chance or accident—with its correlative idea of a meaningless or perverse universe—saturates the content of "A Woman's Kingdom." It is only when this theme is perceived that the real inner structure and meaning of this story—philosophical, social, and psychological—emerges. Strictly speaking, nothing "happens" in this story; yet in the course of twenty-four hours, held as within the classical unities, the fate of the heroine is determined; put in other words, she (and the reader) discover that fate that is already embodied in her character but that has not yet crystallized in consciousness. The story—and it is largely a psychological one—is the account of the feeble inner struggle (turning centrally on a chance encounter but involving the heroine's Christmas charity activities) that results in the defeat for self-determination.

4. Citations from *The Republic* are from *The Portable Plato*, ed. Scott Buchanan, trans. Benjamin Jowett (New York: The Viking Press, Inc., 1948).

CHEKHOV'S *THE SEAGULL* AND MAUPASSANT'S *SUR L'EAU*

BY JEROME H. KATSELL

I

Chacun de nous, sentant le vide autour de lui, le vide insondable où s'agite son coeur, où se débat sa pensée, va comme un fou, les bras ouverts, les lèvres tendues, cherchant un être à étreindre. Et il étreint à droite, à gauche, au hasard, sans savoir, sand regarder, sans comprendre, pour n'être plus seul. [1]

—*Sur l'eau*

From the viewpoint of genre and the reputations of the respective authors, one would not expect a Maupassant travel sketch and a major Chekhov play, the first of the great quartet of plays which brought him world recognition, to have much in common. True, the French author is mentioned in the first act of *The Seagull* when Konstantin invokes Maupassant's flight of disgust before the vulgarity of Eiffel's famous tower, this as part of his assertion of the necessity to turn away from dead artistic routine and to search for new aesthetic forms. True, the travel sketch *Sur l'eau* (1888), is named and quoted from in the opening scenes of the second act of Chekhov's play. At first glance, however, the connection between the two works might appear slight indeed. But it should be remembered that like his use of telling detail in his stories Chekhov's employment of literary allusions in his plays is integral to an overall appreciation of central thematic concerns. Thus, an understanding of *Sur l'eau*, its themes, and its philosophical ruminations may well be useful in further illuminating *The Seagull*.

Maupassant's series of travel sketches has, for the most part, been over-looked in the criticism of *The Seagull*. It is clear, of course, that the passage read by Arkadina in Act II from *Sur l'eau* comments ironically on the relationship between Trigorin and herself. It has been asserted, however, that there are many elements in the second, Cannes chapter of *Sur l'eau* "crucial to an understanding of *The Seagull*." [2] The worship of rank, the superficial ife of the idle rich in hotels, pessimism about human beings to the point of misanthropy—these are some of the elements in the second chapter of *Sur l'eau*. Many other features, some of them common to both works—the mysterious power of the moon is an example—function to the same purpose to "constantly puncture illusions, constantly remove the veneered cover of falsity to expose the deflated reality." [3]

There is much, to be sure, in Chekhov and Maupassant that is predicated on the ironic gap between illusions and reality. But it is more important, I believe, to go to the texture, the ever repeated motifs and structures within *Sur l'eau* to capture the deeper levels shared by the two texts. Here we find a central concern in both works fo the nature of art, the essence of the artistic personality, and beyond that a groping toward an understanding of the nature of freedom. *Sur l'eau* and especially *The Seagull* are not works of profound pessimism, although the former bristles with facile despair; they are, rather, works that center on oppositions such as pessimism-optimism, youth-age, capture-freedom, restriction-bound-less space that have in common a concern for human potentialities. Many of the cadences and arguments throughout *Sur l'eau* may be seen to find echoes, perhaps reincarnations in the very texture of *The Seagull*. There are, without doubt, significant differences among the two works, and these will be pointed out.

Arkadina refuses to read further in *Sur l'eau* because the Maupassant text describes the actions of society women intent upon capturing and dominating a writer; "the rest is both uninteresting and false," she asserts. [4] The travel sketch then continues to render an account of how such a woman turns a writer into a mere social fixture of her drawing room. [5] It would be well to remember that Dorn, in the presence of Arkadina and Masha, has been reading Maupassant's work *before* the beginning of the second act and that the content of *Sur l'eau* might in fact explain Arkadina's need to demand acknowledgment of her youthfulness,

expressed through a display of insecure behavior. She asserts that she
never thinks of death, does not look to the future, that she is stylish and
careful, and always dressed and groomed, as she puts it, *comme il faut.*

When we turn to the passages Dorn, Masha, and Arkadina have in
fact been reading in turn—they must have been at it for some time—we
see that the Maupassant text concerns the dangers for a woman of society
to become involved with a novelist. There is much about the novelist as
described by Maupassant that reminds us of Trigorin, much that might
put Arkadina on the defensive about the vulnerability of her position.
Here is what Maupassant writes:

> The poet has more delicate charm, the novelist often possesses more wit.
> But the novelist presents dangers not encountered in the poet—he preys
> upon, ruins and exploits everything that enters his field of vision. With him
> there is no tranquility, no assurance that he won't, one day, expose you
> quite nude [*toute nue*] in the pages of his book. His eye is like a pump that
> sucks in everything, like the hand of a thief always working away. Nothing
> escapes him; he ceaselessly amasses and gathers things; he remarks the move-
> ments, the gestures, the intentions, everything that occurs about him; he
> notices the least words, the smallest actions, the least little thing. From
> morning till night he stores these varied observations of which he creates
> salable stories, stories that make their way around the world, which will be
> read, discussed, and commented on by countless thousands of people. And
> the most terrible thing of all is that the wretch can't help executing striking
> portraits, unconsciously, in spite of himself, because he sees things clearly,
> and he must tell of what he sees. (30–31)

The passage that Arkadina has been reading and listening to, in contrast
to the main thrust of the passage read aloud onstage, concerns the power
of the writer, his ability to destroy through the use of words, the sense of
dominance over others that the novelist's sensitivity and perspicacity give
him. She has noticed how Nina reacted to Trigorin—it is probably not
the first time the female admiration Trigorin provokes has come to her
attention—and now, perhaps, she gets her own back through Masha.
The truth of her relationship with Trigorin contained in the passages
subsequent to the one read onstage, the ones Arkadina wants to avoid,
concerns the woman who, in Maupassant's opinion, neutralizes the
writer by her wiles and social position. She draws him into her circle to
be admired and shown off, but always under close scrutiny and guard; he
becomes the caged literary lion.

If Arkadina does in fact see her portrait in the description of the society

woman who must emasculate the novelist in order to control and dominate, it might well help us understand her relationship to Trigorin, and
beyond that give us an insight into her relationship to art. Both relationships are intertwined with, and based on, fear. Trigorin must be kept
docile, his art not allowed to go beyond his own characterization of it as
"charming, talented," but far below the level of a Tolstoy or a Zola. It
might be noted parenthetically that Maupassant would neatly fit the description Trigorin applies to himself. This attitude on the part of Arkadina perhaps explains her indulgence of Trigorin's fishing as well as her
casual attitude toward his books. She unwittingly allies herself with the
middle if not the lowbrow in art, and by the end of the play we see her
offering gossipy arty talk to Shamrayev.[6]

More important, Arkadina's fear of real art and forms she cannot understand plays into her relationship with Konstantin. There is more than
an oedipal relationship here. In view of Arkadina's reaction to the Maupassant passage in the second act, we might reconsider her reaction to
Konstantin's play in Act I. His claims to new artistic form in a play that
deals with essences and ultimate states of being/nonbeing threaten Arkadina in the potential for power-as-artist that it might portend for Konstantin. She fears the power of potentially genuine art she does not understand in Konstantin. Thus, she rejects the description of the writer's lady
who, Maupassant insists, is in danger of finding herself "toute nue" between the pages of a story. There is no indication within *The Seagull*, in
fact, that Arkadina *reads* Trigorin. We know that she never reads a word
of Konstantin's work after he begins to publish. Could it be that she fears
an unflattering portrait of herself in Trigorin's fiction? All the while that
she is not supportive of, or interested in, Trigorin's work, she is forcing
her own bad art upon him. Not only does he have to put up with her
flamboyant acting in some good but mostly second-rate plays—we do
have the feeling that Konstantin is right about her level of acting—but he
must also accept her bad melodramatic acting as real feeling in their
personal relationship.[7] Of course Trigorin has exchanged his loftier am-
bitions, those of which he speaks to Nina in the second act, for the
comforts and social position his liaison with Arkadina afford. The adop-
tion by Arkadina of a melodramatic role in her life is underscored by her
hysterical wooing back of Trigorin in Act III, even to the point of her
saying to herself, "Now he's mine!"

An important aspect of Maupassant's *Sur l'eau* concerns social conventions. The focus on travel and contact with the pure elemental forces of the ocean is part of an obsession with attempted escape from the charade of society, highlighted each time the narrator comes to port by devastating criticisms of social customs. Within these sketches, one of the most important oppositions is that between the naturalness of the ocean and the unnaturalness, the role playing, the acting at the heart of society. It is this moving backward and forward from the world of natural perfection to the world of human limitations and corruptions that represents a structural and thematic commonality between *Sur l'eau* and *The Seagull*. Nina embodies such naturalness, especially in contrast to Arkadina. Although she is naïve and impressionable, she is not afraid to seek after real people and real art. It might thus be deemed significant that she does find herself, to an extent, in Trigorin's books. That Trigorin's art, in spite of what Konstantin tells Sorin in the first act about its being "charming, talented, but . . . ," may be more than either the self-depreciating Trigorin or Konstantin claim is highlighted by the latter's admission of its superiority to his own efforts in Act IV. Trigorin initially responds to Nina, as to his own lost potential and to that part of him that is the genuine artist, which Nina unconsciously recognizes despite her lack of worldliness.

Sur l'eau begins with Maupassant's escape on the *Bel Ami* for a sailing trip along the Mediterranean coast. "What joy not to speak for fifteen whole days!" (15). It ends with the author's plunging back into society to meet a friend at Monte Carlo's gambling tables. In *Sur l'eau* land consistently represents imprisonment and the sea potential freedom. Thus, in the story of Paganini's death told by Maupassant, the great musical personality is scorned by the very society that had adored him above all mortals. He can find a resting place for a time only on a tiny island out to sea, Saint-Ferreol.

For Maupassant, it appears, society cannot be avoided, but ideally it should be.

Sur l'eau is saturated with images and accounts of imprisonment. There is reference, for example, to the Man in the Iron Mask, (also mentioned in *The Seagull* in Act IV when Trigorin pointedly notes that Petersburg and Moscow literary people consider Konstantin "mysterious, like the Iron Mask"), an account of a condemned man, a story about a couple secluded from society for decades in self-imposed exile because they are in love, locked into a dependence on each other that severely limits their possibilities. There are other images of imprisonment as well. Maupassant concentrates on imprisonment that is socially engendered and his own general disgust with humanity. Chekhov, on the other hand, concentrates on the emotional imprisonment involved in relationships between people who have not developed independence. The tons of love in *The Seagull* do in fact exist. All the triangles in the play rest upon dependence, with the dependent person in an emotional prison, condemned to a life sentence: Konstantin, Masha, Polina, Trigorin, and even Arkadina fit into this category. There is partial escape into indifference, as displayed, for example, in Dorn's attitude to Polina or Konstantin's toward Masha. Nina, of all the characters in *The Seagull*, although she does not escape emotional dependence and involvement, goes beyond it.

Maupassant escapes from the claims of society to the open sea, to a primeval world that for him is both chaos and simultaneously an emblem of health. The essential element of this chaotic benevolence is the sea, itself at the mercy of the omnipotent wind. "What a personage the wind is for sailors! They speak of it as if of a man, of an all-powerful sovereign who is at times terrible and at times kindly" (16). The wind is both the energy that carries the ship and also the emblem of nature's potentially destructive forces. Like life itself, and like death, the wind represents a reality that must be faced and accepted as man comes to know his existence and function. "No enemy, no woman gives us so intense a sensation of combat, nor forces us to so much foresight, for it is the sea's master; we may avoid it, use it, or flee from it, but we can never subdue it" (17). In the last act of *The Seagull* it is just this master element with which Nina seems to have merged. The storm raging outside is the element from which she comes and to which she returns. Nina's lack of fear of the wind and rain outside is but one of the ways by which Chekhov indicates her independence and facing of life in all its manifestations. Other examples of this include her rejection of Konstantin's offer of dependent love and her declaration of her feelings for Trigorin, despite his total neglect of her.

Konstantin's play deals with the end of time, the end of change, the approach of absolute stasis. If Nina appears to represent the real possibility of change as she battles through chaos, disruption, time's passage, and personal loss, the other characters in *The Seagull* embody only lack of change. Act IV of Chekhov's play is designed to show that in fact nothing changes. We are teased with Konstantin's putative success as a new writer, but soon it is obvious that all the relationships of the central characters are a spinning of wheels into the same, deeper ruts. Even Konstantin's suicide is a repeat performance; we assume a "success." Although Maupassant does not portray any of the inner struggle to overcome routine, but rather the disgust of his narrator at the lack of creativity and expansiveness in man, in *Sur l'eau* he is strikingly in accord with the underlying currents of Chekhov's drama. "Happy are those who do not perceive with immense disgust that nothing changes, nothing passes and that all remains the same" (41).

Although the fin de siècle elements of *Weltschmertz*, sentimental pessimism, misogyny, and misanthropy found in *Sur l'eau* are foreign to Chekhov, *The Seagull* shares with it the presentation of attempted escape from mature and responsible life through vanity, superficiality, loneliness, emotional dependence, and the dead routine of bureaucratic work. For Chekhov, harmony and reconciliation can come, if ever, through hard work and the transcendence of art. For Maupassant, the question of art does indeed surface many times in *Sur l'eau*, in the important second chapter and elsewhere. It is connected for Maupassant, like Chekhov, with man's loneliness and isolation and his inability to overcome. "Console yourself, they say, in the love of science and the arts" (42). Reconciliation for Maupassant is *never* possible, because man cannot be released from the self within which he is enchained. It is, therefore, possible to read *The Seagull* as Chekhov's answer to the world weariness of *Sur l'eau*, where the artist flees from the ordinary world to get close to the basic elements of sea and wind in order to create the journal we have in front of us. "But isn't it perfectly clear that we are always locked up within ourselves, without being able to come out, condemned to drag along the chains of our hopeless dream" (42).

We have now come to a basic difference of approach between Chekhov and Maupassant. In *The Seagull* we are presented with a series of life failures, failure in the deepest needs for love and recognition in virtually all of the characters; the striving to change this situation, especially through art, must be seen as the central problematic about which the play revolves. In *Sur l'eau*, conversely, the possibility of a breakthrough, either from science or art, is seen as the grossest of illusions. Maupassant's travel sketch consists in fact of a series of sorties back and forth from the sea to the shore, from the empty posturing and ineffectual contortions of society to the silence, peace, beauty, and truth of the ever changing and ever unchanged sea. Man can escape neither himself nor the incredible emptiness within Maupassant's world view. After a short rumination on the failure of science to solve fundamental questions there follows perhaps the most devastating sentence in *Sur l'eau:* "We know nothing, we see nothing, we can do nothing, we divine nothing, we imagine nothing, we are shut up in ourselves, imprisoned in ourselves" (43).

This imprisonment of the individual within the self of which Maupassant writes so passionately prevents communication with the other. In *Sur l'eau* the narrative stance is that of the individual who may be excellent at passing pleasantries with his fellows—Maupassant has a longish encomium to the genius of the French nation in making the ordinary in life into something stylish and pleasant, of turning history itself, through the use of well-placed words and phrases, into an elegant diversion—but who is essentially cut off and alone.[8] Chekhov's characters are known to be caught within themselves, too, and are typically subject to the pains of mutual incomprehension. The fundamental difference between Chekhov and Maupassant in this regard is that Chekhov will not give up the idea that man is capable of change, despite his nature.

II

Personne, jamais, n'appartient à personne. On se prête, malgré soi, à ce jeu coquet ou passionné de la possession, mais on ne se donne jamais. L'homme, exaspéré par ce besoin d'être le maître de quelqu'un, a institué la tyrannie, l'esclavage et le mariage. Il peut tuer, torturer, emprisonner, mais la volonté humaine lui échappe toujours, même quand elle a consenti quelques instants à se soumettre.

—*Sur l'eau*

Maupassant does indeed show the other side of the coin as well. The individual's isolation, his inescapable destiny, can be a source of strength if not salvation. The human will is capable of getting around institutions and superstitions based on fear. Built into the individual, along with all that is negative and self-destructive, is the will to fulfill a brighter and more harmonious existence. There is a touching story in the seventh, penultimate chapter of *Sur l'eau* about a young woman who runs away with a young officer below her social rank from a regiment commanded by her father. For thirty years the couple live in isolation far from the mainstreams of society. The man, it eventually turns out, has been keeping a mistress from a nearby village the whole time. His bride, by now an old lady, throws herself from a bedroom window in despair. The human will can cut many ways. It can lead to great happiness, to despair, and even to death. Its function here appears to be the maintaining of the individual's integrity, whatever the cost. One might even see in Maupassant's depiction of a woman's suicide from lost love a parallel with the fate of Konstantin in *The Seagull.*

The impossibility of submitting to something less than the destiny conceived for the individual by the will is central to virtually all the characters in *The Seagull.* Sorin, for example, despite his age, his dozing, and his infirmity, despite his nearly thirty years in a job to which he was indifferent, despite the dosing of valerian drops given him by Dorn, is still searching for the free life of the artist and lover in the exciting city. He identifies with Konstantin's youthful romantic struggle to become the great artist; he has an eye for feminine beauty and even has self-insight. So, in spite of physical decrepitude and the pincers of senility, Sorin's very human will to harmony, independence, and creativity still struggles on. There is even a rearguard action, hopeless as it is, against the outrages of Shamrayev, that embodiment of blunt voracious vulgarity.

This ineluctable thrust of the will is evident in other characters in *The Seagull.* Masha's identification with the creative triumph so poorly actualized by Konstantin stays with her despite all her efforts to "tear it out by the roots." Arkadina, too, wills herself to be a great actress. She has no clear idea of what a great actress should be, but she knows what the popular conception of a great actress is and goes after that. Trigorin is the kind of man that a great actress should have for a lover and so she has him. Her will is directed to fulfilling a highly visible role. Shamrayev is her true audience. We come to know this during the course of the play and the fourth act confirms what we are deeply aware of by the end of Act III. Will is also involved in the actions of Polina and Medvedenko;

and even Dorn, satisfied as he is, throws away his last savings on a trip abroad.

Maupassant's statement beginning the epigraph at the start of this section that "no one, ever, belongs to another," is certainly borne out in *The Seagull*. The will of one individual can involve the suppression of others, and it is true that all love is spurned in *The Seagull* because the object of love has a will demanding something else. Masha rejects Medvedenko; Konstantin, Masha; Nina, Konstantin; Trigorin, Nina; and so on. Maupassant has hit upon something in his statement that was not news to Chekhov but that, given the striking thematic parallels in *The Seagull* and *Sur l'eau*, may have reinforced an important element in the play.

Will exercised presumes subordination of others and the relationship of belonging. Here power and money play an important role. In this sense Nina belongs to her father, who, ironically, has set her on to the road to freedom by disinheriting her. Konstantin is given the same treatment by Arkadina but reacts in an entirely different way. In fact, this role of money and other social conventions that fix individuals in relationships of superiority and inferiority is prominently displayed in *Sur l'eau* and *The Seagull*. Even though no one may own the other, Chekhov knows that the will, even though it struggles on to express its higher needs of love and integration, can be buried by the nets of social necessity.

Independence is an attribute that is a given to nature. Society corrupts or blocks off man from his elemental merging with nature. For Maupassant in *Sur l'eau* there is only temporary respite from the relentless destruction to man caused by human society, and it is to be found in the virtual isolation—Maupassant is of course well tended by a pair of capable sailors who see to his needs—of the sea. For Chekhov the picture is somewhat different. The isolation of the individual is there, the will to independence as well, but not the misanthropy, the revulsion, and the turning away from the frivolous and inane in society. The paradox in *The Seagull* is that true humanity and independence can be found by the individual only through and for the human community with all its grotesque perversions and gaucheries. This is perhaps illustrated by Dorn, who cherishes the tumult and dense humanity of the Italian crowd above all his memories of a recent trip to Western Europe. It is also Dorn, the best obstetrician for miles around, who has worked hard all his adult life for the general good of the community. It is a saving grace in the instance of Trigorin that he realizes as a writer, "I'm also a citizen. I love my country, my people. And I feel that if I am a writer, I must speak of the people, of their sufferings, of their future" (30).

The community is at the center in *The Seagull*. The problem of self-actualization is shared by all, and the triangular nets of love that bind virtually all the characters underscore this fact. The central problematic, finally, in all of Chekhov's work regardless of genre, is to find a way of merging the individually attained victories of wholeness and independence into a stronger and more cohesive community. Without the support of the community the individual withers. And here we may have come upon a key to the overexaggerated devastation experienced by Konstantin when his play proves a failure in the first act. He has been slighted by his mother, whom he had wanted to impress not only with the fact that he has talent but by the fact that he is grown up, but he has also been a failure in front of the entire community surrounding the country estate of his uncle Sorin—Dorn, the doctor and friend of many years; Nina, the girl he loves, a famous writer, Trigorin; and even the servants and estate stewards, the Shamrayevs.

The content of Konstantin's play is also a measure of his alienation from the community and its central striving. His play within the play in *The Seagull* is set at the very end of time when the possibility of community no longer exists, when the human spirit is subjected to the most absolute of all possible isolations. The setting of Konstantin's play could be rivaled in its depiction of the deadened waste of the world's end only by Chekhov's contemporary, H. G. Wells, in his description of time's last phase in *The Time Machine*. Wells's novel was published in 1895, the year in which Chekhov wrote *The Seagull*. Of course, Konstantin's play expresses not only his despair and underlying alienation from those around him but also his need for love. The human spirit still somehow does live in the fruitless dead world he presents, and it takes on the devil himself.

Such a primitive cry of despair and the need for love comes close to escaping the lips of Maupassant. On one of his forays back onshore from the *Bel Ami*, he notices a pair of lovers in a pine forest. He feels sad and happy at once. Later he sees them again at an inn, from the distance and

in profile. "Then I was overcome with my loneliness, and in the mild-
ness of that spring night, at the soft sound of the waves on the sand,
under the slender crescent moon tumbling its light into the sea, I experienced in my heart such an intense desire to love, that I nearly cried out
in my distress of longing" (69). In many ways Maupassant's *Sur l'eau*
presents an artist unhappy with himself and disgusted with society, wandering around without fixed destination for himself or for his art. Could
Chekhov, to some extent, have found here a portrait of one of the possible variants of the artistic personality, a Trigorin, or even a Konstantin?
One may only speculate, but the possibility is intriguing.

The difference between Konstantin and Trigorin, however, goes beyond the question of forms. Trigorin might in fact depend on well-estab-
lished techniques, and Konstantin might on the surface be fiddling with
new devices. But the important difference is that Trigorin, no matter how
unsuccessfully, directs his work toward an attempt to understand the
community and the group personality of which it is ultimately made. His
failure to achieve greatness as a writer lies in the fact that he does not
possess the energy and drive, the will, to dig for the complexity of human
relationships and processes that he *knows* are at the heart of the matter of
art. In this sense he could be very much like the writer Chekhov understood Maupassant to be. If so, this would add yet another layer of interest
to the fact of Arkadina's reading Maupassant and her rejection of his
importance. One has a feeling that Arkadina does not respect Trigorin as
a writer, and therefore as a person, either.

Arkadina's lack of respect for Trigorin on several levels is a reflection
of the basic instability of their relationship. One of the outward manifestations of this instability is the fact that they have no permanent place of
residence. They live in hotels. They are perpetual tourists. The possibility
of getting involved in the local community does not exist for them. Their
lives are based on their selfish and individual needs. This lack of per-
manence goes some way to explain and illustrate the kinds of relationships they do have. Arkadina, distanced from her brother and son, and
Trigorin, lover for nothing better to do and professional colleague because he knows of nothing else to do. Well, going fishing perhaps.

In *Sur l'eau* hotels and the life of the tourist is most strongly associated
with the sense of death and dying, with the idea of life wasted. Maupassant speaks of the tubercular patients who come to the south of France

for treatment and describes the region as "this charming and fearful country, this antechamber of Death" (34). The thrust of his remarks about the frivolous life of tourists in hotels is that it represents a mere sprinkling of perfume over the stench of death, the ultimate reality of human life. In this attitude he is astonishingly close to the subject matter and tone of Ivan Bunin's story, "The Gentleman from San Francisco." "A coffin is never seen in the streets, never the funeral draperies, never are heard the funereal tollings. Yesterday's thin sunken walker no longer passes below your window, and voilà, that's all. If you are surprised to no longer see him and make inquiries, the headwaiter and all the servants will tell you with a smile that he is much better and on his doctor's advise has set out for Italy. In effect, in every hotel Death has its secret stairwell, its confidants, and its accomplices" (36).

We know about Arkadina's and Trigorin's unstable life and their poor relationships between themselves and with others. We know that Konstantin, in effect, accuses them both of being dead, of their art being dead. Arkadina and Trigorin poison the devotion and enthusiasm of youth. Their unstable life is in fact *exactly* that which Nina must adopt. It is a measure of her strength and courage just how independent and clear thinking she has become by the fourth act. She is living in hotels, leading the life of the single actress, uncared for, pawed by the local intelligentsia—surrounded, in Maupassant's terms, by empty, dead people and by death itself. And yet she survives and goes on, it appears from her last meeting with Konstantin, to triumph and achievement.

We must ask the question why Nina, seemingly so naïve and vulnerable, is the one person from all the principals in *The Seagull* who makes an *inner* success of her life. Chekhov gives us, at least in outline, the reasons why Nina can succeed, to the extent that people in his world view can ever succeed, in overcoming the impediments to fulfillment. In her early life her mother died. This is her first confrontation with death and sets her on an elemental and childish search for a world of harmony. Her search involves the lake to which she ascribes miraculous powers. She is rejected by her father and stepmother both materially and spiritually. Nina has learned at an early age to overcome that which is negative within herself and to cherish the harmonious and the possibilities for human transcendence. She recognizes that some if not most people lead, as she tells Trigorin in the second act, "dreary, miserable, inconspicuous lives, everyone just like everyone else, and all terribly unhappy" (28). She recognizes in Trigorin's work, however—and this is just what both Konstantin and Arkadina miss because they are mediocre artists—those elements portending artistic excellence that go beyond his own depression and acceptance of himself as less than he could or would have liked to become.

It is Nina's confrontation with death and rejection of it that has formed her character. She wants to seize life in all its aspects, including the negative, and triumph over it. Thus she leaves behind all the material support she has ever had, her father's estate and its beautiful natural surroundings, especially the lake. She goes beyond the deadness in those she knows, recognizing it and overcoming. It is remarkable in Act I when Konstantin asks her if she is nervous about her debut in acting, and in front of a famous actress, too, that Nina replies she is not afraid of Arkadina. She is close to and cheers Sorin, recognizing his humanity and search for harmony in art, no matter how weak and hopeless. She is able to stand up to all that is dead in her environment, a struggling actress without recognition. For Nina even Yelets with its vulgarity and provincial dullness possesses that spark of artistic harmony that she recognizes to be central to all human personality.

Nina's surname is no coincidence either. Beyond the river, Zarechnaya, refers to water, the traditional symbol for life at its essence, and beyond the river the sea to which it flows. Perhaps it is after all the tidal ebb and flow of the primeval sea in all its vastness which connects at the deepest level *Sur l'eau* and *The Seagull*. Chekhov believed in the power of redemption it symbolizes; he believed in man. Maupassant is another story. "Oh, how I would sometimes like not to think, not to feel, how I would like to live like a brute in a warm and bright-clear country, in a golden-yellow country, without our crude and brutal tones of verdure, in a country of the Orient where I could sleep without sadness, where I could awaken without care or regret, where restlessness is without anxiety, where there is no anguish in love, and where existence is not a burden" (92).

We have seen that a wealth of thematic strains is held in common by *The Seagull* and *Sur l'eau*. The universal symbol of water as a life giver and sustainer is deeply present in both works. For Maupassant, there existed a much greater pessimism about the possibilities for human action in the face of the implacable fact of death and decay. When a storm occurs on the ocean all the possibilities the sea holds out to man for peace and serenity are dashed in an instant. In this he is as much a follower of Schopenhauer as of his older Russian contemporary, Turgenev. The will of nature as a unified and total force is uncalculably beyond the power and ken of man, and—here is the point shared by Maupassant with the German philosopher—totally indifferent to human existence and fate. In *The Seagull*, Konstantin, in his play, comes closest to this world view of Schopenhauer in which human will is a microcosm of nature that is seen as a series of arbitrary processes not subject to rational apprehension.

Konstantin's foil is, of course, Nina. She accepts the raging storm and goes beyond it. She accepts the chaotic form of nature and yet believes in something within man that *can* go beyond the given, something that speaks of the possibility and the potential for human integration, harmony, and inner achievement. It is no accident that she quotes these lines from Turgenev: "Happy is he who on a night like this has a roof over his head, a warm corner" (57). She feels her loneliness deeply; she feels the destructive power of deceit and treachery in personal relationships. But yet she proceeds steadily to develop inner confidence. Her weapons are an honest facing of her feelings, her hurts and her desires, and a memory that goes beyond the negative to the potential in herself and others. Thus she is able to quote from memory from Konstantin's play. Trigorin, a failed artist, within several lines of Nina's quotation from Konstantin's play, states his "I can't remember" (55). Memory is used as one of the main tools by Nina to build a structure of dedication and inner resistance to breakdown in the present; it is the essential tool of the real artist and goes beyond, for example, Konstantin's merely formal innovations. The central role of memory, positive memory, from which the artistic personality builds itself from within is a very strong element in *The Seagull*. Its importance here and elsewhere in Chekhov may explain why Nabokov was such a great admirer of Chekhov. Memory plays a similar role for him.

I believe the foregoing speculations have shown that *Sur l'eau* was a reference point for Chekhov in *The Seagull* that goes far beyond the ironic light shed on the Trigorin-Arkadina relationship in the one quote taken from it in the second act of the play. Maupassant's travel sketch represents a rumination on the role of nature in human life. It ultimately rejects society and the possibillty of human harmony with nature. It is a guide to Maupassant's extreme, and often facile, pessimism and misanthropic despair. Maupassant knows what it takes to make a great artist. His real lack of inner confidence and belief in man was his downfall. Chekhov had that confidence and belief in spite of all Russia's primitive woes and injustices. To quote Maupassant: "He has seen all, noticed all, retained all, in spite of himself, because he is above all a man of letters" (81).

NOTES

1. Guy de Maupassant, *Oeuvres complètes de Guy de Maupassant*, (Paris: Louis Conrad, 1908), XXII, 128. This edition of Maupassant's works is used throughout, and all page references herein apply to it. The Russian original of *The Seagull* (*Chayka*) consulted for this essay appears in A. P. *Chekhov, Polnoye sobraniye sochineniy i pisem v tridtsati tomakh*, [N. F. Bel'chikov, chief editor], (Moscow: Nauka, 1978), XIII, 3–60. Translations from Russian and French are my own.

2. Ellen Chances, "Chekhov's *Seagull*: Ethereal Creature or Stuffed Bird?" in Paul Debreczeny and Thomas Eekman, eds., *Chekhov's Art of Writing: A Collection of Critical Essays*, (Columbus: Slavica Publishers, 1977), esp., p. 32.

3. Ibid., p. 33.

4. Simon Karlinsky believes that this statement by Arkadina expresses Chekhov's opinion of Maupassant's artistic merit. This is an interesting speculation, although Chekhov may here just as well have been masking the many points of connection between the two works. See Michael Henry Heim and Simon Karlinsky, *Anton Chekhov's Life and Thought: Selected letters and Commentary* (Berkeley, Los Angeles, London: Univ. of California Press, 1975), p. 282.

5. *Sur l'eau*, p. 31. It should be noted that Maupassant uses *l'homme de lettres* as a generic term for the "writer," and distinguishes between *le poète* and *le romancier*. The Russian translation used by Chekhov, the work of M. N. Timofeyeva, has *romanist*, which signals specifically a novelist as does the second French term.

6. Chekhov underlines the superficiality and lack of true artistic stature characteristic of Arkadina thoughout *The Seagull*. One of her last statements in the play is typical of her self-centered personality. "We shall play [cards] and drink," p. 60.

7. An important irony that gives the lie to Arkadina's pretentions to artistic superiority and her disdainful attitude toward Konstantin's passion for new forms lies in the fact that Alexandre Dumas *fils*' *La Dame aux camélias* in which she

apparently acted frequently was a play that broke extremely important ground in terms of *form* and content, away from the well-made play of Scribe and his imitators. In its subordination of plot to the psychological investigation of a young woman struggling to find herself in difficult social circumstances, *La Dame aux camélias* intriguingly suggests a basic situation in *The Seagull*. Nina's profession of actress carried in Russia some of the connotations that Marguerite's role of prostitute did in France.

8. *Sur l'eau*, pp. 138–46.

UNCLE VANYA'S PREDICAMENT*

BY IEVA VITINS

Overlooked in discussions of Uncle Vanya's ineffectuality as a male protagonist is a textual network of emotional ties which bind him to his dead sister, her family, and his mother. To a great degree these ties serve to repress his masculinity and prevent him from establishing a family of his own or making an imprint on the outside world.[1] Vanya has become a peripheral male figure, a veritable "Uncle Johnnie" who proudly supports his sister Vera's family and experiences the role of husband vicariously. It is only years after Vera's death and the recent remarriage of her husband that he becomes dissatisfied with his secondary role in life.[2] He ceases temporarily to act the uncle and family provider; instead, he vents his hatred for the brother-in-law he formerly admired and assumes the role of self-dramatized suitor of the new wife Yelena. Querulous and aggressive, he suggests a man painfully out of character, whose impotence reflects the sterility of the dying gentry class. This seemingly sudden change was criticized by early readers for its lack of motivation within the play and has been inadequately treated by later critics.[3] When considered within the context of the play's underlying family drama, however, it is psychologically convincing and justified.

Until recently, Vera has been the sole love object in her brother's life, displacing an unresponsive mother in his affections.[4] Idealized in his memory, she emerges as "a beautiful, gentle creature as pure as the blue sky above us, a fine, generous girl" (Act III).[5] When she leaves home to marry the son of a common priest, Serebryakov, who subsequently be-

* Reprinted from *Slavic and East European Journal*, Vol. 22, No. 4 (1978), 454–463, with the kind permission of the editor.

comes a respected professor of art history, Vanya not only gives up his inheritance but also pays the debts on her estate. For twenty-five years he has devoted his energy to its management in order to provide her family with a steady income. Even after Vera's death, ten years before, he continued to send money to Serebryakov, in whose scholarship he took great pride: "I was proud of him and his great learning. I lived, I breathed by him! It seemed to me that everything he wrote and uttered was inspired" (Act II).[6] Vanya's role as self-sacrificing brother so absorbs him that it stifles his desire for other women; he is at a loss to understand why he did not fall in love with Yelena when his sister was still alive:

> . . . To think that ten years ago I used to meet her at my sister's when she was only seventeen and I was thirty-seven. Why didn't I fall in love then and ask her to marry me? It would have been the most natural thing in the world. And she'd be my wife now. Yes. And tonight the storm would have woken us both. She'd be scared of the thunder and I'd hold her in my arms and whisper, "Don't be afraid. I'm here." (Act II)

It appears that even Vanya's high regard for Serebryakov was determined more by Vera's feelings for her husband than by objective considerations of intellectual worth. Since Vera loved the professor "as only angels in heaven can love beings as pure and lovely as themselves," Vanya, by extension, also came to worship him, investing him with the authority and respect due to a father figure. Fear of losing Vera's love and a son's fear of the "castrating" father no doubt also motivated Vanya's unquestioning devotion to the man.[7]

In the past year, however, Vanya has become disillusioned with the now retired professor, and it is the latter's arrival on the estate, accompanied by Yelena, that precipitates the events which bring about the temporary breakdown in the pattern of Vanya's existence. For by remarrying, Serebryakov has abrogated his bond to Vera and set Vanya free from emotional obligation. This in turn triggers long repressed hostility, part of the price of the brother's unrealized love of his sister; the formerly passive uncle displays belligerent qualities suggested in his family name, Voynitskiy (from the Russian word for "war," *voyna*). He openly admits to the envy behind his admiration of the man who, in his "Don Juanish" success with women, has been the victorious rival for his sister's, mother's, and Yelena's love. He no longer regards Serebryakov with the blind worshiping eyes of the sister and mother, but with the equally subjective lenses of the brother-avenger facing his "worst enemy." The professor's contributions as a scholar, though flashy like his name ("silver," *serebro*), now strike Vanya as shallow and insignificant: "Now he's retired you can see exactly what his life is worth. Not a page of his work will survive him. He's totally obscure, a nonentity. A soap bubble! And I've made a fool of myself, I see it now, a complete fool" (Act II).

The boldness of Vanya's attacks on the professor stems, not only from his conviction that the man is an impostor, but also because he is no longer an effective sexual rival. Physically moribund, "a man in a shell," Serebryakov is now instinctively afraid of the physical threat behind Vanya's hatred, and even refuses to be left alone with him: "No, no! Don't leave me alone with him! No. He'll talk my head off" (Act II). Most importantly, Serebryakov's success as a ladies' man has become suspect, for Vanya is aware that the beautiful Yelena no longer loves her husband and that she too has been blinded by the professor's fame.

When considered against the background of his feelings for Vera and his desire for revenge, Vanya's sudden infatuation and pursuit of Yelena suggest the emergence of a hitherto suppressed and forbidden aspect of his love for his sister. By occupying Vera's position as Serebryakov's wife, Yelena becomes, in effect, Vanya's "foster" sister. But whereas in Vera he recognized only spiritual beauty (as implied by her very name, the Russian "Faith"), Yelena (Helen), the lovely disrupter of tranquility and home, appeals to him physically: ". . . but isn't she lovely? Lovely! She's the most beautiful woman I've ever seen" (Act I). Before her, the brother-protector succumbs to the brother as would-be seducer, one who defies the rival he no longer deems worthy of the sister.[8] Chekhov did not ignore the implied incestuous overtones in the situation; although not stated in *Uncle Vanya*, they are alluded to in the earlier play *Wood Demon* where rumor links the uncle in an affair with Yelena.

> Is nothing sacred to you? You might remember, you and the dear lady who's just gone out, that her husband was once married to your sister. And that you have a young girl living under the same roof. Your affair's already the talk of the whole country. You should be thoroughly ashamed of yourselves. (Act III)

Although Vanya professes a strong physical desire for Yelena, psychologically, he is incapable of attaining his goal. Like Vera, Yelena is a woman to behold, worship, and protect, but never possess. The "sister," in both her spiritual and physical aspects, remains inviolate:

> VOYNITSKIY: You are my happiness, my life, my youth. I know there's little or no chance of your loving me, but I don't want anything from you. Only let me look at you, listen to your voice—
>
> YELENA: Sh! Someone might hear you.
>
> VOYNITSKIY: Let me speak of my love. So long as you don't drive me away, that's all I need to be the happiest man on earth. (Act I)

Vanya remains "prisoner of his passivity, the lack of vigor from which he has always suffered."[9]

If Vera gave the household a reason for its existence and cohesiveness, Yelena upsets its established order and refuses to contribute to its proper functioning, admitting that domestic concerns completely bore her. She sees herself accurately as an episodic figure in the house; inevitably she vitiates every family role she undertakes. Her beauty and sexuality endow her with an energy that lends an element of vitality to the monotonous daily life on the estate and threatens to destroy its very core by exposing and exacerbating family tensions:

> We are in a bad way in this house. Your mother hates everything except her pamphlets and the professor. The professor's overwrought, he doesn't trust me and he's afraid of you. Sonya's annoyed with her father and with me too. She hasn't spoken to me for a fortnight. You loathe my husband and openly sneer at your mother, and I'm so much on edge I've been on the verge of tears a dozen times today. We are in a bad way, aren't we? (Act III)

Yelena finds a certain similarity in character between Vanya and herself—both are "abysmal bores." She regards him more as a brother-confidant than a suitor; his declarations of love and physical attentions clearly exasperate her. By telling him that he should not participate in petty squabbles but mend them, she urges him to resume his role as uncle. At the same time, she prevents him from doing so; her idleness is infectious, and her paralyzing beauty unmans him.

Appropriately, it is a glance from his niece Sonya, reminding him of her dead mother, that brings to the foreground Vanya's guilt about his changed behavior:

> SONYA: The hay's cut, there's rain every day, and it's rotting. And you spend your time on illusions. You've completely abandoned the farm. I do all

the work myself and I'm about at the end of my tether. Uncle, you have tears in your eyes.

VOYNITSKIY: The way you looked at me just now, your dead mother used to look like that. My darling—. *Eagerly kisses her hands and face.* My sister, my darling sister—. Where is she now? *If she only knew! Oh, if she only knew!*

SONYA: Knew what? What do you mean, Uncle?

VOYNITSKIY: It's so painful, such a wretched business. Never mind. I'll tell you later. It doesn't latter. I'll go.(Act II)

In one of his outlandish yet revealing bits of hyperbole, the household hanger-on Telegin provides an insight into the nature of the "wretched business" allued to by Vanya. Upset by Vanya's insistence that Yelena should be unfaithful to Serebryakov because she does not love him, Telegin protests that unfaithfulness in marriage is the same as treason to one's country. Vanya immediately squelches him, as if realizing that he himself has committed a kind of "treason" by surrendering his earlier way of life to the pursuit of Yelena, thereby betraying his sister and the life style he maintained out of loyalty to her. Yet he is at the same time aware that such unfaithfulness is perhaps his and Yelena's only escape from the emptiness of their personal lives to some measure of freedom.[10]

In contrast to Vanya, Sonya (the Russian Sophia) has been endowed with a nature which might have enabled her to move outside the narrow confines of the immediate family and establish a life of her own. From her mother she has inherited spiritual strength, from her father, a sense of purpose, and with Vanya she shares her industriousness. Yet like her uncle, she is sexless, lacking in beauty, and "as a woman" fails to attract the doctor, Astrov, whom she loves "more than my own mother." Astrov claims that he might have considered marriage to Sonya, but Yelena's beauty quickly turns his thoughts to seduction. Sonya is blind to the threat presented by Yelena; at first she distrusts her, for she has taken her mother's place, but eventually the stepmother wins her over (ironically, they even drink a *Bruderschaft*), and Sonya confides in her as she would her mother, confessing her love for Astrov. By accepting the role of confidante and even volunteering to serve as matchmaker, Yelena further injures her family image. In truth she acts as Sonya's rival, not mother, and foils whatever chances her stepdaughter might have had with Astrov, thereby destroying the family's sole hope for a future generation.

Just as Sonya fails to see in her beautiful stepmother a rival for Astrov's attentions, Vanya fails to see that Astrov has replaced Serebryakov as his sexual rival. The two men have been longtime friends; they share intelligence, a life of sacrifice and hard work. If Vanya's concern is for his immediate family and the estate, Astrov, a doctor, concerns himself with the larger community and the forest which he admits is his true love. The "family" gratification which Vanya earlier derived from providing for the future of his kin, Astrov finds in planting trees: "When I plant a young birch and later see it covered with green and swaying in the breeze, my heart fills with pride and I—" (Act I). Both men are infected by Yelena's beauty, but for Vanya it is a beauty to behold, whereas for Astrov, feminine beauty is to be savored and enjoyed. Women for Vanya are fated to be sister-friends; for Astrov, friendship between the sexes can be established only after the woman has been the man's mistress. In some sense, the sexually aggressive Astrov realizes in Vanya's stead his would-be aspect as seducer: he is desired by both his friend's "foster" sister and his niece. There is even a vague hint that the relations between Vera and Astrov were not indifferent: the doctor marks the beginning of his physical decline from about the time of her death. Vanya's disillusionment, on the other hand, appeared the previous year, after Serebryakov's remarriage. The difference in the manner of the two rival friends is highlighted when Vanya, by way of an apology, pleads Yelena's favor with a bouquet of fall flowers, while Astrov, weary of a verbal game of sexual innuendoes, embraces her. As Chekhov himself noted, "Uncle Vanya cries, Astrov—whistles." [11]

The final shattering of Vanya's male ego in the play comes, not when he discovers Yelena in Astrov's arms, but immediately following, at the unprecedented family gathering called by Serebryakov. Significantly, both Vanya and Sonya, the most family-conscious members present, are at the outset reluctant to participate in the event. Vanya is stunned by what he has just witnessed, and Sonya, by Astrov's rejection. The meeting does not bring the family its much-needed unity but hastens its disintegration.

In his proposal to sell the family estate, Serebryakov implements his patriarchal authority to bring about the dissolution of the family hearth. Despite his "fall" from favor in the eyes of all but the mother Mariya Vasil'yevna, he continues as head of the household. "No one questions your rights," Yelena tells him earlier, and she submits when he denies her permission to play the piano. Unfeelingly, Serebryakov equates his brother-in-law's life of labor with the amount of cash that the property will bring for Yelena and himself in the city. Since Vanya's remaining identity is so inextricably bound up with the estate, the proposal that it be taken from its lawful owner, Sonya, the last member of the Voynitskiy line, is tantamount to his emasculation. Nor can he tolerate the humiliating prospect of being reduced to the position of Telegin who, deprived of all family rights, is obliged to live out the rest of his days as a sponger on the estate that formerly belonged to his uncle.[12] Consequently, Vanya's dramatic attempt to assert himself by shooting at the professor is as understandable (even in its choice of weapons) as its abortive outcome.[13] At long last the son openly challenges the father, in this case, an impostor; yet as always, from "a habit of missing,"[14] he is doomed to remain ineffectual before him. And tellingly, it is Yelena who tries to wrest the pistol from him after shooting (from Astrov, however, she takes a pencil as a memento). He even blunders his suicide attempt by failing to keep his new rival Astrov from discovering the morphine he has taken from him. (Suicide by morphine would have enabled Vanya to take posthumous revenge on the doctor by implicating him in the act.)

Vanya's failure as a man extends even to his unsuccessful bid for maternal love. When overwhelmed by the import of Serebryakov's plan, he turns in desperation to his mother for comfort; she not only rejects him,[15] but tells him to heed the professor's advice:

VOYNITSKIY: My life's ruined. I'm gifted, intelligent, courageous. If I'd had a normal life I might have been a Schopenhauer or a Dostoyevskiy. . . . But I'm talking nonsense, I'm going mad. Mother dear, I'm desperate. Mother!

MRS. VOYNITSKIY *sternly:* Do as Aleksandr says. (Act III)

She alone continues to idiolize her ex-son-in-law and prefers him to her own son. Her empty and impassioned preoccupation with liberalism and women's emancipation has deprived the family of a viable mother. Instead, the old nanny, Marina, fills the vacuum by answering the family's need for a nurturing and comforting mother figure. She provides a link between the present and the seemingly happier past. Throughout, she is associated with food and drink.[16] The play opens as she urges Astrov to eat and reassures him with her faith in God. Astrov recognizes her as the only being of whom he is fond: "I don't want anything, I don't seem to

need anything, and there's no one I'm fond of. Except just you perhaps.
. . . I had a nanny like you when I was a little boy" (Act I). The demanding professor responds to her alone when he is ailing, for she sym-
pathizes with his pain and attends to him as she would a child:

> MARINA: . . . Old folks are like children, they want a bit of affection, but
> who feels sorry for old folks? . . . Come along to bed, my dear. Come
> on, my lamb, I'll give you some lime-flower tea . . . I'll say a prayer for
> you.
> SEREBRYAKOV *very touched*: Come on then, Marina. (Act II)

Sonya, too, runs to Marina for solace, not to her maternal grandmother;
the nanny is the only person who senses her vulnerability as an orphan:

> SONYA *pressing to the nurse*: Nanny, nanny!
> MARINA: It's all right, my child. The geese will cackle for a while and then
> they'll stop. . . . They'll cackle a bit and then they'll stop their cackling.
> SONYA: Nanny!
> MARINA *stroking her head*: You're shivering as if you'd been out in the cold.
> There, there, little orphan. God is merciful. A cup of lime-flower tea or
> tea with raspberry jam and it will all pass. . . . (Act III)

Because she represents order and domestic tranquility, Marina complains
most about the Serebryakovs' effect on the household. With a few well-
chosen remarks she ridicules and deflates Vanya's emotional outbursts
and flights of self-dramatization. She compares both his and the professor's antics to those of barnyard animals.

By the end of the play, however, Sonya has taken over the central
female role in the family. Like Marina, she offers food (by contrast, Astrov offers himself to Yelena to be eaten!) but never acquiesces, like the
nanny, to serving vodka in order to mask life's realities. In a play which
abounds with imagery of seeing and nonseeing, Sonya initially opts for
clarity of vision. Even when "it's easier when you don't see," she chooses
to learn Astrov's true feelings for her. She refuses to tolerate her father's
silliness, criticizes her uncle's recent drinking habit which he treats as a
substitute for his earlier illusions in regard to Serebryakov ("When one
has no real existence, one lives by illusions"), and she entreats Astrov not
to drink. For the moment, he complies with her request, but his acceptance of vodka and refusal of bread from Marina before departure punc-
tuate his estrangement.

Denied her dream of becoming Astrov's wife, however, Sonya also seeks an alternative to emotional realities. She becomes surrogate wife, mother, and sister to her uncle. He, in turn, will be her sole male companion and loving mate. She embraces and comforts him, urges him to work, and creates a new illusion, turning his thoughts away from the frustrations of this world to work and the peace of an afterlife, much as Marina had earlier done for Astrov. Her concluding words to Vanya after the Serebryakovs and the doctor have fled the estate incorporate Marina's faith in God and Astrov's reliance on a better future.[17]

Despite his numerous failures, Vanya ultimately manages to keep the estate intact and successfully defends his right to resume his role as uncle and family provider. Because the others have always seen him in that role and have chided him for abandoning it, it is not surprising that they readily forgive his violent aberration: "I've just tried to murder somebody, but no one thinks of arresting me or putting me on trial. So they must think I'm mad" (Act IV). He becomes reconciled with the professor and states his intention to return to the status quo:

> SEREBRYAKOV *to* VOYNITSKIY: We'll let bygones be bygones. So much has happened and I've been through so much and thought so many thoughts these last few hours, I could probably write a whole treatise on the art of living for the benefit of posterity. I gladly accept your apologies and beg you to accept mine. Good-bye.
> VOYNITSKIY: You'll be receiving a regular amount as before. Everything will be just as it was. (Act IV)

Yet Vanya has been deeply shamed by his brief interlude on center stage, and he will never regain his former pride, aware as he now is of his own impotence and the falsity of the man he serves. If by the end of *The Wood Demon* Vanya's predecessor commits suicide, thereby neatly bringing to a close the old gentry line, and Sonya, there an attractive woman, is to marry the play's democratic hero, in *Uncle Vanya* both niece and uncle are doomed to live out a sterile existence on the estate. This sterility is underlined in the stage directions for the fourth act: in the rambling twenty-six-room house, Vanya's room "serves as his bedroom and the estate office." He is, in effect, "married" to the family hearth, unable to leave.[18] Astrov, it is noted, has a table in Vanya's room, but significantly, he is an infrequent visitor to the house. For he finds the atmosphere stifling, as do the other "outsiders." Yelena refers to the house as a crypt, a place of exile, while Serebryakov calls it a labyrinth. All three abandon it at the end of the play.

Vanya is perhaps the most poignant example in Chekhov's plays of a man whose lasting attachment to a sister or mother has decisively affected his desire and ability to lead an independent life, but he is only one of several such ineffectual brothers and sons. Treplev's troubled relationship to his mother in *The Seagull* is recognized as a salient factor in his inability to cope with life and offers striking parallels to the family situation in *Uncle Vanya*.[19] Andrey, in *Three Sisters*, is loved and looked up to by his sisters, but is cuckolded soon after his marriage and turns out to be a disastrous paterfamilias. Finally, the tearful Gayev in *The Cherry Orchard* (Lopakhin refers to him as "an old woman") adores his sister but can do nothing to save the family estate, nor lead a productive life. Each of these men, in his overrefined sensitivity and lack of physical and intellectual vigor, is somewhat of an "old woman," or perhaps an affable and harmless "uncle."

NOTES

1. Maurice Valency, *The Breaking String: The Plays of Anton Chekhov* (New York: Oxford Univ. Press, 1966), pp. 181–203, dwells on the neurotic and masochistic aspects of Vanya's character. Harvey Pitcher, *The Chekhov Play: A New Interpretation* (New York: Barnes and Noble, 1973), pp. 75–78, identifies frustration as the "keynote" of the play but does not focus on the role of the family in determining Vanya's behavior. V. Lakshin, *Tolstoy i Chekhov* (Moscow: Sov. pisatel', 1975), p. 413, is sensitive to the play's text, but mentions the family only in passing. Daniel Gillés, *Chekhov: Observer without Illusion*, trans. C. L. Markman (New York: Funk and Wagnalls, 1967), p. 295, recognizes the family as a source of Vanya's dilemma but barely touches on this line of thought: "[Vanya] begins to wonder whether he himself has been the dupe of family feeling." See also V. Yermilov, *Dramaturgiya Chekhova* (Moscow: GIKL, 1954), pp. 138–39.

2. Isaak Gurvich, *Proza Chekhova: chelovek i deystvitel'nost'* (Moscow: GIXL, 1970), pp. 38–39, observes that number of Chekhov's heroes and heroines of the 1890s suffer from disenchantment with their "calling": ". . . at times the juxtaposition of a person as he is with his name becomes the vehicle of a story, gives rise to a special plot interest." In this regard Z. Papernyy, "Syuzhet dolzhen byt' nov . . . ," *Voprosy literatury*, No. 5 (1976), pp. 182–83, notes that Chekhov's titles tend to be pivotal for a work; thus, the change of the play's title from that of the earlier version, *The Wood Demon*, to *Uncle Vanya* points to the new

significance that attaches to Vanya and his family role. It ironically underlines the hero's ill-fated attempt to assume a more central role in life (and onstage). G. Berdnikov, *Chekhov-dramaturg* (Moscow: Iskusstvo, 1972), p. 173, ignores this important shift in emphasis by dismissing the title change as irrelevant and stressing Astrov as the central character.

3. The literary-theatrical committee of the Malyy Theater that first reviewed the play found among its shortcomings that "the change in Voynitskiy's attitude toward the professor, whom he previously worshipped, is incomprehensible" and that it is inexplicable how Voynitskiy could go after Serebryakov with a pistol. See the notes to A. P. Chekhov, *Sobraniye sochineniy*, 12 vols. (Moscow: GIXL, 1963), IX, 689–90. Later critics, including Valency, Pitcher, Yermilov, Lakshin, and Berdnikov, tend to ignore the impact that the disruption of the family circle by the remarriage has had on Vanya, disregarding the information that his disillusionment begins, not with the arrival of the Serebryakovs, but further back. Vanya has been "different" and "unrecognizable" for a year already, from about the time of the marriage.

4. Otto Rank, *Das Inzest-Motiv in Dichtung und Sage* (Wien: Franz Deuticke, 1926), p. 407, writes of the close connection between the sibling complex and the parent complex: ". . . she (the sister) is first considered as the mother's rival, but may shortly take over her position as the ideal substitute. In his fantasy she then assumes the role of the ideal of the pure woman, of which the mother, through her relationship with the father in the eyes of the boy, has for the most part become unworthy."

5. I have used the English version in Anton Chekhov, *Uncle Vanya*, in *The Oxford Chekhov*, trans. Ronald Hingley (London: Oxford Univ. Press, 1961). The canonical Russian text of *Dyadya Vanya* is in *Sobraniye Sochineniy*, IX, 482–532.

6. An echo of Vanya's dilemma, one that underscores the relevance of the dead sister in his life, is heard in the fate of Telegin, godfather of Vanya's niece Sonya. Because of his unappealing appearance, Telegin's wife abandons him the day after their wedding: yet he remains true to her and gives up his property to support her children by another man. When this man dies, the wife, as Telegin understands it, is left with nothing, whereas he himself still has his pride. The parallel between Vanya's devotion to Vera and that of Chekhov's sister to Chekhov is striking. Their relationship is discussed at length by Virginia Llewellyn Smith, *Anton Chekhov and the Lady with the Dog* (London: Oxford Univ. Press, 1973), pp. 165–72. Surprisingly, she says almost nothing about *Uncle Vanya*, although it seems highly relevant for her study.

7. See John T. Irwin, *Doubling and Incest/Repetition and Revenge: A Speculative Reading of Faulkner* (Baltimore: Johns Hopkins Univ. Press, 1975), p. 47: "On the one hand, there is an aggressive reaction of the son toward the castrating father, a desire for the father's death, a desire to kill him. But on the other hand, there is a tender reaction, a desire to renounce the object that has caused the

father's anger by assuming a passive, feminine role in relation to him—in short, to become the mother in relation to the father."

8. See Valency, p. 196, and Irwin, p. 28.

9. Valency, p. 184.

10. See Gurvich, p. 114.

11. Konstantin S. Stanislavskiy, *Sobraniye sochineniy*, 3 vols. (Moscow: Iskusstvo, 1954), I, 232.

12. Karlinsky notes that the loss of the family homestead, a recurring theme in Chekhov's work, has a basis in the writer's own biography. See Simon Karlinsky and Michael Heim, *Anton Chekhov's Life and Thought: Selected Letters and Commentary* (Berkeley, Calif.: Univ. of California Press, 1975), p. 441.

13. An illuminating discussion of the shooting incident and Vanya's failure to commit suicide is to be found in Z. Papernyy, "Rozhdeniye syuzheta," in *Chekhovkoye chteniye v Yalte* (Moscow, 1973), pp. 39–51.

14. Valency, p. 190.

15. Her behavior suggests that of the "terrible," "denying" mother discussed by Erich Newmann, *The Great Mother: An Analysis of the Archetype*, trans. Ralph Manheim (Princeton, N.J.: Princeton Univ. Press, 1972), pp. 66–68.

16. J. L. Styan (*Chekhov in Performance* [Cambridge: Cambridge Univ. Press, 1971], p. 102) takes a harsher view of Marina, referring to her comfort as "dried religious fatalism" and her offer of food as a "comical greeting" to Astrov's longing for human affection.

17. One hardly need view Sonya's resignation as an indication of "deep religiosity," as does David Magarshak, *Chekhov the Dramatist* (New York: Hill and Wang, 1960), p. 224. Nor does the "weight" of the play deny Sonya "her faith before she opens her mouth" (Styan, p. 98). For a summary of J. J. Moran's "poll" of readings of the play's ending, see Styan, pp. 140–41.

18. "From the time of puberty onward the human individual must devote himself to the great task of *freeing himself from the parent*: and only after this detachment is accomplished can he cease to be a child and so become a member of the social community. For a son, the task consists in releasing his libidinal desires from his mother, in order to employ them in the quest of an external love-object in reality. . . . In neurotics, however, this detachment from the parents is not accomplished at all; the son remains all his life in subjection to the father and incapable of transferring his libido to a new sexual object." Sigmund Freud, *A General Introduction to Psychoanalysis*, trans. Joan Rivière (1924; rpt. New York: Pocket Books, 1975), pp. 335–46.

19. For a discussion of Treplev's relationship to his mother, see Thomas G. Winner, "Chekhov's *Seagull* and Shakespeare's *Hamlet*: A Study of a Dramatic Device," *American Slavic and East European Review*, 15 (1956), pp. 103–11, and Robert L. Jackson, "Chekhov's *Seagull*," in *Chekhov: A Collection of Critical Essays*, ed. Robert L. Jackson (Englewood Cliffs, N.J.: Prentice Hall, 1967), pp. 99–111. Of note also is Pitcher's treatment, pp. 51–52, and Valency, p. 195.

DRAMATIC STRUCTURE IN CHEKHOV'S *UNCLE VANYA**

BY PHILIP BORDINAT

Anton Chekhov's *Uncle Vanya* has often been criticized as being aimless, implying a lack of sound dramatic structure. Yet the play confounds these formalist critics by continuing to be successful on the stage. My view is that the play is built on a rigid structural framework and that the play does possess specific direction.

Chekhov was certainly conscious of the need for a basic framework for his plays. The following statement from one of his letters indicates his realization of the importance of climax in a play:

> The first act can go as long as an hour, but the others must not take longer than thirty minutes. The climax of the play must occur in the third act, but it must not be too big a climax to kill the fourth act. [1]

In addition to Chekhov's concern with climax, this passage suggests his interest in proportion. Yet this passage, though it suggests a consciousness of some of the structural problems of the playwright, tells us little about *Uncle Vanya*. It is in the examination of the play in the light of some of the basic rules for constructing a play that the structure becomes clear. We can see, then, that there is an aim and that *Uncle Vanya* adheres to the conventional structural pattern of exposition, dramatic incident, rising action (through a series of complications), climax, and resolution.

For these formal qualities to become evident, however, the reader must accept a unique idea of protagonist in *Uncle Vanya*. The suggestion is here advanced that there is no single protagonist in the play; rather, the protagonist is "the individual." Thus, the protagonist is no one char-

* Reprinted from *Slavic and East European Journal*, Vol. 16 (1958), 195–210, with the kind permission of the editor.

acter throughout the play, but each character during the time when he is attempting to find some value in Chekhov's Russian "wasteland." In other words, the protagonist is "the individual" in the abstract.

The question may be raised at this point: "But what about Vanya? Surely he is the protagonist." It is true that Vanya is onstage for a major portion of the play; it is also true that, when he is not onstage, he is often kept before us through the conversations of the other characters. On the other hand, there are extended periods when the audience is far more concerned with the fate of Astrov, Yelena, or Sonya than they are with Vanya. It is a rule of the drama that the fate of the central character should always be paramount in the minds of the audience. Such is not the case in our reactions to Vanya nor to any other single character in the play. Rather, we are concerned with the series of bids by "the individual," whichever character it might be, for some kind of value or happiness in the provincial Russian "wasteland" that Chekhov pictures for us.

It is well to remember that *Uncle Vanya* is a revision of his early, less controlled play, *The Wood Demon*.[2] Chekhov, in his revision, supports the idea of no single protagonist by, in a sense, leveling the characters relative to their respective interest value for an audience. The fact that the name of the play was changed from *The Wood Demon*, which refers to Khrushchev, Doctor Astrov's counterpart, to *Uncle Vanya* reflects such a change of thinking on the part of the playwright. Consistent with this change of thinking is the omission of Yegor Voynitskiy's (Vanya in *Uncle Vanya*) suicide. Thus, Vanya is carried through to the final curtain. Furthermore, in *Uncle Vanya* Chekhov makes Sonya much more appealing and Yelena more cowardly than either was in *The Wood Demon*. All of these changes suggest that Chekhov was bringing these characters to the level of protagonist, thus enabling each to be "the individual" during a part of the play.

Let us now consider dramatic structure. A basic structure test that is often applied by playwrights to a new play idea is that of the *fighting triad*. Samuel Seldon describes the fighting triad in this way:

> Nearly all successful plays are built around a triad so arranged as to imply a conflict.

PRINCIPAL FORCE   OPPOSING FORCE   DECIDING AGENT

> The Principal Force is that driving desire of the central character which motivates the action. It is his desire for an object or person, or for a change

of condition. The Opposing Force is the desire of someone else—a rival, foe, or other inimical presence—to block the fulfillment of the first character's want. And the Deciding Agent is that thing which finally turns the course of the conflict to the advantage of the first or the second force. The age-old plot involving two men and a girl is a perfect example of the triad.

Principal Force	Opposing Force	Deciding Agent
The desire of the man for the girl.	The desire of the rival for the same girl.	The mind of the girl.[3]

If the fighting triad is applied to *Uncle Vanya* with Vanya or any single character as the central character, the term "principal" could hardly be used because there are similar forces in the other characters which often occupy audience interest for significant periods of the play. On the other hand, if "the individual" is considered as the central character, the triad applies.

Principal Force	Opposing Force	Deciding Agent
The individual's desire for happiness.	The Provincial Russian "wasteland."	The overpowering quality of the Russian "wasteland."

Through the use of "the individual" as protagonist, the playwright avoided the impossible task of having to create an all-encompassing, everyman character to give his play universal significance. Instead, he achieved this appeal through four characters. Two are men, one a doctor and the other a gentleman farmer; and two are women, one married, physically beautiful and spiritually ugly, and the other unmarried, physically unattractive and spiritually beautiful. However, though the introduction of "the individual" as protagonist simplified one problem it intensified another, the problem of exposition.

The major exposition of any play is difficult; but in *Uncle Vanya*, in addition to the usual details of time, place, and situation, four major characters had to be developed in enough detail to make each one of them of central interest to an audience during that portion of the play in which he would represent "the individual."[4] In a sense, it was the problem of introducing four protagonists. In accomplishing this huge task, Chekhov violated a number of fundamental rules; yet the results are rewarding. In the opening scene of the play, Chekhov violated a cardinal rule of dramatic exposition in that he introduced two characters who both know all of the information that must be imparted to the audience. Thus, the questions which Doctor Astrov puts to Marina, the nurse, are unnatural in that he already knows the answers to them:

> MARINA *pours out a glass of tea:* Here, drink it dearie.
> ASTROV *reluctantly accepting the glass:* I don't feel like it somehow.
> MARINA: Perhaps you'd like a drop of vodka?
> ASTROV: No. I don't drink vodka every day. It's too close anyway. *A pause.*
>   By the way, Nanny, how many years is it we've known each other?
> MARINA *pondering:* How many? The Lord help my memory. . . . You came
>   to live around here . . . well, when was it? . . . Sonechka's mother,
>   Vera Petrovna, was still living then. You came to see us for two winters
>   when she was alive. . . . That means that at least eleven years have gone
>   by. . . . *After a moment's thought.* Maybe more. . . .
> ASTROV: Have I changed a lot since then?
> MARINA: Yes, a lot. You were young and handsome then, but you've aged
>   now. And you're not as good looking as you were. There's another thing
>   too—you take a drop of vodka now and again. (I, 93)[5]

At this point, Astrov takes up the story and proceeds to give an extended answer to his own question. In most plays having a major character put two such contrived questions about himself to another character and then having him launch into an extended, inadequately motivated self-analysis in answer to his own question would be the worst kind of dramaturgy. However, in *Uncle Vanya*, Chekhov's violation of convention seems to fit into context, in that he was attempting to create an atmosphere of boredom in which people act without reason. Here people talk about the past because there is little meaning in the present or hope for the future; there is only the past when there was still hope for a good life.

The entrance of Uncle Vanya illustrates another break with dramatic convention, for there is absolutely no preparation for his entrance. He simply appears, yawning, upon the stage, having just awakened from a nap. Then, in answer to the question "Had a good sleep?" he proceeds to given an extended treatment of the upset in his living routine since the professor and his wife came to live with them, thus for the first time mentioning the dramatic incident. The effect of this speech on the audience is much like the feeling produced on an individual who has politely asked another "How are you?" and is forced to listen to an extended analysis of that person's medical history. The information is hardly interesting in itself, but the surprise of the reply holds the audience. In both cases, we have a bore; yet we are compelled to listen. Vanya's speech, in addition to accentuating the utter boredom of the situation, initiates the preparation for the entrance of Professor Serebryakov and his wife, Yelena.

A brief discussion of the professor's upsetting habits precedes his and Yelena's entrance. The entrance seems to come too soon, for we have learned nothing about Yelena. The audience can only assume that she is the right age and type for the professor. Chekhov outraged dramatic convention in getting them onstage, for he had the couple enter with Sonya and Telegin. Vanya (Voynitskiy) draws the attention of the audience to the entrance when he says:

VOYNITSKIY: They're coming, they're coming! Don't fuss!

> *Voices are heard.* SEREBRYAKOV, YELENA ANDREYEVNA, SONYA, *and* TELE-GIN *approach from the farther part of the garden, returning from their walk.*

SEREBRYAKOV: It was beautiful, beautiful! . . . Wonderful scenery!
TELEGIN: Yes, Your Excellency, the views are remarkable.
SONYA: To-morrow we'll go to the plantation, Papa. Would you like to?
VOYNITSKIY: Tea's ready, my friends!
SEREBRYAKOV: My friends, will you be good enough to send my tea to my study? I've something more I must do to-day.
SONYA: I'm sure you will like it at the plantation.

> YELENA ANDREYEVNA, SEREBRYAKOV, *and* SONYA *go into the house.* TELE-GIN *goes to the table and sits down beside* MARINA.

VOYNITSKIY: It's hot and close, but our great man of learning has got his overcoat and goloshes on, and he's carrying his umbrella and gloves.
ASTROV: He's obviously taking care of himself. (I, 95–96)

This apparently premature entrance seems to serve the function of a preview, for three important characters merely pass through. Yet, the brief conversation identifies Professor Serebryakov and his daughter, Sonya, while Telegin stops on stage to contribute to the ensuing discussion. Yelena crosses the stage and exits. Yet, with Sonya identified through her reference to "Papa," the audience would realize that the other woman is Yelena, the professor's wife. This realization would come as a shock to the audience, for she is much too young for the professor, and she is beautiful. Audience curiosity regarding Yelena would be aroused at this point, and Vanya's comments would accentuate this curiosity:

VOYNITSKIY: But how lovely *she* is! How lovely! I've never seen a more beautiful woman in all my life.

Then he adds:

Her eyes . . . a wonderful woman! (I, 96)

These two utterances by Vanya would create a desire in the audience to have another look at the woman, seen only briefly, who could motivate such comments.

The four characters representing "the individual," or the protagonist, have been presented to the audience during the first quarter of the first act. The remainder of the exposition consists of dialogues which elaborate on these characters and on the antagonist, Serebryakov. Some of these speeches are long and often about the speaker, himself. Here again Chekhov reinforced the utter boredom and hopelessness of the situation, for the boring situation is often characterized by people talking at length about themselves and what they might have been. The following speech by Vanya is typical:

Oh, yes! I used to be an inspiring personality who never inspired anybody!
. . . A *pause.* I used to be an inspiring personality! . . . You could hardly have made a more wounding joke! I'm forty-seven now. Up to a year ago I tried deliberately to pull the wool over my eyes—just as you do yourself with the aid of all your pedantic rubbish—so that I shouldn't see the realities of life . . . and I thought I was doing the right thing. But now—if you only knew! I lie awake, night after night, in sheer vexation and anger—that I let time slip by so stupidly during the years when I could have had all the things from which my age now cuts me off. (I, 100–101)

Reflected here is both the boredom and the hopelessness of Vanya's and, for that matter, the provincial Russian's situation. A desert much like T. S. Eliot's "Wasteland" is suggested when Astrov comments on wanton waste, later in the first act:

You can burn turf in your stoves and build your barns out of stones. . . . Well, I would consent to cutting wood when people really need it, but why destroy the forests? The Russian forests are literally groaning under the axe, millions of trees are being destroyed, the homes of animals and birds are being laid waste, the rivers are getting shallow and drying up, wonderful scenery is disappearing for ever—and all this is happening just because people are too lazy and stupid to stoop down and pick up the fuel from the ground. *To* YELENA. Isn't it so, Madam? Anyone who can burn up all that beauty in a stove, who can destroy something that we cannot create, must be a barbarian incapable of reason. Man is endowed with reason and creative power so that he can increase what has been given him, but up to the present he's been destroying and not creating. There are fewer and fewer forests, the rivers are drying up, the wild creatures are almost exterminated, the climate is being ruined, and the land is getting poorer and more hideous every day. (I, 103–4)

Here we have a Russian "wasteland" characterized by boredom, hopelessness, destruction, and lack of creativity. The intellectual sterility is evidenced by the professor, who is described as "a dull old stick, a sort of scholarly dried fish." The reference to dryness is significant in this and in the reference to "the rivers . . . getting shallow and drying up . . ." in the above quotation. Both augment the impression of a "wasteland."

Thus Chekhov effectively acquainted the audience with the major characters, the mood, the setting, and the dramatic incident of the play.[6] It is true that he violated certain dramatic conventions, but he seems to have gained rather than lost from these violations.

Early in the first act, Chekhov began to develop suspense according to the fighting triad, through three dramatic situations each involving an attempt by "the individual" to find a measure of happiness in the provincial Russian milieu. The three situations are as follows:

1. The attempt of Vanya to secure the love of Yelena.
2. The attempt of Astrov to secure the love of Yelena.
3. The attempt of Sonya to secure the love of Astrov.

Each of these situations holds our attention for a part of the play, but no one of them dominates throughout.

The first hint we have of Vanya's desire for Yelena occurs early in the first act when he comments on her loveliness as she is leaving the stage for the first time (I, 96). The situation is finally resolved in the fourth act. Coming between these passages are three other scenes involving Vanya and Yelena, one in each of the first three acts. Each of these scenes ends in complete frustration for Vanya. The scene at the end of the first act is typical:

YELENA: . . . Perhaps, Ivan Petrovich, you and I are such good friends just because we both are such tiresome and boring people. Tiresome! Don't look at me like that, I don't like it!

VOYNITSKIY: How else can I look at you if I love you? You are my happiness,

my life, my youth! I know the chances of your returning my feelings are
negligible, just zero—but I don't want anything—only let me look at you
and hear your voice. . . .
YELENA: Hush, they might hear you! *They go into the house.*
VOYNITSKIY *following her:* Let me talk of my love, don't drive me away—that
in itself will be such great happiness to me. . . .
YELENA: This is a torture. . . . (I, 105–6)

The suspense generated during a scene of this kind is considerable. The
same may be said of the scenes between Astrov and Yelena.

The Astrov-Yelena situation develops possibly more suspense than the
Vanya-Yelena situation because the characters are attracted to each
other. Once more Chekhov initiated suspense by a subtle hint when Yelena says to Vanya in the first act:

The doctor has a tired, sensitive face. An interesting face. Sonya is obviously
attracted by him; she's in love with him, and I understand her feelings. He's
visited the house three times since I've been here, but I'm shy and I haven't
once had a proper talk with him or been nice to him. He must have thought
me bad-tempered. (I, 105)

In the second act, Astrov describes Yelena as "an exceptionally attractive
woman!" (II, 113). Later in the act, he says to Sonya:

What still does affect me is beauty. I can't remain indifferent to that. I
believe that if Yelena Andreyevna wanted to, for instance, she could turn
my head in a day. . . . But that's not love, of course, that's not affection.
(II, 118)

Shortly after this speech, Astrov and Yelena are bracketed together.
Sonya says to Yelena:

Tell me honestly, as a friend. . . . Are you happy?

YELENA: No.
SONYA: I knew that. One more question. Tell me frankly—wouldn't you
have liked your husband to be young?
YELENA: What a little girl you are still! Of course I should. *Laughs.* Well,
ask me something else, do. . . .
SONYA: Do you like the doctor?
YELENA: Yes, very much. (II, 120)

Then Yelena speaks at length in praise of Astrov. Finally, the preparation
for the big scene between Astrov and Yelena is complete. The lines im-

mediately preceding the scene reflect the playwright's skill in bringing his audience up to a high level of expectation. Yelena soliloquizes first about Sonya, and then she continues about Astrov:

> . . . To fall under the fascination of a man like that, to forget oneself.
> . . . I believe I'm a little attracted myself. . . . Yes, I'm bored when he's not about, and here I am smiling when I think of him. . . . Uncle Vanya here says I have a mermaid's blood in my veins, "Let yourself go for once in your life." . . . Well, perhaps that's what I ought to do. . . . To fly away, free as a bird, away from all of you, from your sleepy faces and talk, to forget that you exist at all—everyone of you! . . . But I'm too timid and shy. . . . My conscience would torment me to distraction. . . . He comes here every day. . . . I can guess why he comes and already I feel guilty. . . . I want to fall on my knees before Sonya, to ask her forgiveness and cry. . . . (III, 126–27)

At this moment, when Yelena's mind is full of her feelings for Astrov, he shocks her from her thoughts:

> ASTROV *comes in with chart:* Good-day to you! *Shakes hands.* You wanted to see my artistic handiwork? (III, 127)

From this point, Chekhov increases the suspense by having Astrov bore her with talk about the maps of his reforestation projects. Then, when she admits to being bored, the playwright once more delayed the intimate scene that must come by shifting the conversation to Sonya's love for Astrov. Finally, he shifted the discussion to their own relationship:

> ASTROV: . . . There's only one thing I don't understand: Why did you have to have this interrogation? *Looks into her eyes and shakes his finger at her.* You're a sly one!
> YELENA: What does that mean?
> ASTROV *laughs:* Sly! Suppose Sonya is suffering—I'm prepared to think it probable—but what was the purpose of this cross-examination? *Preventing her from speaking, with animation.* Please don't try to look astonished. You know perfectly well why I come here every day. . . . Why, and on whose account—you know very well indeed. You charming bird of prey, don't look at me like that, I'm a wise old sparrow. . . .
> YELENA *perplexed:* Bird of prey! I don't understand at all!
> ASTROV: A beautiful, fluffy weasel. . . . You must have a victim! Here I've been doing nothing for a whole month. I've dropped everything, I seek you out hungrily—and you are awfully pleased about it, awfully. . . . Well, what am I to say? I'm conquered, but you knew that without an

interrogation! *Crossing his arms and bowing his head.* I submit. Here I am, devour me!

YELENA: Have you gone out of your mind?

ASTROV *laughs sardonically:* You are coy. . . .

YELENA: Oh, I'm not so bad, or so mean as you think! On my word of honor! *Tries to go out.* (III, 130–31)

In spite of Astrov's persistence, Yelena continues to resist him. Thus Yelena's lack of courage, which keeps her from defying convention, forces Astrov back into the utter boredom of his life as a country doctor and dooms her to the boredom of her marriage with the professor. Their bids for happiness are frustrated.

Sonya's attempt at happiness with Astrov is also frustrated. The doctor, who despite his submission to his environment could react to the superficial beauty of Yelena, is dulled to the point of being incapable of reaction to the less obvious but more substantial beauty of Sonya. Chekhov made this situation more poignant by having Sonya confess her love for Astrov to Yelena, who in turn acts as an unsuccessful emissary to Astrov. Chekhov here achieved added suspense, for the audience is concerned not only with Astrov's reaction to Yelena's mission but also with Sonya's reaction to the disappointing news. Here is one of the most emotionally moving scenes in the play, for the playwright arranged to have Sonya learn the unhappy news at the professor's meeting. Thus, she must suffer while in the group rather than alone:

SEREBRYAKOV: But where are the others? I don't like this house. It's like a sort of labyrinth. Twenty-six enormous rooms, people wander off in all directions, and there's no finding anyone. *Rings.* Ask Mar'ya Vasil'yevna and Yelena Andreyevna to come here!

YELENA: I'm here.

SEREBRYAKOV: Please sit down, my friends.

SONYA *going up to* YELENA, *impatiently:* What did he say?

YELENA: I'll tell you later.

SONYA: You're trembling? You're upset? *Looks searchingly into her face.* I understand. . . . He said he wouldn't be coming here any more . . . yes? *A pause.* Tell me: yes? YELENA *nods her head.*

SEREBRYAKOV *to* TELEGIN: One can put up with ill health, after all. But what I can't stomach is the whole pattern of life in the country. I feel as if I had been cast off the earth on to some strange planet. Do sit down, friends, please! Sonya!

SONYA *does not hear him; she stands and hangs her head sadly.* Sonya! A *pause.* She doesn't hear. *To* MARINA. You sit down too, Nanny. (III, 132–33)

At this point, shortly before the climax of his play, Chekhov introduced a flash of humor. The professor facetiously informs the group that "the Inspector General is coming." This attempt at humor, coming while the audience is still reacting to Sonya's suffering and contrasting with the mood pervading the theater at the moment, helps to emphasize Sonya's suffering. The laugh evoked is a cruel trespass upon Sonya in her grief.

The professor's proposal brings our attention back to Vanya and, therefore, justifies the name of the play. The professor, in an effort to escape completely from the discouraging provincial atmosphere by selling this Russian country estate, endangers the material security of Vanya and Sonya. Furthermore, there is the danger of Vanya's having Yelena drift completely out of his life. This danger, however, relates only to the first of the three dramatic situations mentioned earlier in the discussion. Yet, the professor's proposal is a threat to "the individual" in each of the other two dramatic situations, as well; for Yelena would also be removed from Astrov's life; and Astrov, without a place to visit, would be removed from Sonya's life. Furthermore, Astrov would have no escape from his day-to-day routine and, as a result, no one with whom to discuss his theories of lost opportunity. However, it is Vanya who protests indignantly and then accuses the professor of ruining him:

I will not be silent! *Barring* SEREBRYAKOV'S *way.* Wait, I haven't finished yet! You've ruined my life! I haven't lived. I have not lived! Thanks to you I've destroyed, I've annihilated the best years of my life! You've been my worst enemy! . . . My life is ruined! I have talent, courage, intelligence. . . . If I had had a normal life, I might have been a Schopenhauer, a Dostoyevskiy. . . . Oh, I'm talking rubbish! . . . I'm going out of my mind. . . . Mother, I'm in despair! Mother! (III, 136–37)

Yet, in his protest, Vanya is outlining not only his own lost opportunities but those of "the individual"—Sonya, Astrov, Yelena, and even the professor—all whose hopes are crushed in the Russian provinces. The climax, which follows immediately with Vanya's abortive attempt to shoot his "worst enemy," symbolically reflects the frustration of "the individual," his inability to carry through to completion any plan requiring decisive action.

In the final act, Chekhov resolved each of the three dramatic situations in a way that shut out hope for value or happiness for "the individual." First, Astrov and Yelena say good-bye forever:

> ASTROV: It is strange somehow. . . . Here we've known one another, and all at once for some reason . . . we shall never see each other again. That's the way with everything in this world. . . . While there's no one here— before Uncle Vanya comes in with a bunch of flowers, allow me . . . to kiss you . . . good-bye. . . . Yes? *Kisses her on the cheek.* There . . . that's fine.
>
> YELENA: I wish you every happiness . . . *Looks around.* Well, here goes— for once in my life! *Embraces him impulsively, and both at once quickly step back from each other.* I must be off.
>
> ASTROV: Go as soon as you can. If the horses are ready, you'd better be off!
>
> YELENA: I think someone's coming. *Both listen.*
>
> ASTROV: Finita! (IV, 146–47)

Following this exchange, Vanya bids farewell to Yelena:

> VOYNITSKIY *warmly kisses* YELENA'S *hand.* Good-bye. . . . Forgive me. . . . We shall never see one another again.
>
> YELENA *moved:* Good-bye, dear Ivan Petrovich. *Kisses him on the head and goes out.* (IV, 147–48)

Finally, Sonya and Astrov part:

> SONYA: When shall we see you again?
>
> ASTROV: Not before next summer, I expect. Hardly in the winter. . . . Naturally, if anything happens you'll let me know and I'll come. *Shakes hands with them.* Thank you for your hospitality, your kindness . . . for everything, in fact. *Goes to the nurse and kisses her on the head.* Goodbye, old woman!
>
> MARINA: So you're going before you've had tea?
>
> ASTROV: I don't want any, Nurse.
>
> MARINA: Perhaps you'll have a drop of vodka?
>
> ASTROV *irresolutely:* Perhaps. . . . (IV, 149)

Chekhov quickly resolved the three dramatic situations and, at the same time, brought his play back to the point where it opened, that is, with Marina's offering Astrov "a drop of vodka." It is as if nothing has happened; yet something has happened. "The individual," represented by Vanya, Astrov, Sonya, and Yelena, has been defeated; nor is there hope for "the individual," whether it be Yelena committed to a life of boredom with the professor or the others doomed to the unrelieved lethargy of the Russian provinces. Astrov has already spoken the epitaph:

> The people who come a hundred years or a couple of hundred years after us and despise us for having lived in so stupid and tasteless a fashion—perhaps they'll find a way to be happy. . . . As for us. . . . There's only one hope for you and me. . . . The hope that when we're at rest in our graves we may see visions—perhaps even pleasant ones. *With a sigh.* Yes, my friend! In the whole of this province there have only been two decent, cultured people—you and I. But ten years of this contemptible routine, this trivial provincial life has swallowed us up, poisoned our blood with its putrid vapors, until now we've become just as petty as all the rest. (IV, 143)

Chekhov has, in *Uncle Vanya*, written a play that obeys the rules of dramatic construction if the reader will accept the idea of the protagonist's being "the individual." Without the idea of "the individual" in *Uncle Vanya*, our interest shifts from one character to another in a way that implies not a single motivating force, but a separate force for each of the three important dramatic situations in the play. Thus, these three situations seem unrelated dramatically. However, when "the individual" is accepted, the "individual's" desire for happiness becomes the central motivating force in the play. At this point it can be seen that the three important dramatic situations are related dramatically to each other; and the structural framework of exposition, dramatic incident, rising action, climax, and resolution becomes clear.

NOTES

1. David Magarshack, *Chekhov the Dramatist* (New York: Hill and Wang, 1952), p. 46.

2. *The Wood Demon* was completed in October 1889 and first produced on December 27 of the same year. *Uncle Vanya* was completed before the end of 1896 and first produced on September 30, 1899. Chekhov achieved far greater economy and polish in *Uncle Vanya* than he had in *The Wood Demon*. In characterization, for example, he secured greater concentration by cutting the number of characters from thirteen in *The Wood Demon* to nine in *Uncle Vanya*.

3. Samuel Seldon, *An Introduction to Playwriting* (New York, 1946), p. 41.

4. In 1900 Chekhov was faced with a similar problem of exposition in *Three Sisters*. He says in a letter to Gor'kiy, dated October 16, 1900, "It has been very difficult to write *Three Sisters*. Three heroines, you see, each a separate type and

all the daughters of a general." See Constance Garnett, trans., *Letters of Anton Chekhov* (New York: Macmillan, 1920), p. 400.

5. All quotations from *Uncle Vanya* have been taken from Elisaveta Fen, trans., *The Seagull and Other Plays* (London: Penguin Classics, 1954).

6. The dramatic incident is the entrance of Professor Serebryakov and his wife, Yelena. The impact of the professor and Yelena upon the several protagonists of the play causes each of these protagonists to make one last attempt to find happiness. The suspense of the play depends upon audience concern as to the outcome of these attempts.

THREE SISTERS, OR
TAKING A CHANCE ON LOVE

BY KARL D. KRAMER

For all the talk about *Three Sisters*, it is still extraordinarily difficult to determine exactly what the play is about. One prominent school places the emphasis on the sisters as inevitably ruined creatures. Beverly Hahn, for instance, speaks of the "inbuilt momentum towards destruction" in the sisters' world.[1] Another commentator claims that we cannot avoid contrasting the success of Natasha and Protopopov with the failures of the sisters.[2] We might do well to examine just what the first two do achieve: a house, an affair, and a businesslike manipulation of the professional positions of the others. It would, of course, be absurd to suggest that the sisters have in some way failed because they do not aspire to such heights of crass avarice as Natasha and Protopopov. But there is still the claim that the sisters continually yearn for a quality of life that they do not possess, and yet do very little, if anything, to make their dreams come true. Chekhov invited this response by initiating the to Moscow line. That goal remains unattained, while the desires of Natasha and Protopopov are richly fulfilled. This seems to present an opposition between those who get what they want and those who don't, as if the goals were equivalent, but abilities not. Natasha wants the big house on the hill and a union with the man who runs things in town—the boss. These may be attainable prizes, and certainly Natasha does wrestle their house away from the sisters, but the sisters never really enter into combat with her over such issues. If they did, they would themselves be transformed into first-class Natashas, an extremely dubious achievement at best. Natasha sees living in the big house at the top of the hill as an end in itself. The sisters' aspirations go considerably beyond this. Moscow as destination is equally illusory. Natasha, incidentally, isn't even up to that aspiration on the fanciful scale; she's quite content with a good view in a city much like Perm. The questions the sisters seek answers to are considerably more basic: how to seize and properly evaluate one's own experience, how to cope with experience, and when all one's delusions have been cast aside how to go on somehow from there. The particular area of experience around which the majority of the action in the play revolves is the question of love. The stance of nearly every character is determined by his ability to establish a close relationship with another. Love gone awry is in most instances the pattern. Ol'ga seems to have the least chance of finding a mate—a situation to which she has become largely reconciled, though in Act I she chides Masha for failing to value the man she does have. Kulygin himself—aware of the failure of his own marriage—pathetically suggests to Ol'ga in the third act that if he hadn't married Masha, he would have married her. Irina ultimately admits that her desire to reach Moscow is directly connected with her desire to find her true love. Masha is the only one of the sisters who does at least temporarily find real love, and in this sense her experience is the standard against which the experience of nearly all the other characters is to be measured. Chebutykin once loved their mother but has long since lost that love, and with it his involvement in actual experience. Solenyy, on the other hand, capitalizes on his inability to inspire love by deliberately creating hostile relationships. But to determine the structure of the play as a whole and the way in which the experience depicted adds up to a statement about human capabilities, we must look in considerably more detail at the variety of responses to love among the main characters.

It is Andrey's fate to make the most ghastly miscalculation of them all in believing he loves Natasha. How could he, an educated man, brought up in the same environment as his sisters, believe he has fallen in love with her? Masha in the first act discounts the possibility that he could be serious about her. The answer seems to lie in a recognition that he has been constantly living under pressures he can't bear. "Father . . . oppressed us with education. . . . I grew fat in one year after he died, as if my body were liberated from his oppression," he tells Vershinin.[3] He has been preparing for a university career, bowing to his father's wishes— a course he abandons immediately after his marriage. Since the father's death, Andrey has been under constant pressure from his sisters to deliver them from this provincial town. His love for Natasha is simply a means of escaping these various responsibilities, which have been thrust upon him. But a relationship based on such motivation becomes a trap from which Andrey desperately wishes to escape. In some dialogue that Chekhov eventually deleted from the play, Andrey dreams of losing all his money, being deserted by his wife, running back to his sisters, crying, "I'm saved! I'm saved!"[4] In the finished play, Andrey and Chebutykin argue about the efficacy of marriage, Andrey maintaining it is to be avoided, Chebutykin asserting loneliness is worse. But by the end of the play, even Chebutykin admits that the best course for Andrey is to leave, "leave and keep going, don't ever look back" (XI, 295). This is, indeed, the course Chebutykin himself adopts at the end of the play. Andrey's escape from responsibility through love thus seems to lead only to an entrapment from which he would be only too happy to flee by the end of the play. His predicament stems not so much from Natasha's nature as from his own desire to avoid experience by hiding behind a very illusory kind of love.

Chebutykin's problems turn equally on love. He had at one time known a real love for the sisters' mother. That has long been in the past, but the only vaguely positive way he can deal with immediate experience is by the illusion that this love can be sustained through his relationship with the sisters, particularly Irina. His other protective screen is his growing insistence that nothing and nobody really exists and that therefore nothing matters. In his first appearance at stage center, he is talking sheer nonsense about a remedy for baldness and duly noting down this trivia. Shortly thereafter in Act I he displays his tender—almost sentimental—affection for Irina by presenting her with a silver samovar on her name day. The fact that the silver samovar is the traditional gift on the twenty-fifth wedding anniversary surely suggests that he is honoring the memory of the woman he loved and is exploiting the occasion of Irina's name day for this purpose. During the first two acts he alternates between these two poles—the attempt to sustain a lost love and an abiding interest in trivia. The chief sign of the latter is his constant reading of old newspapers, a device for distracting himself from the actuality of the present moment.

In Act III his failure to handle his experience reaches a crisis when, drunk, realizing he is responsible for the death of a woman who was under his care, he retreats into a pretense that nothing and nobody exists.

It may be a measure of his feeling that he so retreats, but I would suggest that he associates this recent death with that death in the past of the woman he loved. Death has denied him his love, and the recent event vividly reminds him of his own earlier loss. Within moments of this breakdown he smashes the clock which had belonged to the sisters' mother. This may of course suggest that he is trying to destroy time itself, which separates him from his love, but he is also deliberately destroying a material object that belonged to her; it may also be a gesture of denial— a denial that his love ever existed. He tries to cover this by suggesting that perhaps there was no clock to break, and he accuses the others of refusing to see that Natasha and Protopopov are having an affair. The assumption is that if others don't see what's right before their eyes, why shouldn't Chebutykin refuse to recognize anything in the world that may hurt him? In any case, what comes out of this episode is our discovery that Chebutykin cannot deal with a death that takes away his love. His final stance in the play—"The baron is a fine fellow, but one baron more or less, what difference does it make?" (XI, 294)—is a pathetic indication of the lengths he is driven to in trying to cope with a love long since lost.

Solenyy is the only character in the play who turns away from love— turns away so completely that he commits himself to murder instead. He has an uncanny knack for turning a situation that is initially friendly into one of enmity. In Act II Tuzenbakh attempts to bury the hatchet with Solenyy, who immediately denies that there is any animus between them, thus provoking an argument and indirectly testifying to the correctness of Tuzenbakh's view of their relationship. Their discussion ends with Solenyy's "Do not be angry, Aleko" (XI, 271), which distorts Tuzenbakh's friendly overtures into a rivalry, presumably over Irina. Dissatisfied in his exchange with Tuzenbakh, Solenyy seizes upon the first opportunity for further quarrel. Chebutykin enters, regaling Irina with an account of a dinner given in his honor. He is particularly pleased with the *chekhartma* (lamb). Solenyy insists that *cheremsha* (an onion) is totally disagreeable. This pointless argument ends with a victory on Chebutykin's side when he says: "You've never been to the Caucasus and have never eaten *chekhartma*" (XI, 271). Chebutykin is the clear victor here, because Solenyy prides himself on being a reincarnation of Lermontov, the nineteenth-century Russian romantic poet whose setting is regularly the Caucasus Mountains. To suggest that Solenyy has never been there totally undercuts his stance as a hero in the Lermontov mold. Having lost the argument with Chebutykin, Solenyy immediately proceeds to avenge himself in the best Lermontov tradition by picking a quarrel with Andrey over the number of universities in Moscow. It is true that he declares his love for Irina toward the close of Act II, but one senses that he had expected a cool reception from her. In any case, the scene ends with what seems to be Solenyy's real message—that he will brook no rivals. To put it another way, Solenyy employs his declaration of love to establish a hostile relation with Tuzenbakh. We might also view the episode as a parody of the opening scene in Act II, where Vershinin declares his very real love to Masha. The initial exchange between Masha and Solenyy in the first act suggests that we are to view them as polar extremes in some sense. Solenyy's first speech implies a $1 + 1 = 3$ equation: "With one hand I can lift only fifty-five pounds, but with two hands I can lift a hundred and eighty—two hundred, even. From that I deduce that two men aren't twice as strong, they're three times as strong as one man . . . or even stronger . . ." (XI, 244). Masha's opening speech implies a retort to Solenyy: "In the old days, when Father was alive, there'd be thirty or forty officers here on our name days, there was lots of noise, but today there's a man and a half . . ." (XI, 247). In view of the fact that the only officers present are Solenyy, Tuzenbakh, and Chebutykin, Masha's equation is apparently $3 = 1.5$. Solenyy immediately picks up on this banter, if that's what it is, and compares one man philosophizing with two women trying to philosophize, the latter being equal to sucking one's thumb. Masha thereupon cuts him off: "And what is that supposed to mean, you terribly dreadful man?" (XI, 247). This exchange between Masha and Solenyy in the opening moments of *Three Sisters* is a vitally important one because, on the question of love, they represent polar extremes within the play: Masha is willing to take a chance on love; Solenyy can only capitalize on love as a pretense for a duel.

The wooing scenes between Vershinin and Masha are masterpieces in Chekhov's whimsical art. The process is initiated in the first act as Ol'ga and Irina laugh together over recollections of Moscow. It is Masha who suddenly pins down a real moment of connection in their lives when she recalls that they used to tease Vershinin as the lovesick major. In the first of his rather protracted philosophical speeches, Vershinin offers a justification for existence in response to Masha's statement that the sisters' lives will go unnoticed. She immediately responds to his attention by announcing she'll stay to lunch after all. This exchange initiates that special relationship between them. Shortly after this, Vershinin offers Masha another view with which she must be wholly in sympathy: ". . . if I were to begin life over again, I wouldn't get married. . . . No! No!" (XI, 254). This is the precise moment Chekhov chooses for Kulygin's entrance.

In Act II, Vershinin's speech on what life will be like in two or three hundred years is clearly directed toward Masha; indeed, his philosophical ramblings are primarily a way of wooing her. She understands this and laughs softly during his speech. Tuzenbakh is clearly not privy to this particular form of lovemaking. He believes he is engaged in a serious discussion with Vershinin and cannot understand why Masha is laughing. Vershinin, of course, has no reason to ask. It is interesting to note, incidentally, that in his musings about the future Vershinin almost never responds to Tuzenbakh's attempts to join in the discussion. Indeed, Chekhov revised the text of *Three Sisters* at a number of points to eliminate Vershinin's responses to Tuzenbakh's remarks.[5] In the first act Tuzenbakh announces Vershinin's arrival to the assembled company; Vershinin ignores the introduction and proceeds to identify himself by name. In his first monologue on the future, Vershinin dismisses Tuzenbakh's attempt to enter the discussion with a curt "Yes, yes, of course" (XI, 251). In the musings about life in two or three hundred years in Act II, Vershinin suggests the theme and Tuzenbakh offers his opinion about the future. Vershinin is apparently ruminating on his own views as Tuzenbakh speaks—the stage direction reads: "*After a moment's thought*" (XI, 266). His subsequent remarks bear no relation to Tuzenbakh's; we get the distinct impression that Vershinin has not the slightest interest in a debate, thus emphasizing the real motive for his musings, to converse indirectly with Masha. The ostensible discussion continues with Masha's observations on the necessity for meaning in life:

It seems to me a man must believe, or search for some belief, or else his life is empty, empty. . . . To live and not know why the cranes fly, why children are born, why there are stars in the sky. . . . Either you know what you're living for, or else it's all nonsense, hocus-pocus. (XI, 267)

In effect, her words confirm her need for the kind of reassurance Vershinin has been offering her, that what man is presently doing is creating the possibility for future happiness and understanding. Vershinin's next line—"Still it's a pity our youth has passed" (XI, 267)—is almost a reproach to Masha: since youth has passed and each of them is set in his respective relationship, their mutual happiness is impossible for any protracted period of time. Masha greets his reproval with the famous line from Gogol': "It's dull in this world, gentlemen." Tuzenbakh, not comprehending the private dialogue, answers with a paraphrase of Masha's reference to Gogol', expressing his frustration over a conversation he was never meant to follow. Chebutykin does apparently follow at least the drift of the conversation—love—as he notes that Balzac was married in Berdichev. Irina, either consciously or unconsciously, picks up on this drift as she repeats Chebutykin's observation. Tuzenbakh, now attentive to one strand in the discussion—what can we do with our lives?—announces he's leaving the service. Having argued that life will always be pretty much the same, he now asserts that he will change the direction of his own. This is an important aspect of that contradiction of position so characteristic of Tuzenbakh and Vershinin. It is highly ironic that Vershinin consistently denies there is any happiness for us now, while achieving at least a momentary happiness with Masha. Tuzenbakh, on the other hand, argues that he is happy right now, in his love for Irina, while he is denied any return of that love. Masha, characteristically, disapproves of his determination to change, feeling herself denied any such opportunity.

In the third act, Vershinin's musings on life in the future are a direct response to Masha's arrival on the scene. After Chebutykin's rather shocking references to Natasha having an affair, perhaps partly to distract everyone's attention from the assumption that he and Masha are, too, Vershinin launches into a peroration on what his daughters have yet to go through in their lives. When Masha enters, he almost immediately shifts theme from daughters to life in the future, as though the topic has already become a secret code between them. His musings are intermixed with his laughter and expressions of happiness. Everybody has fallen asleep except Masha and Vershinin, making clear that his philosophizing *is* a way of talking about love. The episode ends with their strange love duet from Chaykovskiy's *Yevgeniy Onegin*.

Near the end of the third act Masha has her frank talk with her sisters. Ol'ga refuses to listen; Irina listens most attentively, as she presumably longs for a love of her own. Despite Ol'ga's disclaimers, Masha's confession of love brings the sisters closer together than they have been at any point in the play thus far and prepares the way for their final scene of coming together in the finale.

In the fourth act Masha speaks to Chebutykin of her love, implicitly comparing her own position with his at an earlier time:

MASHA: . . . Did you love my mother?
CHEBUTYKIN: Very much.
MASHA: Did she love you?
CHEBUTYKIN *after a pause:* That I don't remember anymore.
MASHA: Is mine here? That's the way our cook Marfa used to speak of her policeman: mine. Is mine here?
CHEBUTYKIN: Not yet.
MASHA: When you take happiness in snatches, in little pieces, and then lose it as I am, little by little you get coarse, you become furious. . . . (XI, 293)

The ambiguity in Chebutykin's reply to Masha's question about her mother is remarkable. Is he trying to protect the honor of the woman he loved? Did she perhaps not return his love? Or is his reply part of his attempt to deny the past experience itself? We have no way of knowing. Masha's use of "mine" must refer to Vershinin, and Chebutykin so understands it. If he thought she were speaking of her husband, he could not reply "Not yet," for he has just seen Kulygin go in the house. Masha's remarks on happiness contain little joy, and yet she is admitting she has now known love, and the indications are that it will not turn her away from experience as it has Chebutykin. We shall see more of this in the finale.

As far as love is concerned, Irina would seem to be in the best position of the three sisters. She is unattached; two suitors pursue her; and yet she is unhappy because there is an imaginary third lover, whom she associates with Moscow. It is the dream of going to Moscow that animates her in the first act, and, although it is not clear why Moscow is so important to her at this point, it does become clear by the end of Act III. Still, there are hints, even in the opening scene, that it is love Irina seeks.

When Tuzenbakh reports the arrival of the new battery commander, it is Irina who pricks up her ears, inquiring, "Is he old? . . . Is he interesting?" (XI, 244). Her desire to work looks like a second choice, and Tuzenbakh is at his most pathetic as he tries to ingratiate himself with her by sharing her desire for work: "That longing for work, Oh Lord, how well I understand it!" (XI, 245). Tuzenbakh seems to use the work theme to promote his standing with Irina in very much the way Vershinin talks of the future to woo Masha. Irina's cry at the end of Act II—"To Moscow! To Moscow! To Moscow!"—suggests that it is an appeal to love, if we look at the context out of which it arises. Solenyy has just made his rather ridiculous and thoroughly repulsive declaration of love to her; Vershinin has just returned bearing the news that his wife didn't poison herself after all; Kulygin is unable to find his wife; Natasha has just left with Protopopov; Ol'ga makes her first appearance in the act, complaining of professional responsibilities and of Andrey's gambling losses. Each situation suggests an abortive love relationship, including the absence of a love for Ol'ga. If all this is what provokes Irina's cry, it may well mean she is looking to Moscow for the kind of love that is simply unavailable to her here.

Her association of Moscow with love becomes explicit in the third act when she says: "I always expected we would move to Moscow, and there I would meet my real one, I've dreamed of him, I've loved him. . . . But it seems it was all nonsense, all nonsense . . ." (XI, 285). In the final lines of Act III she agrees to marry the baron, but still wants to go to Moscow: ". . . only let's go to Moscow! I beg you, let's go! There's nothing on earth better than Moscow! Let's go, Olya! Let's go!" (XI, 288). These words come after Masha's declaration that she loves Vershinin and would seem to suggest that though Irina has agreed to marry Tuzenbakh, she looks forward to finding her real love elsewhere, as Masha has.

Ol'ga has had the least opportunity to find happiness through love, and yet Ol'ga seems to cope with her situation better than the other two. She has very nearly reconciled herself to a single life even at the opening of the play, and during the course of it she expresses her love in an entirely different fashion. We see her love in her readiness to help with both clothing and lodging for those who have been left homeless by the fire;

we see it in her comforting Irina in the third act and in the way she silently acquiesces to Masha's love for Vershinin, as she steps aside to allow them their last moment alone together.

Finally, we must compare the situations at the opening of the play and at its end to gather some measure of just what the intervening experience has meant for the sisters, how it has altered their conceptions of human possibility. Harvey Pitcher has observed that the fourth act is very nearly an "inversion" of the first.[6] He lists any number of actions and situations that occur in Act I and again in altered form in the fourth. He makes a convincing argument for seeing the finale as a negation of most of the positive elements that appeared in the opening, but I think that in addition to such negations, we see a number of positive elements in the finale that invert the hopeless and desperate attitudes of the opening. In one sense, the play moves from both naïve faith and despair to a heightened awareness of possibilities in life and a more solidly rooted ability to endure. At the opening, the sisters are both physically and temporally separated; Ol'ga is primarily oriented to the past as she recollects the death of their father a year ago and comments on how the last four years at the high school have aged her. Irina disclaims any interest in this past, as she remarks to Ol'ga: "Why talk about it?" (XI, 243). She also shares some of Irina's naïve faith in a future in Moscow, but even Moscow is in part a past orientation; certainly for Ol'ga it must be, since she is the eldest and would have the clearest memory of what their life had been like there. Irina's Moscow, on the other hand, is the land of the future; she can look only forward to Moscow and to going to work. Masha restricts her observations to an occasional whistle, is not particularly interested in either Ol'ga's sense of the past or Irina's hopes for the future; she is, as she sees it, buried in a present without hope. When Ol'ga suggests that Masha can come up to Moscow every summer to visit them, Masha's only comment is to whistle, as if, knowing her own present, she recognizes Ol'ga's wishful thinking as a mere whistling in the wind. Perhaps Masha's only departure from a present orientation is her remark about her mother: "Just imagine, I've already begun to forget her face. Just as they won't remember us. They'll forget" (XI, 250). But even here she seems to exploit both past and future to affirm the worthlessness of present existence. Thus, at the opening the sisters are totally at odds, as they contemplate three different perceptions of reality. Perhaps the only common strain here is their shared dissatisfaction with the present.[7] Spatially, there is some sense of their occupying a restricted area, particularly with Ol'ga, who either sits at her desk correcting papers or walks to and fro about the room. Even Masha seems initially restricted to her couch. Temperamentally, they are also separated from one another here, each involved in her own activity—Ol'ga correcting, Masha reading, Irina lost in thought, their dresses dark blue, black, and white.

Ol'ga's opening speech is full of strands connecting past, present, and future:

> Father died exactly a year ago on this very day, the fifth of May, your name day, Irina. It was very cold then, snow was falling. I thought I couldn't bear it, you lay in a dead faint. But a year has passed and we remember it easily; you're wearing a white dress now, your face is radiant. *The clock strikes twelve.* And the clock was striking then. *Pause.* I remember, when they were carrying Father, there was music playing and they fired a volley at the cemetery. (XI, 242–43)

The play opens with the recollection of a death, just as it will end with the news of a death at the present moment. At the same time, Ol'ga's recollection of death is associated with birth; it is also Irina's name day. Ol'ga's reflections next focus on the difficulty of facing the loss of a father whom both Ol'ga and Irina presumably loved, but, as if in anticipation of their stance at the end of the play, Ol'ga notes that they did survive the calamity. In short, Ol'ga's speech is a kind of summary of their reactions to calamitous experience: it is both unendurable and endurable, and calamity itself is mixed with elements of joy. The contrast between the weather a year ago and the weather today ("sunny and bright") underscores a recurrent cycle of anguish and joy. The funeral music of the military band of a year ago will be transformed at the end of the play into music that is played "so gaily, so eagerly, and one so wants to live" (X, 303).

The process of redressing natural relationships which were at the very least strained in Act I gets under way near the end of Act III. First, there is Masha, who refused to join in the sisters' conversation at the opening. In Act III she draws the sisters together, although against Ol'ga's better judgment, in her frank discussion of her love for Vershinin. This is followed shortly by Andrey's confession to at least two of his sisters that he is desperately unhappy, which constitutes a considerably more honest response to the family than his rapid departure from the scene as early as possible in Act I. The setting in Act IV is the garden attached to the house. On the one hand, it is true that Natasha dominates the house, but at the same time, if we recall that sense of the sisters' confinement in the living room of Act I, there is a compensatory feeling of openness in Act IV. The garden is unquestionably preferable to the living room now, and one is uncertain whether the sisters have been evicted or liberated— perhaps a combination of the two. The final tableau certainly contrasts the separation the sisters felt in the opening scene with their physical closeness at the end—"*The three sisters stand nestled up to one another*" (XI, 302). But the physical closeness reflects a far more basic sense of unity. Harvey Pitcher has quite justly commented on this scene: "The sisters feel perhaps closer to one another now than they have ever done before."[8] In the departure of the regiment and the death of Tuzenbakh, they give themselves to one another as they have not done earlier. They give themselves to their love for one another and discover a strength in this to endure.

Masha has the first of the sisters' final speeches, and I would like to look at her words, not as they are printed in texts today, but as they appear in Chekhov's original version of the speech, which, unfortunately in my view, has never been restored to the play. The speech was cut at the request of Ol'ga Knipper, who found the lines difficult to speak.[9] It would appear that Chekhov silently acquiesced. I've indicated the deleted lines by brackets:

> Oh, how the music is playing! They are leaving us, one has really gone, really and forever; and we'll stay here alone to begin our lives anew. I shall live, sisters! We must live. . . . [*Looks upward.* There are migratory birds above us; they have flown every spring and autumn for thousands of years now, and they don't know why, but they fly and will fly for a long, long time yet, for many thousands of years—until at last God reveals to them his mystery. . . .][10]

The reference to migratory birds connects a series of images that run through the play and that have two reference points for their meaning. The first is the rather familiar metaphor of birds' flight as man's passage through life. Irina is the first to use the image in Act I: "It's as if I were sailing with the wide blue sky over me and great white birds floating along" (XI, 245). Chebutykin picks up on this metaphor in Act IV when he tells Irina: "You have gone on far ahead, I'll never catch up with you. I'm left behind like a migratory bird which has grown old and can't fly. Fly on, my dears, fly on and God be with you" (XI, 291). Chebutykin makes the metaphorical meaning clear here: he may be too old a bird to continue the flight himself, but Irina must of necessity be engaged in her passage through life. Shortly after this Masha refers to the birds, apparently with reference to Vershinin: "When Vershinin comes, let me know. . . . *Walks away.* Migratory birds are leaving already. . . . *Looks upward.* Swans, or geese. . . . My dear ones, my happy ones . . ." (XI, 294). Like Chebutykin, Masha here refers to others whose lives go on, but in her final speech her "we must live" is connected with the bird imagery so that it becomes a positive image for her as well; her life—the life of all the sisters—will go on.

There is a second reference point for her speech, however, and that occurs in Act II when Tuzenbakh, as well, invokes the image. It comes in the midst of that scene in which Vershinin muses about the future, as a way of wooing Masha—a scene in which Tuzenbakh is largely left out of the proceedings. He says: "Migratory birds, cranes, for instance, fly and fly and whatever great thoughts or small may wander through their heads, they'll go on flying, knowing neither where nor why. They fly and will fly whatever philosophers may appear among them; and let them philosophize as much as they like, so long as they go on flying . . ." (XI, 267). Masha's last speech is equally a tribute to Tuzenbakh. In paraphrasing his lines she both acknowledges his conception of experience and reconciles it with her own point of view, that eventually we must have some understanding of why we do what we do. Irina's betrothed— whatever the degree of affection she may have had for him—has just died. Masha has just parted with the man she loves, but she transforms their shared sorrow into a virtual panegyric to Tuzenbakh and finds in it a reason why the sisters must go on living.[11] In any case, the sisters have clearly come a long way from that point a year before the play began when death seemed unendurable.

In Ol'ga's final speech she answers that remark of Masha's in Act I— "they'll forget us too"—when she says: ". . . They'll forget us, forget our faces, our voices, and how many of us there were, but our sufferings will be transformed into joy for those who live after us, happiness and peace will reign on the earth and they will remember with a kind word and bless those who are living now" (XI, 303). Essentially, she is reiterating Masha's appeal that we must go on living because the experience is worth the effort, and reaffirming that the purpose will be revealed in the future. But whether it is or not, the continuation of living is essential.

The sisters' final speeches are interspersed with Chebutykin's nihilistic observations on the total indifference of the universe to anything that happens. The interchange may be read as an ultimately ambivalent attitude toward the nature of experience, or it may be read as a final tribute to the sisters' faith. They have not retreated to Chebutykin's fatalism, though their experience of love has been no more encouraging. The final interchange between Chebutykin and the sisters may suggest not an either/or response to life, but a measure of their capacity for endurance. After all, love is largely a matter of faith.[12]

NOTES

1. *Chekhov: A Study of the Major Stories and Plays* (New York: Cambridge Univ. Press, 1977), p. 289. Hahn also offers a representative discussion of Natasha's role in ruining the sisters (p. 301).

2. Harvey Pitcher, *The Chekhov Play: A New Interpretation* (New York: Harper and Row, 1973), p. 123.

3. A. P. Chekhov, *Polnoye sobraniye sochineniy i pisem* (Moscow: Ogiz, 1944–51), XI, 253. Further references to the play will be cited by volume and page number in the text.

4. *Literaturnoye nasledstvo: Chekhov*, ed. V. V. Vinogradov et al. (Moscow: Akademiya Nauk, 1960), LXVIII, 69.

5. In *Literaturnoye nasledstvo* two earlier redactions of the play are included (pp. 1–87; see esp. pp. 27, 30, and 41.)

6. *The Chekhov Play*, pp. 119–20.

7. See J. L. Styan, *Chekhov in Performance: A Commentary on the Major Plays* (Cambridge: Cambridge Univ. Press, 1971), p. 162, for some further comments on the sisters' temporal orientation.

8. *The Chekhov Play*, p. 151.

9. See A. R. Vladimirskaya's introduction to the two earlier redactions of *Three Sisters* in *Literaturnoye nasledstvo*, pp. 13–14.

10. *Literaturnoye nasledstvo*, p. 86.

11. To delete the majority of Masha's final remarks may be a tribute to Chekhov's admiration, even love, for Ol'ga Knipper, but I see no reason why modern directors need bow to the actress' difficulties. They might well consider restoring this crowning link in the play's bird imagery.

12. Many of the views expressed in this essay have emerged from interchanges between director, actors, and myself during work on a production of *Three Sisters* in Seattle in the summer of 1978 by the Intiman Theatre Company, Margaret Booker, artistic director.

CIRCLES, TRIADS, AND PARITY IN
THE THREE SISTERS

BY EUGENE K. BRISTOW

Even a casual reading of *The Three Sisters* reveals that the concept of three is somehow intertwined in the fabric of the play. And so it is. No matter what is seen or what is heard, the answer is usually three—or its multiple. Let's begin with, say, the number of characters. Fourteen characters are named in the dramatis personae;[1] there is, however, a fifteenth character—Protopopov, the chairman of the District Council—who never sets foot onstage, but his presence offstage touches or ensnares all members of the Prozorov family, including the three sisters, their brother Andrey, and his wife (after the first act) Natasha. Five of the fifteen are female; the remaining two thirds, male. If Protopopov, his old watchman Ferapont, and the old Prozorov nurse Anfisa are set aside momentarily, the remaining twelve characters divide evenly into soldiers and civilians.

The concept of three shows up in the ages of the characters. For example, at the beginning, Irina, the youngest of the three sisters, is in her twenty-first year. Baron Tuzenbakh is almost thirty; Vershinin is forty-two; Chebutykin is almost sixty; Anfisa is seventy-eight and has been with the family twenty-seven years.[2] All are multiples of three. The calendar time—from the beginning to the end—is three and a half years. The second act takes place twenty-one months after the first; the third, eighteen months later; the last, three months later. The time of day follows a similar pattern. At the beginning, the clock strikes twelve—it is noon. During the second act, the hour of nine in the evening rolls by; during the third, three in the morning; and the last act takes place at twelve noon. Not only is the time of each act three or its multiple, but also the diurnal/nocturnal time span could conceivably total twenty-four hours—

again, a multiple of three. Moreover, even though four acts divide the play, only three settings define the locale: drawing room/ballroom; bedroom; garden.

The basic architecture of the play is apparently constructed in terms of three; that is, three characters, three parts of a triangle, three time orientations (past, present, future), and so on. As the first act begins, so does the last act end. At the beginning, for example, three female characters are downstage, and three male characters are upstage. At the close of the play, three female characters are downstage, and three male characters are upstage.[3] The close of the play is arranged like the beginning, not only to illustrate the circular effect, but also to emphasize the precise balance, or parity, of a six-part conclusion on the meaning of existence. Both concepts of the circle and parity are closely associated with the concept of three in the play.

The effect of Chekhov's opening and closing in *The Three Sisters* is similar to that of the chorus in ancient Greek tragedy; that is, two groups, separated in space, sing and dance their choral odes; the first is called a strophe; the second, antistrophe.[4] At the beginning, the answering group upstage consists of three military officers, Tuzenbakh, Solenyy, and Chebutykin, who are talking together. What is heard by the audience, however, is an ironic comment on what the downstage group (the sisters Ol'ga, Masha, and Irina) is doing and saying. That Chekhov deliberately arranged this opening in terms of the Greek chorus is verified by a comparison of the Yalta manuscript (an early version) with the Moscow manuscript (a late version).[5] The three verbal combinations of the upstage group have been added (*LN*, 20), including Tuzenbakh's apparent comment to Solenyy (in reality, a summary conclusion on the optimistic dreams of the sisters): "You're talking so much nonsense I'm sick of listening to you" (XI, 244). It should be noted that not one character in either group is aware of the chorus device. The aspirations expressed in the downstage odes are consistently denied by the negative comments in the upstage odes. The result is an appropriate stalemate in which the downstage three sisters are perfectly balanced by the upstage three military officers.

The grouping of characters in threes occurs throughout; moreover, membership in one group does not exclude membership in another, since both members and groups are constantly in flux. The Prozorov family is a good example.

Ol'ga

Irina   Masha

Andrey

The family quartet is viewed as a foursome only for a few moments in the first act, when Andrey is called in to meet Vershinin (XI, 251–53), and for a single moment in the third act, just before Masha leaves to meet Vershinin (XI, 286–87). Combinations of these four Prozorovs into threesomes, however, take place on six or perhaps seven occasions. For example, in addition to the opening and close, the sisters share important scenes with Vershinin in Act I (XI, 248–51) and Natasha in Act IV (XI, 301–12) and develop one of their own in Act III (XI, 284–86). Andrey, Masha, and Irina are together for the party in Act II (XI, 271–73), and Ol'ga and Irina behind their screens apparently listen to Andrey's confession near the end of Act III (XI, 287–88). It might be argued that this last scene—the seventh—is not really a threesome, since Andrey is the only visible character onstage, and neither sister acknowledges his presence or his words once they have escaped behind the screens.

The concept of three pervades the stories, particularly the love stories, in the play. Love triangles, with varying combinations, complicate the action, adding interest and suspense. Three triangles are apparently the most important. Baron Tuzenbakh loves Irina, as does Solenyy who tells Irina his feelings in Act II (XI, 273–74).

Irina, however, does not love either one, but is persuaded by Ol'ga in Act III (XI, 285–86, 288) to become the fiancée of Tuzenbakh (Act IV). In the first act, Kulygin loves his wife Masha, who, in turn, is falling in love with Lieutenant Colonel Vershinin (XI, 255, 259). Vershinin declares his love in Act II (XI, 263–64), and in the following act, Masha tells her sisters that she has fallen in love with Vershinin (XI, 286). Masha does not love her husband, nor does Vershinin love his wife. At the end of Act

I, Andrey declares his love to Natasha, and between Acts I and II they marry and Natasha births a son, whom she calls Bobik (XI, 260). Her affair with Protopopov is discussed later in this essay. Andrey, who is very much aware of Natasha's adultery, inexplicably still loves her, as he tells the doctor in Act IV (XI, 294).

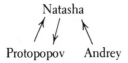

Three subsidiary love triangles exist; one seems more important than the others; and, in terms of parenting, the result is probably conjecture, perhaps even surmise. For example, the old doctor Chebutykin could easily be seen as the surrogate father to the Prozorov children, and perhaps in his special relationship with Irina as her biological father. Both the mother and her husband the general are dead by the time the play begins, and thus their relationship depends solely on Chebutykin's memory. Chebutykin professes his love for their mother on three separate occasions (Acts I, II, IV). As to evidence pertaining to biological parenting, however, whatever conclusion is reached can only be the result of guesswork. In the last act, when Masha asks Chebutykin if their mother loved him, he confesses, after a pause, "That I don't remember anymore" (XI, 293). The other two love triangles are Tuzenbakh-Irina-the man of her dreams and Vershinin-Masha-Vershinin's wife. In terms of the six love triangles, if the Chebutykin-Mother-General triangle of the past is excluded, three characters participate in adulterous affairs (Natasha, Masha, Vershinin), and, if Irina's dream man and Vershinin's wife are included, a total of seven characters experience unrequited love (Irina, Tuzenbakh, Solenyy, Andrey, Kulygin are the five seen onstage).

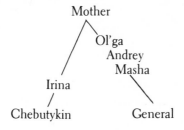

Trios abound throughout, and in keeping with Chekhov's striking a balance, parity is consistently observed. In the first act, for example, Vershinin waxes eloquently on the loss of personal identity, the mutability of human mores, and the essence of culture and education. The three sisters are enchanted, but three other characters are not. Solenyy snarls insults at Tuzenbakh for joining in the philosophical discussion; Chebutykin tries to turn it all into a joke; and Andrey wanders off to his room to play the violin (XI, 250–53).

Linking characters in groups of three is a common technique in *The Three Sisters*. For example, three characters thoroughly enjoy mulling over metaphysical matters, as is evidenced in Act II, when Vershinin, Masha, and Tuzenbakh perform a musical trio on the meaning of life (XI, 265–67). Ol'ga, Kulygin, and Irina (Act IV) are linked by their occupation of teachers and potential teacher. Natasha, Solenyy, together with Protopopov, form another group of three who have been characterized as "the forces of darkness," in opposition to "the forces of life and culture," such as the sisters, Andrey (Act I), Tuzenbakh, and Vershinin.[6] Although three characters play the paino, only Tuzenbakh (Acts I and II) and Natasha (offstage in Act IV) are heard. In Act III, Tuzenbakh claims that Masha is an exceptional pianist, which is denied by Irina's assertion that Masha has forgotten how to play, since she "hasn't played in three years . . . or four" (XI, 280). To illustrate the superiority of Tuzenbakh over Natasha in terms of talent and training, their playing (in performance) reveals a significant contrast between Tuzenbakh's better-than-average rendition of his waltz (Act II) and Natasha's inept thwacking of "A Maiden's Prayer."

In the language itself, Chekhov constructed sets of three. That is, three subjects, verbs, predicates, attributes, and so on, have been carefully threaded into a multitude of words, phrases, clauses, sentences. Indeed, the opening line of dialogue illustrates the basic ternary formula:

Otéts úmer róvno god nazád,	Father died exactly one year ago,
kak raz v étot den',	on this very day,
pyátogo máya,	the fifth of May,
v tvoí imeníny,	on your saint's day,
Irína (XI, 242).	Irina.

The three adverbial modifiers stress in rhythm (accent marks) and sounds (assonance italicized) the ternary construction. What Chekhov begins at the very opening is consistently practiced, with variations, throughout. At times, a word is simply repeated, and a new word added to conclude the threesome.

Vprochem, byl *dozhd'* togda. Sil'nyy *dozhd'* i *sneg.* (XI, 243)[7]

Or perhaps two verbs have been chosen, and one of the two is repeated to make three.

Segodnya utrom *prosnulas'*, *uvidela* massu sveta, *uvidela* vesnu. (XI, 243)[8]

Sometimes a word or phrase is said and then twice repeated by a character, as in the following famous exchange in Act III.

KULYGIN: Ya dovólen, ya dovólen, ya dovólen!
MASHA: Nadoyélo, nadoyélo, nadoyélo . . . (XI, 284)

Kulygin's "I am satisfied" is musically matched by his wife's "[I am] bored." The sense in the exchange (Kulygin's contentment versus Masha's ennui) vies with rhythm (anapests) and sound (Kulygin's *yada* rhymes with Masha's *nada*) to gain control, and the result is a perfect balance at this moment between husband and wife.

Recurring phrases between two characters occur here and there. For example, in the opening moments Ol'ga begins a thought, Irina continues it, and Ol'ga finally concludes it.

OL'GA: I tol'ko rastet i krepnet odna mechta . . .
IRINA: Uyekhat' v *Moskvu.* Prodat' dom, pokonchit' vse zdes' i v *Moskvu* . . .
OL'GA: Da! Skoreye v *Moskvu.* (XI, 243)[9]

It is also apparent that, besides the three instances of v *Moskvu,* Irina's second sentence incorporates three action verbs (the last is missing but is understood as the first word[10] in her speech). As the example illustrates, the unity of the three sisters as a family group is explained in part by Chekhov's subtle use of ternary construction in the dialogue.

Chekhov's preoccupation with trinominal combination in language was not restricted to *The Three Sisters.* In examining the syntax of his stories, both Derman[11] and Yefimov[12] verify the ternary formula and note that it occurs regularly enough in prose written early as well as late in his career to pass muster as a consistent feature of Chekhov's writing style.[13] Moreover, it seems that Chekhov frequently chose this device, according to Derman, "especially in dramatic, lyric, and generally 'touching' places"[14] in the stories. A great share of the lyric and compassionate moments assigned to *The Three Sisters* by critic after critic[15] may be attributed to the trinominal combinations in the dialogue.

Tuzenbakh's farewell scene with Irina in the last act is a good example. In the space of less than a page and a half of printed text, almost a dozen separate sets of trinominal combinations develop contrapuntally elaborations (in rhythms and sounds) on the theme of unrequited love. The scene begins appropriately with Tuzenbakh and Irina commenting on Kulygin, who crosses the stage calling for his wife Masha. Both understand that Kulygin is happy at seeing the soldiers leave, since his wife's lover, Vershinin, is marching away, too.

Tuzenbakh, like Kulygin, is experiencing unrequited love. Tuzenbakh's chief rival in his love triangle, however, is not Solenyy, who is waiting across the river for their forthcoming duel; instead, his chief rival is the unknown man in Irina's dreams. Although Irina and Tuzenbakh plan marriage the next day, she does not love him and tells him so, explaining that her soul "is like a beautiful piano that has been locked up and the key is lost" (XI, 296). This is the second time in the play that a key is mentioned; the first "lost" key apparently prompts Andrey at the end of the third act to seek out Ol'ga and ask for a replacement (XI, 287).[16]

It is apparent that Irina, like Tuzenbakh, is experiencing unrequited love, in that she has not yet met in actuality the man of her dreams. What Tuzenbakh desperately seeks is "only that lost key" (the third and last time a "lost" key is mentioned) that torments his soul and gives him no sleep (XI, 296). He continues:

TUZENBAKH: Skazhí mne chtó-nibud'.	Tell me something.
Pauza. Skazhí mne chtó-nibud' . . .	*Pause*. Tell me something . . .
IRINA: Chto? Chto skazát'? Chto?	What? What (can I) say? What?
TUZENBAKH: Chtó-nibud'.	Something.
IRINA: Pólno! Pólno! *Pauza*.	Enough! Enough! *Pause*.

Occurring as it does in the central moments of their final duo, the sextet of *chtos*—evenly divided between the pair—aptly illustrates their inability to assuage the other's pain. Tuzenbakh's threefold request for "something," or "anything," [17] is crisply denied by Irina's impersonal "what." [18] Even their choice of rhythms is appropriate. Tuzenbakh's dactylic *chtó-nibud'* is countered by Irina's trochaic *chtó skăzát'* and, subsequently, *Pólno! Pólno!*

In Tuzenbakh's long speech following this exchange, he at first tries to explain the events and attitudes leading to the duel. Irina apparently does not understand what he is saying, since he couches his remarks in Aesopian language. Tuzenbakh then turns to the here and now. And to the ternary formula, as well. "As if [it's] the first time in [my] life I [actually] see these *firs, maples, birches*, and everything is *looking* at me, *questioning*, and *waiting*" (XI, 296). His plea that a beautiful life should go hand in hand with the beautiful trees is punctuated by Skvortsov's shout, "Au! Gop-gop!"—a signal reminding Tuzenbakh of the impending duel. Before he goes, however, he sees the dried-up (dead) tree swaying in the wind with the live trees and concludes that he, if he should die, will participate in life (like the dead tree), "in one way or another" (XI, 297). Kissing Irina's hand, he speaks in threes once more.

Tvoi bumagi,
    chto ty mne dala,
    lezhat u menya na stole,
        pod kalendarem. (XI, 297)
	Your papers,
	    that you gave me,
	    are lying on my table,
	        under a calendar.

Their scene breaks off abruptly when Tuzenbakh "quickly leaves" (XI, 297). His departure follows his piddling request that coffee be prepared since, "not knowing what to say," he lamely explains that he had not "drunk coffee today" (XI, 297). Tuzenbakh knows, as does the reader, that he will probably die in the duel. It is, after all, Solenyy's "third duel" (XI, 294), and Solenyy himself predicted three years earlier that Tuzenbakh "will die of a stroke," or Solenyy would lose his temper "and plant a bullet" in his forehead "in about two or three years" (XI, 246). Irina's inability to respond to Tuzenbakh's request that coffee be prepared perhaps only clarifies their understanding that the *coffee* is simply a substitute for her *declaration of love*. In short, the two end their final scene in the same way that Tuzenbakh begins his long speech in it—with Aesopian dialogue.

As the example of the final duo scene between Irina and Tuzenbakh illustrates, the trinominal combinations in the language itself contribute to an understanding of structure, character, and thought. In fact, the duo scenes of Irina and Tuzenbakh in the remainder of the play reveal that the uses of three are subtle, consistent, and—above all—numerous.

Irina and Tuzenbakh have three duo scenes (Acts I, II, IV) where the two are alone; their duo scene in Act III is monitored by Masha, although Tuzenbakh—in the beginning—believes that he and Irina are alone and thus speaks to Irina "tenderly" (XI, 283). Their duo scene in Act II is confined to Irina's complaint of being tired and to Tuzenbakh's ternary statements about his three surnames, the dominance of his Russian qualities over the German, and his persistent attention to Irina's welfare (XI, 264). Their next-to-the-longest duo scene alone, lasting about a half page of printed text, takes place near the end of Act I, when the other characters are upstage in the ballroom. Their conversation is limited to three topics: Solenyy, love/life, and work (XI, 256–57). Their duo scene in Act III, although Masha keeps telling Tuzenbakh to leave the bedroom, is also focused on three topics: work, love/life, and erosion by time (XI, 283).

Not only are trinominal combinations interlaced in the Russian language, but they are also apparent in the other two languages, Latin and French. In keeping with Chekhov's addiction to the concept of three, *The Three Sisters* is indeed trilingual. Latin is spoken by Kulygin who teaches that language in the school; French, by Natasha who is apparently trying to "better" herself. How ironic that the Prozorov family admit their knowledge of three languages (XI, 253) and in reality know twice that number[19] but speak only Russian, whereas Natasha whose origins are socially inferior to the Prozorovs, coming as she does out of the *meshchane* (an estate next to the peasantry in Old Russia), persists in speaking French. She speaks it badly,[20] of course, enough so that Tuzenbakh must suppress his laughter (XI, 270), but she speaks it only two times—once in the second act (XI, 270), and once in the fourth act[21] (XI, 293). French is, however, spoken a third time in the play—by Chebutykin in the second act when he asks Irina to come into the ballroom (XI, 265).

Kulygin's Latin phrases and sentences (two in every act except the second when only one is spoken) can be viewed as annotations, injunctions, or even Chekhovian signatures as to action and character. Two examples may suffice to illustrate the device. In the first act, Kulygin presents Irina with a copy of his book on the history of the school and concludes his presentation speech with a Latin injunction, which reads (in translation): "Do what you can, let those who are able to do it better" (XI, 254). Apparently, he is referring to the result (his book) of his own efforts as historian. When Irina points out that she had already received a copy from Kulygin last Easter, Kulygin then makes a gift of the book to Vershinin—an ironic action, since the book still carries with it the Latin injunction. In a short while, Vershinin and Masha fall in love, and it is apparent that Masha considers Vershinin far superior to Kulygin. Moreover, the Latin injunction pervades other stories in the play, as well as the Kulygin-Masha-Vershinin love triangle. For example, Natasha apparently believes her lover Protopopov abler than her husband Andrey. Irina picks the man of her dreams over both Tuzenbakh and Solenyy. Vershinin prefers Masha to his own wife. And so on throughout the play. In terms of control of the house, for example, both Natasha and Protopopov are superior to the Prozorov family by the end of the play. So is Solenyy topmost when it comes down to dueling.

A second example of Kulygin's Latin takes place in the third act. Chebutykin is drunk and, in a touching speech, excoriates himself and others for their hypocrisy, ignorance, and philistinism (XI, 279–80). Shortly thereafter, Kulygin slaps Chebutykin on the shoulder, thereby appointing to the doctor Cassandra's gift for prophetic truths as he announces, "*In vino veritas*," or "In wine there is truth" (XI, 280). Whatever the doctor says and does in this third act may be considered the truth, or close to the truth, and like Cassandra, the doctor is scarcely listened to. For example, he drops mama's clock, smashing it to pieces—an appropriate action that depicts time itself as going to pieces, or the Prozorov family's dream of Moscow as falling apart, or the very house in which they live as no longer belonging to them. The doctor repeats his nihilistic avowal of nonexistence.[22] And he reports that Natasha is having an affair with Protopopov (XI, 281). Since the rules of linear time no longer apply (mama's clock is smashed to pieces), the doctor's statement about the affair is not only current, but travels back into the past and forward into the future, as well. In fact, Natasha's sexual affair with Protopopov ostensibly begins with their sleigh ride at the end of Act II (XI, 274–76), since Natasha's new child, Sofochka, announced at the beginning of Act III, is probably Protopopov's (XI, 277). It is possible, of course, that the affair began much earlier; for example, Masha—at the beginning of the play—

reports the rumor of their forthcoming "marriage" (XI, 251). Thus, the "truthful" messages—blessed with Kulygin's Latin—that Chebutykin drunkenly brings into the third act reveal incontinence, putridity, even manslaughter.

In addition to the trilingual explorations in sound and sense, three instances of nonsense sounds have been selected, since they permeate certain characters and their actions: Solenyy's barnyard irritant; the love duet between Masha and Vershinin; and the doctor's nihilistic song. Solenyy comes up with the nonsense sound *tsip* three times on each occasion, and since there are five occasions (four in Act I, one in Act III), the sound is heard fifteen times—a multiple of Chekhov's three. It is an irritating sound—high pitched, piercing, grating—and designed by Solenyy to needle his rival Tuzenbakh. Not until act III, when Solenyy quotes from Krylov's "The Geese," is the sound clarified, its origin discovered, and the threat to Tuzenbakh's welfare intensified (XI, 283).

The famous love duet in nonsense sounds occurs in three separate instances in the third act. The first comes after Vershinin sings a line or two from Pushkin's *Yevgeniy Onegin* (the music is probably Chaykovskiy's).

MASHA: Tram-tam-tam . . .
VERSHININ: Tam-tam . . .
MASHA: Tra-ra-ra?
VERSHININ: Tra-ta-ta. *Laughs.* [23]

The three-syllable exchange of vows is undoubtedly their mutual declaration of love, and Masha's agreement to a consummation of their affair probably takes place in their second interaction a few moments later as Vershinin prepares to leave.

VERSHININ: Tram-tam-tam.
MASHA: Tram-tam. (XI, 283)

And their final exchange is heard near the close of Act III.

VOICE OF VERSHININ *offstage:* Tram-tam-tam!
MASHA *Rises, loudly:* Tra-ta-ta!

This last three-syllable interaction is an appropriate culmination of the previous scene between Masha and her two sisters, during which Masha describes her profound, abiding, inexplicable love for Vershinin. When he finally calls her from offstage, she answers boldly and then leaves, knowing full well that she is replacing her reputable marriage state with the life of an adulteress. Her farewell moments with her sisters and brother are impeccable Chekhovian signatures as to the end of one role and the beginning of the next.

The doctor's nihilistic song occurs only in the last act (twice in the early part, twice at the end). It consists of twelve syllables (a multiple of Chekhov's three); the first six are nonsense sounds; the last six essentially mean "Sitting on a curbstone am I" (XI, 290). The entire line, composed in almost perfect dactyls and aptly punctuated with Chekhov's trinary series of three dots, runs: *Tarara . . . bumiya . . . sizhu na tumbe ya . . .* Its apparent purpose is chiefly to help balance the six-part ending of the play.

Another word that seems to be a nonsense sound is the interjection *gop* that appears only in the last act. In Chekhov's day, the sound was used to spur animals into jumping or leaping,[24] and its choice is effective. It is first used at the beginning by Rode.

> *Takes in the garden at a glance.* Farewell, trees! *Shouts.* Gop-gop! *Pause.*
> Farewell, echo! (XI, 289)

As produced at the Moscow Art Theater, there is a third *gop*, that is, the echo itself that is heard in place of the *pause*, and thus Rode's youthful, lyric, compassionate moment of farewell is carefully constructed in threes. A few moments later, Rode repeats his farewell *gop-gop* upstage (XI, 290), and in production the third *gop* is heard. The same interjection, combined with another sound for attracting attention—"Au! Gop, gop!"—occurs three times in the act. In place of the touching effect witnessed with Rode, this phrase is designed to sound a note of impending doom. When it is first heard, for example, Irina "shudders," explaining that "Everything somehow frightens me today" (XI, 291). When it is repeated, it follows Chebutykin's comment on the baron's chances in the duel: "The Baron is a fine person, but one Baron more, one Baron less— what does it matter, anyway! Let them! It doesn't matter!" After the sounds are heard, Chebutykin explains, "That's Skvortsov shouting, he's the second. He's sitting in a boat" (XI, 294). And the last time the phrase occurs, it signals Tuzenbakh to the duel.

Musical instruments and their sounds apparently go in threes, too. In

Act I, three instruments are heard: onstage piano (Tuzenbakh); offstage violin (twice played by Andrey); onstage humming top (Fedotik's gift to Irina). In Act II, three instruments: offstage accordion (heard at the beginning and end of the act); onstage guitar(s) played by Fedotik and/or Rode; onstage piano (waltz by Tuzenbakh). In Act III, the only "musical" instrument is the fire alarm bell that is struck three times (beginning, middle, end). In Act IV, however, a piano and two groups of instruments are heard: offstage piano (Natasha playing "The Maiden's Prayer"); offstage and onstage violin and harp; offstage military band.

Embedded firmly in the play are numerous threads of folksong, poems, folklore, literary allusions and names, and rituals that stitch point to patterns of meaning that are easily understood or felt only by audiences familiar with the Russian language and environment. A partial listing includes writers such as Dobrolyubov, Gogol', Griboyedov, Lermontov; poems such as Krylov's "The Geese" or Pushkin's "Gypsies"; literary concepts like superfluous (*lishniy*), freeloader (*prizhival*), or the universal concept of *poshlost'*.[25] The daily rituals of eating, drinking, and interacting combine with the larger rituals associated with individual rites of passage: celebration of a saint's day in Act I; births (Bobik and Sofochka); and death (Tuzenbakh in Act IV). Group rituals occur throughout, including a rite of intensification in Act II (Carnival Week), as well as that of fighting the town fire in Act III, and the arrival (Act I) and departure (Act IV) of the soldiers. In most of these instances, the concepts of the circle, triads, and parity clarify the patterns and complicate the action of the play. Two examples should illustrate Chekhov's technique.

Early in Act I, the first words spoken by Masha are the opening lines of the prologue to *Ruslan and Lyudmila* (1820) by Aleksandr Pushkin.

> By the curved seashore stands an oak tree green;
> A golden chain to that oak is bound . . . (XI, 246)

Masha then repeats the second line. These lines are appropriate in all aspects: structure, character; thought; diction; music; spectacle. They introduce a long fairy tale that, in turn, is based on seventeenth-century popular narrative, and thus in *The Three Sisters* clarify the beginning of the Vershinin-Masha-Kulygin triangle in terms of awe, mystery, ecstasy of new love. Having introduced Pushkin's poetic image, Masha returns to that image twice. At the end of Act I, these same two lines are repeated by Masha, who then adds, "Now, why on earth do I keep saying this? Those lines have been bothering me since early morning . . ." (XI, 259). What is not said, but is well known to all educated Russians, are the third and fourth lines.

> And linked to the chain with a scholarly mien
> A tomcat is seen going round and round and. . . .[26]

The poetic image of the tomcat chained to, and circling round, the oak tree underscores both the repetition (Act I) and the final effect (Act IV) of Masha's two loves: first, for her husband Kulygin (about four years before the play begins); second, for Vershinin during the course of the play. The cyclical effect of Masha's love is stressed at the end of the first act when Fedotik gives a spinning (and humming) top to Irina, and thus the images of the cat circling the tree, as well as that of Masha and the love cycle, are reinforced both visually and aurally (XI, 259). At this point in Russian productions, all the actors onstage (except Masha) usually "freeze" into a tableau, and only the humming sound of the top and Pushkin's lines, reinforced by the sight of the spinning top and the slight movement of Masha, are heard and seen. Masha's third and last reference to Pushkin's poem occurs immediately following the farewell scene with Vershinin in Act IV. There, of course, she is so distraught, she scrambles the poem and refers to "A tomcat green . . ." (XI, 300). At no point in the play is Masha ever consciously aware of the subtle connections between Pushkin's poem and the complex of emotions, meanings, and action.

A second example of Chekhov's craftsmanship occurs shortly after the introduction of the Pushkin poem in Act I, and like the earlier image, the second is twice repeated; unlike the first, however, the second image exemplifies the action of several characters. Solenyy overhears the sisters in conversation, makes a stupid remark, and is quickly ripped apart by Masha. "What is it you wanted to say, you loathsome, terrible person?" Masha asks, and Solenyy replies, "Nothing at all" (XI, 247). He then adds two lines.

| On akhnut' ne uspel, | Before he had time to let out a yell, |
| kak na nego medved' nasel. | The bear was squeezing him to hell. |

The lines are from *The Peasant and the Workman* (1815), a well-known

fable by Ivan Krylov. By quoting these lines, Solenyy refers to the sud-
denness of Masha's attack; the *he* in the fable is Solenyy himself; and the
bear is Masha. In the last act, Solenyy arrives to take Chebutykin to the
duel and repeats the Krylov lines.[27] Then Chebutykin repeats the same
lines, and it is clear that Chekhov has linked Solenyy and his action to
the action of the bear (XI, 295). The *he* in the fable is associated with
Tuzenbakh. Both the fable and the Pushkin poem meld in the last act.
At the very moment Kulygin forgives Masha for her love affair with Vershinin, the gunshot that kills Tuzenbakh is heard.

> KULYGIN: She's stopped crying . . . she is a good woman . . .
>
> *There is heard a faint shot, far off.*
>
> MASHA: By the curved seashore stands an oak tree green;
>   A golden chain to that oak is bound . . .
>   A tomcat green . . . an oak tree green . . .
> I'm getting it all mixed up . . . (XI, 300)

Not only does Chekhov link the fable and its bear to Solenyy and his
action, but he also links it to Protopopov and his. In Act I, immediately
after Solenyy quotes from Krylov, the nurse Anfisa and Ferapont enter
with a cake—a gift to Irina on her saint's day. Anfisa says, "From the
District Council, from Protopopov, Mikhail Ivanych . . . A cake (XI,
247). It is tempting to associate Protopopov with the two lines in the
fable, particularly with the bear in the fable. The common nicknames of
Mikhail (Protopopov's first name) are *Misha* and *Mishka*, which are also
common nicknames for the Russian bear (*medved'*). The action of Protopopov from beginning to end, as David Magarshack points out, resembles the swift action of the bear in the fable.[28] The *he*, in this instance,
is associated with the three sisters, who have been forced out of their
home by Act IV, whereas Protopopov is comfortably seated inside—a
guest of his paramour Natasha. The last verbal reference to the image of
the bear occurs in French, when Natasha at the window shouts at Andrey: "It's you, Andryusha? You'll wake up Sofochka. *Il ne faut pas faire
du bruit, la Sophie est dormée déjà. Vous êtes un ours*" (XI, 298). In
translation, "Don't make a noise, Sophie is already asleep. You are a
bear." The baby Sofochka at this moment is in the carriage Andrey has
been wheeling outdoors. Natasha then orders Ferapont to take the carriage from Andrey. Natasha's accusation and decision are—unwittingly

for her—ironic comments on the condition of Andrey. He, too, resembles the bear in Krylov's fable. His marriage to Natasha is the beginning of a downward glide that ends in cuckoldry and alienation from his sisters. On the way he mortgages the house to pay his gambling debts, and Natasha holds the money (XI, 284, 288). Andrey is as much the bear as is his rival Protopopov. Moreover, when Natasha shouts, "You are a bear," the *you* can refer not only to Andrey outside but also—unwittingly for Natasha—to Protopopov sitting next to her inside. It may be that the removal of Sofochka from Andrey is perhaps a symbolic gesture of emasculation—as much as it is symbolic of Natasha's drive for order. That is, at the end of the play, Andrey is outside, wheeling his son Bobik, while Protopopov is inside, holding his daughter Sofochka—an effective ironic conclusion, in keeping with Natasha's manipulation of persons. To each child, her or his own father. Both actions are the result of Natasha's own decision (XI, 301).

All these moments grow—not only linearly but also geometrically—into clusters of ideas, feelings, and images that recur, multiply, and strike consistent balances. *The Three Sisters*, perhaps more than any other Chekhovian play, is centrally concerned with the meaning of existence. What goes into the making of happiness? How should we live out our lives? Why do people suffer? "Nothing happens," Ol'ga concludes in Act IV, "the way we want it to" (XI, 299).

Chekhov's questions that he raises throughout the play come together at the very end. Just as the seasons change (each of the four acts takes place during one of the four seasons), the life cycle starts over again at the end. And the ending resembles the beginning. Only a strophe and a half, separated by an antistrophe, conclude the play. It begins with the three sisters downstage, "pressing next to one another," and each sings and dances her own song. Masha begins, and borrowing from Tuzenbakh's ideas, she stresses the necessity of simply to keep on living. Repeating Vershinin's faith in the future, Irina returns to her own beliefs (first expressed in Act I) that personal salvation can be realized only through work. Ol'ga, cribbing too from Vershinin's ideas pertaining to the loss of personal identity and optimism in the future, searches for the raison d'être: "The band plays so joyfully, so happily, and it seems that in a little while we shall know the reason we live, the reason we suffer . . ." (XI, 303). And then Ol'ga adds her famous dactyl plea, "*Yesli by znat'*," which is repeated. The statement, usually translated "If only we knew," is a hypothetical conditional statement, so constructed without a stated subject but with an infinitive. Any subject could be added—*I, you, he, she, one, they*, in place of *we*, or, more to the point—all subjects could be added, thus encompassing everyone in listening range. And so ends the first ode, a three-part harmony on existence.

The antistrophe, consisting of two mute male characters (Kulygin and Andrey) and the speaking doctor, is a three-part answer to the sisters' ode. Kulygin, carrying Masha's hat and cape, is "happy, smiling" (XI, 303), apparently convinced that everything will return to the way it was before Masha's affair with Vershinin. The Latin teacher had previously expressed his belief that life is very real, by no means an illusion, and like the Romans, a person's life style must be ordered, following its routine, regimen, rules (XI, 255). Andrey, emasculated by his wife and neglected by his sisters, wheels the carriage, in which Bobik is sitting, a consistent reminder of his vanished dreams. Earlier in the act, he condemns the town (audience) for their indifference, deceit, and philistinism (XI, 297), charges that could perhaps be leveled at the speaker himself. The third member of the upstage chorus, Chebutykin, sits on a bench and denies the optimism expressed by the sisters. He *"sings quietly."*

"Tara . . . ra . . . boom-di-yah . . . sitting on a curb today . . ." *Reads newspaper.* It doesn't matter! It doesn't matter![29]

The antistrophe ends, and Olga begins the second strophe: "If only we knew, if only we knew!" (XI, 303).

And the curtain falls on two choruses. In each chorus are embodied three characters, each singing and dancing her and his viewpoint on the nature of existence. The play has come full circle, in keeping with the persistent cyclical patterns. Moreover, it has consistently followed the ternary construction from beginning to close. And the characters, usually cast in groups of threes, together with their ideas, emotions, and images, have been carefully balanced to reveal an equivalence rarely seen in the drama since the Renaissance.

NOTES

1. A. P. Chekhov, *Polnoye sobraniye sochineniy i pisem v dvadtsati tomakh* (Moscow: GIKHL, 1944–51), XI, 242. All further references to this work appear in the text with citation of volume and page(s).

2. Anfisa's age is probably unknown; in the dramatis personae, she is listed as eighty; in the third act, however, three years following the beginning, she says she is eighty-one (XI, 277).

3. In his *Chekhov the Dramatist*, David Magarshack inexplicably argues that "only the three sisters take part" in the chorus at the end of the play ([New York: Hill and Wang, 1960], pp. 172, 262–63). His conclusion may be derived from Soviet productions since 1940. That is, in order to stress that a happy, new life is on its way and will be realized with the Revolution in October 1917, some Russian productions of the play since 1940 eliminate the male characters (Chebutykin, Kulygin, Andrey) in the final scene of Act IV and thereby cut out the balancing effect of Chekhov's antistrophe. Such Russian productions therefore create the effect of an optimistic future for the three sisters.

4. David Magarshack examines in detail the beginning of Act I in terms of the Greek chorus convention (pp. 168–73).

5. Both the Yalta MS. and the Moscow MS. (*belovaya redaktsiya*) are reprinted in *Literaturnoye nasledstvo*, (Moscow: Izd-vo Akademii Nauk SSSR, 1960), LXVIII, 1–86. All further references to this work appear in the text with citation *LN* and page number(s). For a discussion in English of the two manuscripts, see Ronald Hingley, *The Oxford Chekhov*, Vol. III (London: Oxford Univ. Press, 1964), pp. 305–12.

6. Robert Brustein, "Chekhov's Dramaturgy in *The Three Sisters*," in *Anton Chekhov's Plays*, trans. and ed. Eugene K. Bristow (New York: W. W. Norton, 1977), pp. 372–80.

7. Of course, (there) was *rain* at the time. (A) heavy *rain* and *snow*.

8. This morning I *woke up*, I *saw* (*at once*) the sunlight everywhere, I *saw* (*at once*) the springtime. . . .

9. *Ol'ga.* And only grows and becomes stronger one dream . . . *Irina.* To leave *to Moscow.* To sell the house, to have done with everything here and (off) *to Moscow* . . . *Ol'ga.* Yes! As soon as possible (off) *to Moscow.*

10. Chekhov added the first sentence in Irina's speech (*LN*, 20), thereby completing the ternary construction in this exchange.

11. A. B. Derman, *Tvorcheskiy portret Chekhova* (Moscow: Izd-vo "Mir," 1929), pp. 250–51.

12. A. I. Yefimov, *Stilistika khudozhestvennoy rechi* (Moscow: Izd-vo Moskovskogo Universiteta, 1961), p. 425.

13. Derman claims that the first Russian critic to discuss ternary language construction in Chekhov's stories was Professor N. N. Sretenskiy (p. 250). Peter Rossbacher notes the ternary language construction in the opening three sen-

tences of *The Seagull* and concludes that those lines are related to the theme. "The Thematic Significance of Four of Chekhov's Stylistic Devices," in *Proceedings: Pacific Northwest Conference on Foreign Languages,* Twenty-First Annual Meeting, April 3–4, 1970, ed. Ralph W. Baldner (Victoria, B.C.: Univ. of Victoria, 1970), p. 141.

14. Derman, p. 252.

15. Among critics who describe Chekhov's music and lyricism are: Charles du Bos, "The Chekhovian Sense of Life: From the *Journal* of Charles du Bos," in *Chekhov; A Collection of Critical Essays,* ed. Robert Louis Jackson (Englewood Cliffs, N.J.: Prentice-Hall, 1967), pp. 184–94; Nicholas Moravčevich, "Chekhov and Naturalism: From Affinity to Divergence," in *Anton Chekhov's Plays,* pp. 286–309; Simon Karlinsky, *Anton Chekhov's Life and Thought: Selected Letters and Commentary* (Berkeley: Univ. of California Press, 1973), pp. 285–88; Nils Åke Nilsson, "Intonation and Rhythm in Chekhov's Plays," in *Anton Čechov: 1860–1960, Some Essays,* ed. T. Eekman (Leiden: E. J. Brill, 1960), pp. 168–80; A. Skaftymov, *Stat'i o russkoy literature* (Saratov: Saratovskoye Knizhnoye Izd-vo, 1958), pp. 313–15.

16. Andrey has "mislaid" (*zateryal*) his key to the cupboard; whereas, Irina's key has been "lost" (*poteryan*). Irina's "lost" key clarifies Andrey's "mislaid" key; what Andrey wants from Ol'ga is, of course, the recovery of their sibling understanding, respect, and love that Andrey himself forfeited by marrying Natasha.

17. The word *chto-nibud'* an also mean "anything." Thus, Tuzenbakh's request for some kind of answer, however minuscule, stresses his feelings of desperation, torment, even insomnia.

18. Irina's question, *Chto skazat'?* is an impersonal construction, meaning not only "What can you," or "What can he," etc. "say?" but also "What can be said?"

19. Andrey claims that his sisters and he know French, German, English, and that Irina also knows Italian; add to his three languages the knowledge of Greek and Latin from their school days and Russian.

20. Natasha's word order is Russian, not French.

21. In each instance, Natasha has three topics. In Act II, she begs to be excused; she tells Masha she is slightly uncouth; and she says that Bobik is awake. In Act IV, she tells Andrey to be quiet; she points out that Sofochka is asleep; and she says, "You are a bear!"

22. On three occasions Chebutykin flatly states his nihilistic stance. He says it first in Act III, using trinominal combinations: "Perhaps I am not really a person, but only pretend that I have *hands,* and *feet,* and a *head.* Perhaps I don't even exist at all, but it only seems to me that I *walk, eat, sleep*" (XI, 279). The doctor repeats it shortly after he drops mama's clock (XI, 281). His third and final direct statement of nonexistence occurs in the last act shortly before he leaves for the duel (XI, 294).

23. Anton Chekhov, *P'esy*, in *Polnoye sobraniye sochineniy* (SPb: A. F. Marks, 1910), VII, 343–44.

24. Institut Yazykoznaniya Akademii Nauk SSSR, *Slovar' russkogo yazyka* (Moscow: Gos. Izd-vo Inostr. I Nats. Slovarey, 1957), I, 443.

25. Vladimir Nabokov, "A Definition of *Poshlost'*," in *Anton Chekhov's Plays*, pp. 322–26.

26. The Prologue in Russian may be found in *The Oxford Book of Russian Verse*, ed. Maurice Baring and D. P. Costello (Oxford: Clarendon Press, 1961), pp. 74–75.

27. In keeping with Chekhov's three, when Solenyy arrives in Act IV he is accompanied by two officers (XI, 295).

28. Magarshack, pp. 234–36.

29. Chebutykin's last words, "It doesn't matter," is a translation of the most frequently employed phrase, *vse ravno*, in *The Three Sisters*. The phrase and its variants are said over thirty times, and almost every major character says it at least once. Chebutykin repeatedly returns to it, saying it ten times alone in the last act, until it becomes one of the chief musical themes. That Chekhov considered the phrase significant is indicated by his adding it six times to Chebutykin's fourth-act dialogue during his preparation of the 1902 edition of the play (XI, 590). For a brief discussion of Chebutykin's nihilistic position in Acts III and IV, see note 22, above.

THE CHERRY ORCHARD:
A THEATER-POEM OF THE
SUFFERING OF CHANGE*

BY FRANCIS FERGUSSON

THE PLOT OF *THE CHERRY ORCHARD*

The Cherry Orchard is often accused of having no plot whatever, and it is true that the story gives little indication of the play's content or meaning; nothing happens, as the Broadway reviewers so often point out. Nor does it have a thesis, though many attempts have been made to attribute a thesis to it, to make it into a Marxian tract, or into a nostalgic defense of the old regime. The play does not have much of a plot in either of these accepted meanings of the word, for it is not addressed to the rationalizing mind but to the poetic and histrionic sensibility. It is an imitation of an action in the strictest sense, and it is plotted according to the first meaning of this word which I have distinguished in other contexts: the incidents are selected and arranged to define an action in a certain mode; a complete action, with a beginning, middle, and end in time. Its freedom from the mechanical order of the thesis or the intrigue is the sign of the perfection of Chekhov's realistic art. And its apparently casual incidents are actually composed with most elaborate and conscious skill to reveal the underlying life, and the natural, objective form of the play as a whole.

---

* "The Plot of *The Cherry Orchard*"/"Chekhov's Histrionic Art: An End and a Beginning," in Francis Fergusson, *The idea of a Theater: A Study of Ten Plays. The Art of Drama in Changing Perspective* (copyright 1949 © 1977 by Princeton University Press; Princeton Paperback, 1972), pp. 161–177. Reprinted by kind permission of the Princeton University Press.

In *Ghosts*, . . . the action is distorted by the stereotyped requirements of the thesis and the intrigue. That is partly a matter of the mode of action which Ibsen was trying to show; a quest "of ethical motivation" which requires some sort of intellectual framework, and yet can have no final meaning in the purely literal terms of Ibsen's theater. *The Cherry Orchard*, on the other hand, is a drama "of pathetic motivation," a theater-poem of the suffering of change; and this mode of action and awareness is much closer to the skeptical basis of modern realism, and to the histrionic basis of all realism. Direct perception before predication is always true, says Aristotle; and the extraordinary feat of Chekhov is to predicate nothing. This he achieves by means of his plot: he selects only those incidents, those moments in his characters' lives, between their rationalized efforts, when they sense their situation and destiny most directly. So he contrives to show the action of the play as a whole—the unsuccessful attempt to cling to the cherry orchard—in many diverse reflectors and without propounding any thesis about it.

The slight narrative thread which ties these incidents and characters together for the inquiring mind, is quickly recounted. The family that owns the old estate named after its famous orchard—Lyubov', her brother Gayev, and her daughters Varya and Anya—is all but bankrupt, and the question is how to prevent the bailiffs from selling the estate to pay their debts. Lopakhin, whose family were formerly serfs on the estate, is now rapidly growing rich as a businessman, and he offers a very sensible plan: chop down the orchard, divide the property into small lots, and sell them off to make a residential suburb for the growing industrial town nearby. Thus the cash value of the estate could be not only preserved, but increased. But this would not save what Lyubov' and her brother find valuable in the old estate; they cannot consent to the destruction of the orchard. But they cannot find, or earn, or borrow the money to pay their debts either; and in due course the estate is sold at auction to Lopakhin himself, who will make a very good thing of it. His workmen are hacking at the old trees before the family is out of the house.

The play may be briefly described as a realistic ensemble pathos: the characters all suffer the passing of the estate in different ways, thus adumbrating this change at a deeper and more generally significant level than that of any individual's experience. The action which they all share by analogy, and which informs the suffering of the destined change of the cherry orchard, is "to save the cherry orchard": that is, each character sees some value in it—economic, sentimental, social, cultural—which he wishes to keep. By means of his plot, Chekhov always focuses attention on the general action: his crowded stage, full of the characters I have mentioned as well as half a dozen hangers-on, is like an implicit discussion of the fatality which concerns them all; but Chekhov does not believe in their ideas, and the interplay he shows among his dramatis personae is not so much the play of thought as the alternation of the characters' perceptions of their situation, as the moods shift and the time for decision comes and goes.

Though the action which Chekhov chooses to show onstage is "pathetic," i.e., suffering and perception, it is complete: the cherry orchard is constituted before our eyes, and then dissolved. The first act is a prologue: it is the occasion of Lyubov''s return from Paris to try to resume her old life. Through her eyes and those of her daughter Anya, as well as from the complementary perspectives of Lopakhin and Trofimov, we see the estate as it were in the round, in its many possible meanings. The second act corresponds to the agon; it is in this act that we become aware of the conflicting values of all the characters, and of the efforts they make (offstage) to save each one *his* orchard. The third act corresponds to the pathos and peripety of the traditional tragic form. The occasion is a rather hysterical party which Lyubov' gives while her estate is being sold at auction in the nearby town; it ends with Lopakhin's announcement, in pride and the bitterness of guilt, that he was the purchaser. The last act is the epiphany: we see the action, now completed, in a new and ironic light. The occasion is the departure of the family: the windows are boarded up, the furniture piled in the corners, and the bags packed. All the characters feel, and the audience sees in a thousand ways, that the wish to save the orchard has amounted in fact to destroying it; the gathering of its denizens to separation; the homecoming to departure. What this "means" we are not told. But the action is completed, and the poem of the suffering of change concludes in a new and final perception, and a rich chord of feeling.

The structure of each act is based upon a more or less ceremonious social occasion. In his use of the social ceremony—arrivals, departures, anniversaries, parties—Chekhov is akin to James. His purpose is the same: to focus attention on an action which all share by analogy, instead of upon the reasoned purpose of any individual, as Ibsen does in his drama of ethical motivation. Chekhov uses the social occasion also to reveal the individual at moments when he is least enclosed in his private rationalization and most open to disinterested insights. The Chekhovian ensembles may appear superficially to be mere pointless stalemates—too like family gatherings and arbitrary meetings which we know offstage. So they are. But in his miraculous arrangement the very discomfort of many presences is made to reveal fundamental aspects of the human situation.

That Chekhov's art of plotting is extremely conscious and deliberate is clear the moment one considers the distinction between the stories of his characters as we learn about them, and the moments of their lives which he chose to show directly onstage. Lopakhin, for example, is a man of action like one of the new capitalists in Gor'kiy's plays. Chekhov knew all about him, and could have shown us an exciting episode from his career if he had not chosen to see him only when he was forced to pause and pathetically sense his own motives in a wider context which qualifies their importance. Lyubov' has been dragged about Europe for years by her ne'er-do-well lover, and her life might have yielded several sure-fire erotic intrigues like those of the commercial theater. But Chekhov, like all the great artists of modern times, rejected these standard motivations as both stale and false. The actress Arkadina, in *The Seagull*, remarks, as she closes a novel of Maupassant's, "Well, among the French that may be, but here with us there's nothing of the kind, we've no set program." In the context the irony of her remark is deep: she is herself a purest product of the commercial theater, and at that very time she is engaged in a love affair of the kind she objects to in Maupassant. But Chekhov, with his subtle art of plotting, has caught her in a situation, and at a brief moment of clarity and pause, when the falsity of her career is clear to all, even herself.

Thus Chekhov, by his art of plot-making, defines an action in the opposite mode to that of *Ghosts*. Ibsen defines a desperate quest for reasons and for ultimate, intelligible moral values. This action falls naturally into the form of the agon, and at the end of the play Ibsen is at a loss to develop the final pathos, or bring it to an end with an accepted perception. But the pathetic is the very mode of action and awareness which seems to Chekhov closest to the reality of the human situation, and by means of his plot he shows, even in characters who are not in themselves unusually passive, the suffering and the perception of change. The "moment" of human experience which *The Cherry Orchard* presents thus corresponds to that of the Sophoclean chorus, and of the evenings in the *Purgatorio*. *Ghosts* is a fighting play, armed for its sharp encounter with the rationalizing mind, its poetry concealed by its reasons. Chekhov's poetry, like Ibsen's, is behind the naturalistic surfaces; but the form of the play as a whole is "nothing but" poetry in the widest sense: the coherence of the concrete elements of the composition. Hence the curious vulnerability of Chekhov on the contemporary stage: he does not argue, he merely presents; and though his audiences even on Broadway are touched by the time they reach the last act, they are at a loss to say what it is all about.

It is this reticent objectivity of Chekhov also which makes him so difficult to analyze in words: he appeals exclusively to the histrionic sensibility where the little poetry of modern realism is to be found. Nevertheless, the effort of analysis must be made if one is to understand this art at all; and if the reader will bear with me, he is asked to consider one element, that of the scene, in the composition of the second act.

ACT II: THE SCENE AS A BASIC ELEMENT IN THE COMPOSITION

Jean Cocteau writes, in his preface to *Les Mariés de la Tour Eiffel*: "The action of my play is in images (*imagée*) while the text is not: I attempt to substitute a 'poetry of the theater' for 'poetry in the theater.' Poetry in the theater is a piece of lace which is impossible to see at a distance. Poetry of the theater would be coarse lace; a lace of ropes, a ship at sea. *Les Mariés* should have the frightening look of a drop of poetry under the microscope. The *scenes* are integrated like the *words* of a poem."

This description applies very exactly to *The Cherry Orchard*: the larger elements of the composition—the scenes or episodes, the setting, and the developing story—are composed in such a way as to make a poetry of the theater; but the "text" as we read it literally, is not. Chekhov's method, as Stark Young puts it in the preface to his translation of *The Seagull*, "is to take actual material such as we find in life and manage it in such a way that the inner meanings are made to appear. On the surface the life in his plays is natural, possible, and at times in effect even casual."

Young's translations of Chekhov's plays, together with his beautifully accurate notes, explanations, and interpretations, have made the text of Chekhov at last available for the English-speaking stage, and for any reader who will bring to his reading a little patience and imagination. Young shows us what Chekhov means in detail: by the particular words his characters use; by their rhythms of speech; by their gestures, pauses, and bits of stage business. In short, he makes the text transparent, enabling us to see through it to the music of action, the underlying poetry of the composition as a whole—and this is as much as to say that any study of Chekhov (lacking as we do adequate and available productions) must be based upon Young's work. At this point I propose to take this work for granted; to assume the translucent text; and to consider the role of the setting in the poetic or musical order of Act II.

The second act, as I have said, corresponds to the agon of the traditional plot scheme: it is here that we see most clearly the divisive purposes of the characters, the contrasts between their views of the cherry orchard itself. But the center of interest is not in these individual conflicts, nor in the contrasting versions for their own sake, but in the common fatality which they reveal: the passing of the old estate. The setting, as we come to know it behind the casual surfaces of the text, is one of the chief elements in this poem of change: if Act II were a lyric, instead of an act of a play, the setting would be a crucial word appearing in a succession of rich contexts which endow it with a developing meaning.

Chekhov describes the setting in the following realistic terms. "A field. An old chapel, long abandoned, with crooked walls, near it a well, big stones that apparently were once tombstones, and an old bench. A road to the estate of Gayev can be seen. On one side poplars rise, casting their shadows, the cherry orchard begins there. In the distance a row of telegraph poles; and far, far away, faintly traced on the horizon, is a large town, visible only in the clearest weather. The sun will soon be down."

To make this set out of a cyclorama, flats, cut-out silhouettes, and lighting effects would be difficult, without producing that unbelievable but literally intended—and in any case indigestible—scene which modern realism demands; and here Chekhov is uncomfortably bound by the convention of his time. The best strategy in production is that adopted by Robert Edmond Jones in his setting for *The Seagull*: to pay lip service only to the convention of photographic realism, and make the trees, the chapel, and all the other elements as simple as possible. The less closely the setting is defined by the carpenter, the freer it is to play the role Chekhov wrote for it: a role which changes and develops in relation to the story. Shakespeare did not have this problem; he could present his setting in different ways at different moments in a few lines of verse:

> Alack! the night comes on, and the bleak winds
> Do sorely ruffle; for many miles about
> There's scarce a bush.

Chekhov, as we shall see, gives his setting life and flexibility in spite of the visible elements onstage, not by means of the poetry of words but by means of his characters' changing sense of it.

When the curtain rises we see the setting simply as the country at the sentimental hour of sunset. Yepikhodov is playing his guitar and other hangers-on of the estate are loafing, as is their habit, before supper. The dialogue which starts after a brief pause focuses attention upon individuals in the group: Sharlotta, the governess, boasting of her culture and complaining that no one understands her; the silly maid Dunyasha, who is infatuated with Yasha, Lyubov''s valet. The scene, as reflected by these characters, is a satirical period-piece like the "Stag at Eve" or "The Maiden's Prayer"; and when the group falls silent and begins to drift away (having heard Lyubov', Gayev, and Lopakhin approaching along the path) Chekhov expects us to smile at the sentimental clichés which the place and the hour have produced.

But Lyubov''s party brings with it a very different atmosphere: of irritation, frustration, and fear. It is here we learn that Lopakhin cannot persuade Lyubov' and Gayev to put their affairs in order; that Gayev has been making futile gestures toward getting a job and borrowing money; that Lyubov' is worried about the estate, about her daughters, and about her lover, who has now fallen ill in Paris. Lopakhin, in a huff, offers to leave; but Lyubov' will not let him go—"It's more cheerful with you here," she says; and this group in its turn falls silent. In the distance we hear the music of the Jewish orchestra—when Chekhov wishes us to raise our eyes from the people in the foreground to their wider setting, he often uses music as a signal and an inducement. This time the musical entrance of the setting into our consciousness is more urgent and sinister than it was before: we see not so much the peace of evening as the silhouette of the dynamic industrial town on the horizon, and the approach of darkness. After a little more desultory conversation, there is another pause, this time without music, and the foreboding aspect of the scene in silence is more intense.

In this silence Firs, the ancient servant, hurries on with Gayev's coat, to protect him from the evening chill, and we briefly see the scene through Firs's eyes. He remembers the estate before the emancipation of the serfs, when it was the scene of a way of life which made sense to him; and now we become aware of the frail relics of this life: the old gravestones and the chapel "fallen out of the perpendicular."

In sharpest contrast with this vision come the young voices of Anya, Varya, and Trofimov, who are approaching along the path. The middle-aged and the old in the foreground are pathetically grateful for this note of youth, of strength, and of hope; and presently they are listening happily (though without agreement or belief) to Trofimov's aspirations, his creed of social progress, and his conviction that their generation is no longer important to the life of Russia. When the group falls silent again, they are all disposed to contentment with the moment; and when Yepikhodov's guitar is heard, and we look up, we feel the country and the evening under the aspect of hope—as offering freedom from the responsibilities and conflicts of the estate itself:

YEPIKHODOV *passes by at the back, playing his guitar.*
LYUBOV' *lost in thought:* Yepikhodov is coming—
ANYA *lost in thought:* Yepikhodov is coming.
GAYEV: The sun has set, ladies and gentlemen.
TROFIMOV: Yes.
GAYEV *not loud and as if he were declaiming:* Oh, Nature, wonderful, you gleam with eternal radiance, beautiful and indifferent, you, whom we call Mother, combine in yourself both life and death, you give life and take it away.
VARYA *beseechingly:* Uncle!

Gayev's false, rhetorical note ends the harmony, brings us back to the present and to the awareness of change on the horizon, and produces a sort of empty stalemate—a silent pause with worry and fear in it.

All sit absorbed in their thoughts. There is only the silence. Firs is heard muttering to himself softly. Suddenly a distant sound is heard, as if from the sky, like the sound of a snapped string, dying away, mournful.

This mysterious sound is used like Yepikhodov's strumming to remind us of the wider scene, but (though distant) it is sharp, almost a warning signal, and all the characters listen and peer toward the dim edges of the horizon. In their attitudes and guesses Chekhov reflects, in rapid succession, the contradictory aspects of the scene which have been developed at more length before us:

LYUBOV': What's that?
LOPAKHIN: I don't know. Somewhere far off in a mine shaft a bucket fell. But somewhere very far off.
GAYEV: And it may be some bird—like a heron.
TROFIMOV: Or an owl—
LYUBOV' *shivering*: It's unplesant, somehow. *A pause.*
FIRS: Before the disaster it was like that. The owl hooted and the samovar hummed without stopping, both.
GAYEV: Before what disaster?
FIRS: Before the emancipation.
    A pause.
LYUBOV': You know, my friends, let's go. . . .

Lyubov' feels the need to retreat, but the retreat is turned into flight when "the wayfarer" suddenly appears on the path asking for money. Lyubov' in her bewilderment, her sympathy, and her bad conscience, gives him gold. The party breaks up, each in his own way thwarted and demoralized.

Anya and Trofimov are left onstage; and, to conclude his theatrical poem of the suffering of change, Chekhov reflects the setting in them:

ANYA *a pause*: It's wonderful here today!
TROFIMOV: Yes, the weather is marvelous.
ANYA: What have you done to me, Petya, why don't I love the cherry orchard any longer the way I used to? I loved it too tenderly; it seemed to me there was not a better place on earth than our orchard.
TROFIMOV: All Russia is our garden. The earth is immense and beautiful. . . .

The sun has set, the moon is rising with its chill and its ancient animal excitement, and the estate is dissolved in the darkness as Nineveh is dissolved in a pile of rubble with vegetation creepng over it. Chekhov wishes to show the cherry orchard as "gone"; but for this purpose he employs not only the literal time-scheme (sunset to moonrise) but, as reflectors, Anya and Trofimov, for whom the present in any form is already gone and only the bodiless future is real. Anya's young love for Trofimov's intellectual enthusiasm (like Juliet's "all as boundless as the sea") has freed her from her actual childhood home, made her feel "at home in the world" anywhere. Trofimov's abstract aspirations give him a chillier and more artificial, but equally complete, detachment not only from the estate itself (he disapproves of it on theoretical grounds) but from Anya (he thinks it would be vulgar to be in love with her). We hear the worried Varya calling for Anya in the distance; Anya and Trofimov run down to the river to discuss the socialistic *Paradiso Terrestre*; and with these complementary images of the human scene, and this subtle chord of feeling, Chekhov ends the act.

The "scene" is only one element in the composition of Act II, but it illustrates the nature of Chekhov's poetry of the theater. It is very clear, I think, that Chekhov is not trying to present us with a rationalization of social change *à la* Marx, or even with a subtler rationalization *à la* Shaw. On the other hand, he is not seeking, like Wagner, to seduce us into one passion. He shows us a moment of change in society, and he shows us a "pathos"; but the elements of his composition are always taken as objectively real. He offers us various rationalizations, various images, and various feelings, which cannot be reduced either to one emotion or to one idea: they indicate an action and a scene which is "there" before the rational formulations, or the emotionally charged attitudes, of any of the characters.

The surrounding scene of *The Cherry Orchard* corresponds to the significant stage of human life which Sophocles' choruses reveal, and to the empty wilderness beyond Ibsen's little parlor. We miss, in Chekhov's scene, any fixed points of human significance, and that is why, compared with Sophocles, he seems limited and partial—a bit too pathetic even for our bewildered times. But, precisely because he subtly and elaborately develops the moments of pathos with their sad insights, he sees much more in the little scene of modern realism than Ibsen does. Ibsen's snow-peaks strike us as rather hysterical; but the "stage of Europe" which we divine behind the cherry orchard is confirmed by a thousand impressions derived from other sources. We may recognize its main elements in a cocktail party in Connecticut or Westchester: someone's lawn full of voluble people; a dry white clapboard church (instead of an Orthodox chapel) just visible across a field; time passing, and the muffled roar of a four-lane highway under the hill—or we may be reminded of it in the final section of *The Wasteland*, with its twittering voices, its old gravestones and deserted chapel, and its dim crowd on the horizon foreboding change. It is because Chekhov says so little that he reveals so much, providing a concrete basis for many conflicting rationalizations of contemporary social change: by accepting the immediacy and unintelligibility of modern realism so completely, he in some ways transcends its limitations, and prepares the way for subsequent developments in the modern theater.

CHEKHOV'S HISTRIONIC ART: AN END AND A BEGINNING

Purgatorio, CANTO VIII—[1]

> Era già l'ora che volge il disio
> ai naviganti e intenerisce il core,
> lo dì ch'han detto ai dolci amici addio;
> e che lo nuovo peregrin d'amore
> punge, se ode squilla di lontano,
> che paia il giorno pianger che si more.

The poetry of modern realistic drama is to be found in those inarticulate moments when the human creature is shown responding directly to his immediate situation. Such are the many moments—composed, interrelated, echoing each other—when the waiting and loafing characters in Act II get a fresh sense (one after the other, and each in his own way) of their situation on the doomed estate. It is because of the exactitude with which Chekhov perceives and imitates these tiny responses, that he can make them echo each other, and convey, when taken together, a single action with the scope, the general significance or suggestiveness, of poetry. Chekhov, like other great dramatists, has what might be called an ear for action, comparable to the trained musician's ear for musical sound.

The action which Chekhov thus imitates in his second act (that of lending ear, in a moment of freedom from practical pressures, to impending change) echoes, in its turn, a number of other poets: Laforgue's "poetry of waiting-rooms" comes to mind, as well as other works stemming from the period of hush before the First World War. The poets are to some extent talking about the same thing, and their works, like voices in a continuing colloquy, help to explain each other: hence the justification and the purpose of seeking comparisons. The eighth canto of the *Purgatorio* is widely separated from *The Cherry Orchard* in space and time, but these two poems unmistakably echo and confirm each other. Thinking of them together, one can begin to place Chekhov's curiously nonverbal dramaturgy and understand the purpose and the value of his reduction of the art to histrionic terms, as well as the more obvious limitations which he thereby accepts. For Dante accepts similar limitations at this point but locates the mode of action he shows here at a certain point in his vast scheme.

The explicit coordinates whereby Dante places the action of Canto VIII might alone suffice to give one a clue to the comparison with *The Cherry Orchard:* we are in the Valley of Negligent Rulers who, lacking light, unwillingly suffer their irresponsibility, just as Lyubov' and Gayev do. The *antepurgatorio* is behind us, and Purgatory proper, with its hoped-for work, thought, and moral effort, is somewhere ahead, beyond the night which is now approaching. It is the end of the day; and as we wait, watch, and listen, evening moves slowly over our heads, from sunset to darkness to moonrise. Looking more closely at this canto, one can see that Dante the Pilgrim and the Negligent Rulers he meets are listening and looking as Chekhov's characters are in Act II: the action is the same; in both, a childish and uninstructed responsiveness, an unpremeditated obedience to what is actual, informs the suffering of change. Dante the author, for his elaborate and completely conscious reasons, works here with the primitive histrionic sensibility; he composes with elements sensuously or sympathetically, but not rationally or verbally, defined. The rhythms, the pauses, and the sound effects he employs are strikingly similar to Chekhov's. And so he shows himself—Dante "the new Pilgrim"—meeting this mode of awareness for the first time: as delicately and ignorantly as Gayev when he feels all of a sudden the extent of evening, and before he falsifies this perception with his embarrassing apostrophe to Nature.

If Dante allows himself as artist and as protagonist only the primitive sensibility of the child, the naïf, the natural saint, at this point in the ascent, it is because, like Chekhov, he is presenting a threshold or moment of change in human experience. He wants to show the unbounded potentialities of the psyche before or between the moments when it is morally and intellectually realized. In Canto VIII the pilgrim is both a child and a child who is changing; later moments of transition are different. Here he is virtually (but for the Grace of God) lost; all the dangers are present. Yet he remains uncommitted and therefore open to finding himself again and more truly. In all of this the parallel to Chekhov is close. But because Dante sees this moment as a moment only in the ascent, Canto VIII is also composed in ways in which Act II of *The Cherry Orchard* is not—ways which the reader of the *Purgatorio* will not understand until he looks back from the top of the mountain. Then he will see the homesickness which informs Canto VIII in a new light, and all of the concrete elements, the snake in the grass, the winged figures that roost at the edge of the valley like night-hawks, will be intelligible to the mind and, without losing their concreteness, take their place in a more general frame. Dante's fiction is laid in the scene beyond the grave, where every human action has its relation to ultimate reality, even though that relation becomes explicit only gradually. But Chekhov's characters are seen in the flesh and in their very secular emotional entanglements: in the contemporary world as anyone can see it—nothing visible beyond the earth's horizon, with its signs of social change. The fatality of the *Zeitgeist* is the ultimate reality in the theater of modern realism; the anagoge is lacking. And though Ibsen and Chekhov are aware of both history and moral effort, they do not know what to make of them—perhaps they reveal only illusory perspectives, "masquerades which time resumes." If Chekhov echoes Dante, it is not because of what he ultimately understood but because of the accuracy with which he saw and imitated that moment of action.

If one thinks of the generation to which Anya and Trofimov were supposed to belong, it is clear that the new motives and reasons which they were to find, after their inspired evening together, were not such as to turn all Russia, or all the world, into a garden. The potentialities which Chekhov presented at that moment of change were not to be realized in the wars and revolutions which followed: what actually followed was rather that separation and destruction, that scattering and destinationless trekking, which he also sensed as possible. But, in the cultivation of the dramatic art after Chekhov, renewals, the realization of hidden potentialities, did follow. In Chekhov's histrionic art, the "desire is turned back" to its very root, to the immediate response, to the movements of the psyche before they are limited, defined, and realized in reasoned purpose. Thus Chekhov revealed hidden potentialities, if not in the life of the time, at least in ways of seeing and showing human life; if not in society, at least in the dramatic art. The first and most generally recognized result of these labors was to bring modern realism to its final perfection in the productions of the Moscow Art Theater and in those who learned from it. But the end of modern realism was also a return to very ancient sources; and in our time the fertilizing effect of Chekhov's humble objectivity may be traced in a number of dramatic forms which cannot be called modern realism at all.

The acting technique of the Moscow Art Theater is so closely connected, in its final development, with Chekhov's dramaturgy, that it would be hard to say which gave the more important clues. Stanislavskiy and Nemirovich-Danchenko from one point of view, and Chekhov from another, approached the same conception: both were searching for an attitude and a method that would be less hidebound, truer to experience, than the cliché-responses of the commercial theater. The Moscow Art Theater taught the performer to make that direct and total response which is the root of poetry in the widest sense: they cultivated the histrionic sensibility in order to free the actor to realize, in his art, the situations and actions which the playwright had imagined. Chekhov's plays demand this accuracy and imaginative freedom from the performer; and the Moscow Art Theater's productions of his works were a demonstration of the perfection, the reticent poetry, of modern realism. Modern realism of this kind is still alive in the work of many artists who have been more or less directly influenced either by Chekhov or by the Moscow Art Theater. In our country, for instance, there is Clifford Odets; in France, Vildrac and Bernard, and the realistic cinema, of which *Symphonie Pastorale* is an example.

But this cultivation of the histrionic sensibility, bringing modern realism to its end and its perfection, also provided fresh access to many other dramatic forms. The Moscow technique, when properly developed and critically understood, enables the producer and performer to find the life in any theatrical form; before the revolution the Moscow Art Theater had thus revivified *Hamlet, Carmen,* the interludes of Cervantes, neoclassic comedies of several kinds, and many other works which were not realistic in the modern sense at all. A closely related acting technique underlay

Reinhardt's virtuosity; and Copeau, in the Vieux Colombier, used it to renew not only the art of acting but, by that means, the art of playwriting also. . . .

After periods when great drama is written, great performers usually appear to carry on the life of the theater for a few more generations. Such were the Siddonses and Macreadys who kept the great Shakespearian roles alive after Shakespeare's theater was gone, and such, at a further stage of degeneration, were the mimes of the Commedia dell'Arte, improving on the themes of Terence and Plautus when the theater had lost most of its meaning. The progress of modern realism from Ibsen to Chekhov looks in some respects like a withering and degeneration of this kind: Chekhov does not demand the intellectual scope, the ultimate meanings, which Ibsen demanded, and to some critics Chekhov does not look like a real dramatist but merely an overdeveloped mime, a stage virtuoso. But the theater of modern realism did not afford what Ibsen demanded, and Chekhov is much the more perfect master of its little scene. If Chekhov drastically reduced the dramatic art, he did so in full consciousness, and in obedience both to artistic scruples and to a strict sense of reality. He reduced the dramatic art to its ancient root, from which new growths are possible.

NOTE

1. It was now the hour that turns back the desire of those who sail the seas and melts their heart, that day when they have said to their sweet friends adieu, and that pierces the new pilgrim with love, if from afar he hears the chimes which seem to mourn for the dying day.

COUNTERPOINT OF THE
SNAPPING STRING:
CHEKHOV'S *THE CHERRY ORCHARD**

BY JEAN-PIERRE BARRICELLI

To the author of *The Cherry Orchard*, to be a member of the human race meant to be a confused victim of oppositions or paradoxes, of counterpoints. For this reason, paradox is inherent in Chekhov's concept of dramaturgy, and something provoking bewilderment does not necessarily constitute an extraneous element in a play. A case in point is the unexpected and vaguely disconcerting sound of a snapping string that is heard in the distance and from the sky twice in *The Cherry Orchard*, once toward the end of Act II, and again at the conclusion of the fourth and final act. Critical bewilderment before the sound has persisted since the first rehearsals in Moscow, attended by the author during December and January of 1903–4.[1] To our way of thinking, the two counterpoising soundings, symmetrically placed, are central to the play: to its structure and symbolism and therefore to its innermost meaning. More than a psychological device for the audience, the double sounding is a substantive and structural device embedded deep in its heart, though all too often it has not been considered in this light. J. L. Styan declares correctly that "To interpret that sound is to interpret the play,"[2] although his interpretation follows that of many others who simply relate the sound to the passing of time, to the demise of the old social order, and the

* Reprinted from *California Slavic Studies*, vol. x (1977), 121–136, with the kind permission of the University of California Press. Throughout this essay, the term "counterpoint" is used more to denote opposition or counterpoising than simultaneity (essential in musical use), though the quality of simultaneity is never absent. Even at the end of the play, where the sounds of the string and the ax are heard in succession, they sound together psychologically.

ushering in of a new one. H. Pitcher contends that by it Chekhov did not intend "one specific meaning,"[3] and F. Fergusson hears it as a "sharp, almost warning signal,"[4] but nothing more. And C. B. Timmer, in an otherwise enlightening article on Chekhov's use of the bizarre, the grotesque, and the absurd—that is, in an article which, by drawing careful distinctions among these aspects of his art, would seem, therefore, to lend itself somewhere to a consideration of the weird, bizarre, and potentially absurd sound—makes no mention of it.[5]

As might be expected, Soviet criticism, which eschews the exploration of metaphysical or symbolical forms that are not directly related to "social realism" and that may in fact controvert its goals, engages in no discussion of the meaning of the snapping string. Vsevolod Meyerkhol'd once came close when in criticizing Stanislavskiy's interpretation he sought the key to the play in its acoustics and inner rhythm (comparing it to a symphony of Chaykovskiy!), and concluded that the producer "must first of all understand it with his hearing."[6] Clearly for Chekhov words are not the best vehicle to express thoughts and feelings. But more recently, Georgiy Berdnikov, who speaks of "devices" as coordinated with the characters, of "pauses" as revealing their inner substance, and of "sounds" as adding to the lyrical idea of the play, is silent on how this special sound may reveal the inner substance of *The Cherry Orchard*.[7] Aleksandr Revyakin merely calls our attention to how the generally sad mood "finds correspondence in the words of Lopakhin, in the melancholy song of Yepikhodov, and is diffused in the sounds of a breaking string," though a few pages later he returns to the sound, suggesting that it has "an especially large, realistico-symbolic meaning"—but only, again, because it "announces a coming catastrophe."[8] Again, no attempt is made to come to grips with the actual sound of the snapping string, which, in this nonformalistic body of criticism, is totally ignored. Abram Derman, whose chapters on "The Structural Elements in Chekhov's Poetics" or "The Poetry of Chekhov's Creativeness" would otherwise be likely places for such a discussion, overlooks it,[9] as do Korney Chukovskiy and Vladimir Yermilov.[10] One of the most striking omissions occurs in Sergey Balukhatyy's study of Chekhov as a dramatist, where a whole chapter is devoted to *The Cherry Orchard* with no mention of the sound despite an important comparison between Act II and Act IV.[11] And we are not farther advanced in our inquiry by consulting the works of Aleksandr Roskin or Vasiliy Golubkov.[12]

Maurice Valency, in his fine study of Chekhov's plays, despite its revealing title (*The Breaking String*) as well as its concluding chapter called "The Sound of the Breaking String," accepts the sound metaphorically, but does not explore its more intimate meanings, either contextually or intextually. While he recognizes that "*The Cherry Orchard* centers upon the sound of the breaking string," he prefers to leave it shrouded in mystery: "The sound of the breaking string remains mysterious, but it has finality. The symbol is broad; it would be folly to try to assign to it a more precise meaning than the author chose to give it. But its quality is unequivocal. Whatever of sadness remains unexpressed in *The Cherry Orchard*, this sound expresses."[13] And later, following up the observation that the sound is heard when the young people, Varya, Anya, and Trofimov find the aging Gayev's lyrical tribute to nature unbearable and force him to silence, Valency explains the metaphor in terms of a generation gap: "The golden string that connected man with his father on earth and his father in heaven, the age-old bond that tied the present to the past, was not to be broken lightly. When at last it snapped, the result . . . was both world-shaking and soul-shaking."[14] While Pitcher finds the interpretation forced,[15] we might nonetheless admit to the logic of its spirit. In any event, no further sense is made of the mysterious occurrence.

To be sure, the sound bespeaks a mood (and as such should not be explained with specifics), what Mirsky would call one of Chekhov's "purely atmospheric creations."[16] For, as the critic remarks, in Chekhov, where no one person seems to listen to his neighbor, there is not straight line but a series of moods. It was reported by Stanislavskiy that during the December rehearsals, one of the actors casually made an imitative sound with his lips of the kind the author had described, and Chekhov turned to him exclaiming: "That's just what we want!"[17] Yet, because of its highly unusual quality—even for Chekhov—Styan believes that he took "an extraordinary risk" in introducing it in Act II,[18] and Mirsky goes even further: ". . . in his search for suggestive poetry he sometimes overstepped the limits of good taste— . . . for instance, the bursting of a string in *The Cherry Orchard*. . . ."[19]

The implication here is that, while Chekhov's world is filled with noises, they are not necessarily strange noises, and that in *The Cherry Orchard* he planned something much out of the ordinary. The apocalyptic sound, as Mirsky describes it, is not typical of Chekhov. It is different from the guitar string which snaps in a dark room in the story *The Dream Fiancée* (1903). It is even different from the *"Takh! t! t! t!"* that reverberates across the steppes' thin air in *Happiness* (1887): it may be equally mysterious and receive a similar explanation ("It must have been a bucket falling in a mine shaft," says Panteley, unperturbed, just as in *The Cherry Orchard* Lopakhin attempts to identify the sound the same way), but it is nowhere near as "apocalyptic," and furthermore it sounds only once. The episode recalls the passage in *A Rolling Stone*, of the same year, where the hero falls to the bottom of a mine when the chain holding his bucket snaps.[20] Hence Hingley's comment about the extraordinary sound which baffles stage directors: "One remarkable sound effect has caused some embarrassment to producers, and illustrates the production of *nastroenie* on a more surrealist level. . . . The play does not make it entirely clear how this noise is supposed to have originated, but Chekhov certainly regarded it as important in evoking the right sort of mood in his audience."[21]

If the enigmatic sound stands out, however, it does so because it does more than provoke the "right sort of mood." Chekhov was too precise and self-conscious an artist to allow a gratuitous or solely mood-setting, isolated incident to enter his work. As we know, he insisted that all specifics in his plays be executed down to the last particular, but, by the same token, not overexecuted.[22] The Chekhovian pattern of understatement obtained even in expressing the significant detail. He used all sound effects in his stage directions with great subtlety, and did not fill his plays with mysterious happenings which require a spectator to turn detective. There are no "secret connotations which must be pieced together like a jigsaw puzzle."[23] The sound in *The Cherry Orchard* cannot be said even to fit the musical dimensions of the play; it may be "a musical sound in its way, but contrasting so strangely with the thoroughly familiar sounds of Yepikhodov's guitar"[24] or the Jewish orchestra that it commands direct attention. The simple fact that Trofimov and Gayev *hear* it suggests that the incident is woven firmly into the fabric of the play. That Chekhov wanted his characters to take note of the sound is best suggested by his change of setting from a river to a chapel, as if to allow the greater quiet to bring out better the distant vibrations: "In the second act I have substituted the river with an old chapel and a well. It is quieter so."[25] Furthermore, Chekhov's direction or description concerning the sound is expressed verbatim both times it is heard—as sure an indication of the importance he placed on it as we might wish to have. So if *ultimately* it is a mere sound effect, *intimately* it has much to say.

The most important thing it has to say, regardless of Chekhov's own paradoxical assertions about his plays being comedies and not tragedies (another counterpoint!), is that the play is not an "undramatic drama" (as Mirsky likes to call Chekhov's dramas) but indeed a tragic drama. It is not a cheerful message the story conveys; yet, strange as it may sound, an optimistic interpretation is not uncommon. For there are those like Yermilov who in good Soviet fashion see the play's ending as bright, as introducing a new, powerful, and decisive force in society, the Russian working class, and who accordingly entitles his chapter on *The Cherry Orchard*: "Welcome, New Life." To put an end to the past: this is the emotional significance of the play. "Laughter, gay and unrestrained, penetrates every situation in the play. . . . Karl Marx expressed a profound thought when he called laughter a way of 'bidding farewell' to the old, exhausted forms of life."[26] Similarly, outside the Soviet periphery, Sophie Lafitte, while recognizing that the basic theme of Chekhov is the "contrast affirmation of inner solitude," insists that at the end of *The Cherry Orchard* (and *Uncle Vanya!*) there "bursts the hope of a better future, of happiness which is not only possible, but certain, though still far off."[27] Pitcher, more cautiously and neutrally, sees no *real* pessimistic or tragic implications.[28]

We believe the opposite, however, and concur with Aimée Alexandre: "*The Cherry Orchard* is the drama of death, the disappearance of a past with all that it contained that was good and bad, with all the nostalgia it will create, with all the sadness over the passage of time."[29] The important concept is the "drama of death," and the snapping string is the surrealistic symbol relating to it, reminiscent of the final snipping of the thread by Atropos. It provides a mood not just of "wonder" but of "regret," stressing nostalgically "time past and time passing"[30] rather than "bidding farewell" to them with "bursts of hope" for time future. Let us not forget, among other indications, that at the end Mme. Ranevskaya and Gayev—not villains in any way—sob in each other's arms, according to the stage directions, *"in despair"* (*v otchayanii*) that the family is dispersed, and that the final posture and situation of good Firs *does* remind us of death. It should not be surprising that, running down the aisle during a rehearsal, Chekhov had insisted that the sound be made "more painful" or dolorous (*zhlobnye*).[31] Therefore, many critics and directors have indeed associated the sound with death, generally relating it, like Styan and Valency, to the death of values and way of life of the older Russian society of the Ranevskayas and Gayevs, symbolized by the cherry orchard—nostalgically "a sort of requiem for the 'unhappy and disjointed' lives of [Chekhov's] characters."[32] But in doing so, they have indicated at best only *what* the sound seems to signify, and if its meaning is tragic, we must still be able to say *how* it got to have this meaning, and *how* it reveals it structurally within the play. Given the dissension over the optimism or pessimism of the message, we should look for clues to validate the latter interpretation *inside* the play, for the former interpretation is little more than a superimposition.

To begin with, and with no intention of detracting from its arcane quality, the background of the snapping string must be sought in folklore. The sound establishes the folklore element inside the play. This possibility is hinted when Mme. Ranevskaya refers to the sound as "ill-omened" (ominous or foreboding: *neschastnyy*). Perhaps this is what led a German critic to claim that it is used "as a symbol for the end of the aristocracy's splendor, as a ghostly omen"[33] (*Menetekel*). There can be no question that Chekhov used the motif in its most widespread folklore application concerning unhappiness associated with the end of life. Its homeopathic aspects appear all over Western and Central Europe, Western Slavic countries included. Though one cannot yet locate immediate evidence of the motif's presence in Russia itself, folklorists find it legitimate (and logical) to suppose its existence in Russian folklore because it is well known, for example, in Slovak folklore which in turn shows frequent links with Russian popular traditions. And Chekhov, being well acquainted with Eastern Slavic folk traditions, was undoubtedly familiar with this motif.

In folklore, a player may leave his instrument behind as a "life token," an extension of himself, and if during his absence a string breaks, this is considered an evil portent. The chord that snaps involves the idea of a separable soul.[34] One may come upon several such examples of a break-ing string: "If a string of an instrument breaks for no special reason, then there will soon be a wedding, or, according to a more widespread super-stition, one must expect a death."[35] With reference to *The Cherry Or-chard*, it is clearly the more common belief, the *Todesfall*, that draws our attention. A typical illustration of the "snapping-chord-of-death" motif is the story of the Swiss fiddler:

> A fiddler living in the wilds of Elvig used to visit his loved one, who used his fiddle, twice a week in the Balmen Lötschenpass. She always knew ex-actly at what time he would walk into her house. Suddenly a chord of an-other violin snapped. "Oh Lord," cried she, "now something unfortunate has happened to my beloved," and correctly, at that exact moment he had been struck dead.[36]

Again, there is the story from Syra of Strong Hans, who could not be made to do anything except play the zither, and who sallied forth one day to fight the ogre (who had ravished the king's daughter), telling his mother: "If you see that the strings of my zither are broken, then come and seek me [for I shall be dead]."[37] Folktales such as these form the tradition underlying the question of how the breaking string got to mean what it means in Chekhov's play.[38]

How this sound reveals its meaning structurally in the play is a ques-tion which leads us to the heart of Chekhov's art in *The Cherry Orchard*, the art of counterpoint. Its ingredients combine in a pattern of opposi-tions, establishing architectural and conceptual relationships, expressively balanced, while retaining a clear individuality of their own at all times. Fundamental are the images of the owl and heron, not only because they appear in the very center of the play (end of Act II) and just before the first instance of the snapping string, but also because of their symbolic significance juxtaposing life and death, the drama's main counterpoint. Furthermore, a number of ancillary contrapuntal motifs come forth in the same scene. Yepikhodov has just crossed the stage, playing his guitar:

GAYEV: Ladies and gentlemen, the sun has set.
TROFIMOV: Yes.
GAYEV *in a low voice, declaiming as it were*: Oh, Nature, wondrous Nature, you shine with eternal radiance, beautiful and indifferent! You, whom we call our mother, unite within yourself life and death! You animate and destroy!

VARYA *pleadingly:* Uncle dear!

TROFIMOV: You'd better bank the yellow ball in the side pocket.

GAYEV: I'm silent, I'm silent . . .

All sit plunged in thought. Stillness reigns. Only FIR's *muttering is audible. Suddenly a distant sound is heard, coming from the sky as it were, the sound of a snapping string, mournfully dying away.*

MME. RANEVSKAYA: What was that?

LOPAKHIN: I don't know. Somewhere far away, in the pits, a bucket's broken loose; but somewhere very far away.

GAYEV: Or it might be some sort of bird, perhaps a heron.

TROFIMOV: Or an owl . . .

MME. RANEVSKAYA *shudders:* It's weird, somehow.

Pause

FIRS: Before the calamity the same thing happened—the owl screeched, and the samovar hummed all the time.

GAYEV: Before what calamity?

FIRS: Before the Freedom. *Pause.*

MME. RANEVSKAYA: Come, my dear friends, let's be going. It's getting dark . . .

Then the poor stranger appears, in a shabby white cap, begs thirty kopecks, and Mme. Ranevskaya, who has no silver in her purse, gives him a gold piece (to Varya's annoyed astonishment).

The break in silence, like the quiet tranquility of the old world that comes to an end, is anticipated by Gayev's words concerning the animating and destructive manner of nature, and what he exclaims literally about life and death is balanced and restated symbolically after the break in silence by the heron and the owl—the former alluded to by Gayev himself, who dreams of his tranquil, older world continuing, and the latter by the representative of the younger generation, Trofimov, who wants its demise (and who strangely, and ironically, it might appear, seems to hoot at the very end of the play, over Anya's happy calls, while the older people leave and the orchard starts falling: "Aoooo" [*Au!*]). In folk literature, the hooting of an owl represents a bad omen, while hearing the heron's cry represents a good one. In the Egyptian systems of hieroglyphs, the owl symbolizes "death, night, cold and passivity" and also pertains to the realm of the dead sun (a sun that has set),[39] and not surprisingly Virgil speaks of the owl's mournful strain when Dido longs for death.[40] Similarly, among the Egyptians, the heron (together with the stork and ibis) symbolized morning and the generation of life,[41] and Homer has Athene send a heron to Odysseus and Diomedes as they set out on a perilous mission, in order to insure their success.[42]

Old Firs had heard an owl years before, while the graciously living society kept minding its cup of tea, after which the bad portent became reality: the emancipation of the serfs in 1861, serfs who became the Lopakhins of the next generation, the one that buys and axes the orchards.[43]

Once the heron-owl pattern is set, the rest of the counterpoint falls into place, and we come to realize that hearing the sound of the snapping string twice underscores the structure.[44] An expressive series of sometimes obvious but more often subtle oppositions between death and life forces makes up this dialectic, as it were, which creates a tension throughout the play, and how the tension is resolved—the chord snaps—can only invite a pessimistic interpretation. But this becomes clear only at the end, because before that the dialectic operates ambiguously on an optical and phonic as well as on an actional and perceptional level.

On the optical level, we note that, as the tombstones of Act II counterpoise the chapel, so do the telephone poles the cherry orchard. The industrial and the natural, the city and the meadow, the skeletal and the rounded, termination and hope, face each other in precarious balance.[45] In addition, the death instruments, the gun Sharlotta carries and the revolver Yepikhodov reveals, act to counterpoise the musical instruments as well as the expressed desires for continued life or the rays of hope emanating from the many telegrams, torn up or not, Mme. Ranevskaya receives every day from that "savage" who needs her and whom she loves in Paris. Yepikhodov's query, "Should I live or should I shoot myself . . . ?" creates more tensions than the words by themselves seem to betray, as does his ominous remark, "Now I know what to do with my revolver," followed by his reassured walking off playing his guitar. In effect, his query does not differ from his double-edged, symbolic observations at the beginning of the play that while "there's a frost this morning—ten degrees below— . . . yet the cherries are all in bloom" (and at the end: "It's devilishly cold here . . . yet it's still and sunny as though it were summer"), or from Mme. Ranevskaya's romantic attempt to poison herself in Paris coupled ambivalently with her sudden magnetic attraction for life in Russia. Even the stage directions, as N. Å. Nilsson points out, are composed of "wholly opposing parts" ("cheerfully through tears [radostno skvoz' slezy]," as an example; the non sequiturs too

[Varya's and Anya's in Act I] amount to "oppositions").[46] Almost everything we see, from tombstones to guitars, exists in dialectical relationship
with other objects. And observations and events follow the same pattern.

The optical level of interpretation is intensified by Chekhov's insistence
on the use of the color white. White pervades the play, not merely as a
refraction of the heron, but as a veritable tonality struck about a dozen
and a half times during the drama: one of Mme. Ranevskaya's two rooms
is white, Firs wears a white waistcoat and puts on white gloves, Sharlotta
appears in a tightly laced white dress, Mme. Ranevskaya imagines her
mother "all in white" in the orchard, and even Pishchik discovers white
clay on his land. Furthermore, the orchard, as Gayev describes it, "is all
white," and Mme. Ranevskaya laughs with joy at its being "all, all
white!" while she visualizes her mother in it in the form of "a little white
tree, leaning over." Then she underscores: "What an amazing orchard!
White masses of blossom. . . ." Chekhov's intent is clear from his correspondence: in his mind, even Lopakhin has a white waistcoat,[47] and
"in Act One cherry trees can be seen in bloom through the windows, the
whole orchard is a mass of whites. And ladies in white dresses." Hardly
any other color is mentioned in the play.[48]

Inside and outside Western folk tradition, white has symbolized the
positive and timeless. It is considered purified yellow; it is the hope of
life. By the same token, yellow is considered impure white, or life in a
state of decay, or, at least, of imperfection. One is reminded of Balzac's
character Poiret, in Old Goriot, whose white ivory cane handle has
turned yellow with age and use, or of the aged countess' yellow gown in
Pushkin's The Queen of Spades. The figurative meaning of yellow as a
color given in Ozhegov's dictionary[49] includes the notions of concilia-
tion, reform, and betrayal of the interests of the working class (used con-
temptuously). One should not overlook, then, Gayev's many, although
eccentric, references to the "yellow ball"[50] bank shot in the side
pocket,[51] for through his very eccentricity Gayev tacitly suggests that he
realizes, at least subconsciously, what is happening to Russia. Despite his
white waistcoat, suggesting the higher-class status he has now attained,
Lopakhin still wears "yellow shoes,"[52] almost as if to suggest his peasant
stock. Thus, the mood of counterpoising oppositions is enforced, shaping
the play with tensions as it develops, and guiding it to its final expression
of the snapping string.

Actional and perceptional levels of interpretation corroborate the optical. In a spatial context, the counterpoint between Mme. Ranevskaya's kissing her "darling bookcase" or Gayev's tearful and impassioned encomium to it on the one hand, and the epidemic of knocking over furniture accidentally or breaking belongings on the other, is quite obvious.[53] Lack of control over the physical world symptomizes the collapse of the spiritual. The spatial context is corroborated in turn by the temporal: in Act I, Mme. Ranevskaya says of Varya what she will also say of Lopakhin, that she is "the same as ever," which at different times is what Yasha says of Gayev and Varya of her mother, like a variation of Lopakhin's phrase to Gayev: "You're as splendid as ever." The phrases "You haven't changed a bit" and "just the same as ever" take on the qualities of a leitmotif by the end of the first act. They imply a desire to hang on to the status quo, to have it continue as splendidly as before, to prolong the "whiteness." But as the play wears on and, let us say, the heron turns owl, we hear the opposite theme sounded, that of change: "How you've aged," exclaims Mme. Ranevskaya to Firs, the way Varya laments to Petya: "How old you look!" Together, the spatial and the temporal dimensions produce a counterpoint of their own: that of the wishful, dreamy, and passive world of the status quo which Mme. Ranevskaya, Gayev, Firs, and Dunyasha live in, epitomized by the latter's remark: "I am daydreaming"; and that of the realistic, pragmatic, and materialistic world of change which Anya and Trofimov look to, or the mercantile logic of Lopakhin prepares. Says Lopakhin: "I'm always handling money. . . . Sometimes I lie awake at night, I think. . . ."

The most encompassing counterpoint, of course, operates on the phonic level, and it climaxes with the sound of the snapping string. The meaning of *The Cherry Orchard* is rooted in a kind of recondite music, or unmusic, contrasting intensely with the clumsiness of the characters or their inability to harmonize (*neskladnyy*), and is expressed on the surface in many ways—the distant sound of a shepherd's piping and the allusion to bells in Act I, the guitar (confused with a mandolin) and the band (four violins, a double bass, and a flute) in Acts II and III, the waltz and the frequent mention of the musicians in Act III, and Yasha's and Sharlotta's humming in Act IV. In point of fact, however, all this music leads to naught; it represents little more than an attempt by the characters to impose happiness artificially—again, to retain the "whiteness." It echoes in an empty shell of vapid desire. The pessimism could not ring more poignantly. For in *The Cherry Orchard* the music, like the whiteness, ultimately becomes an illusion, a pathological form of wishful thinking. These two would-be positive forces resemble the orchard itself—an illusion of a past life that the protagonists perceive more easily than the audience, which sees more poplars and telephone poles through the set windows than anything else. Symbolically, the sprightly sound of a band's music yields to the dull, unmusical clicking of billiard balls— all of which lends significance to the double innuendo that people are like the balls on a billiard table, knocked about in a series of banked shots before being pocketed away, and that they are made to act like melancholy puppets on a string, dancing ritually as if in a state of benumbed dream, not knowing the reason for what they do. This is the forlorn state of those who can say soulfully with Pishchik: "Everything in this world comes to an end."

Out of a simple pair of bird images, then, Chekhov cross-weaves a network of motifs which culminates in the final counterpoint: the sounds of the snapping string and of the felling ax. That both are related intrinsically, and gloomily, is certain from Chekhov's description of them: both ring identically: mournfully and sadly (*grustno, pechal'nyy*). The first instance of the snapping string in the middle of the performance is not accompanied by the thuds of axes against trees, for at this point, like the characters, we do not know whether it is a heron or an owl that we have heard. In the reverberation there is hope rather than finality: at least there is questioning. Life and death hang in the balance, so the counterpoint may continue: the cherry orchard may still not be sold to strangers and leveled for commercial purposes. But the first sounding leads to the second, as if answering the question with death. "A feeling of emptiness" takes over, and in the shell of the house the tunes have vanished, leaving nothing but the faint echoes of humming voices. Since the string's sound and the ax's thud become synonymous (as if the ax had struck the string and broken it), it becomes painfully clear that a breaking string is after all a broken string. Here it does sound with finality, and here the counterpoint ends. This is not a case of "emotional distancing," as has been claimed.[54] *The Cherry Orchard* is written in an emotional key, deeper or more overt, perhaps, than we are used to in Chekhov, and the emotional experience finds its objective correlative in sounds. And the experience is far from optimistic: that the white illusion of life is finally crushed by the axed trees, just as the musical illusion of happiness is finally destroyed, as in the ending of folktales, by the snapped string—all this bespeaks a pessimistic message, a "drama of death." The ending is tragic:

> FIRS: . . . Life has gone by as if I had never lived. *Lies down.* I'll lie down a while . . . There's no strength left in you, old fellow; nothing is left, nothing. Ah, you addlehead! *Lies motionless. A distant sound is heard coming from the sky as it were, the sound of a snapping string mournfully dying away. All is still again, and nothing is heard but the strokes of the ax against a tree far away in the orchard.*

In every other full-length play, Chekhov made a pistol shot dominate the climax. He was well aware that *The Cherry Orchard* represented a departure from this practice: ". . . there's something new about it . . . there's not a single pistol shot in the whole play."[55] But the snapping string is a pistol shot of a different order of magnitude: rather than limit itself immediately and primarily to the physical world, it reverberates throughout the world of the spirit, regardless of whether mortals can make sense out of it. It has contrapuntal associations which the other Chekhov "sounds" do not have, and because of its distant origin in folklore, uniting the light and dark of creation, one could say, its vibrations can be overpowering. Perhaps Chekhov was aware of this potentially deafening resonance when he tried to tone down the enthusiasm for sound effects of his directors, who were trying hard to make acoustic sense out of the enigmatic sound. Chekhov naturally spoke in terms of a simple sound effect, which, after all, is all the snapping string is when it comes to producing the play: "Tell Nemirovich that the sound in Acts Two and Four of *The Cherry Orchard* must be shorter, a lot shorter, and must be felt as coming from a great distance. What a lot of fuss about nothing—not being able to cope with a trifle like this, a mere noise, although it's so clearly described in the play."[56] For us, however, this trifle, or mere noise, well illustrates what Thomas Mann said of Chekhov: that he was one of those major writers who could embrace the fullness of life in a simple incident.

NOTES

1. See Ronald Hingley, *Chekhov: A Biographical and Critical Study* (New York: Barnes and Noble, 1966), p. 230.

124 CHEKHOV'S GREAT PLAYS

2. J. L. Styan, *Chekhov in Performance* (Cambridge: Cambridge Univ. Press, 1971), p. 337.

3. Harvey Pitcher, *The Chekhov Play* (London: Chatto and Windus, 1973), p. 182.

4. Francis Fergusson, "The *Cherry Orchard*: A Theater-Poem of the Suffering of Change," in *Chekhov: A Collection of Critical Essays*, ed. R. L. Jackson (Englewood Cliffs, N.J.: Prentice-Hall, 1967), p. 154.

5. Charles B. Timmer, "The Bizarre Element in Cechov's Art," in *Anton Cechov: Some Essays*, ed. T. Eekman (Leiden: E. J. Brill, 1960), pp. 277–92.

6. Quoted from Nils Åke Nilsson, "Intonation and Rhythm in Čechov's Plays," in *Anton Čhechov: Some Essays*, ed. Eekman, p. 180. The quotation in turn is to be found in S. D. Balukhatyy and N. V. Petrov, *Dramaturgiya Chekhova* (Khar'kov, 1935), p. 120. Meyerkhol'd, of course, predates Soviet criticism. Except for *The Cherry Orchard* itself, for which I have used the translation of Avrahm Yarmolinsky in *The Portable Čhekhov* (New York: The Viking Press, 1968), all translations, unless otherwise noted, are by me. For the original text of the play, I have consulted the following edition: *Vishnevyy sad: komediya v chetyrekh deystviyakh* (Vstup. Statya V. V. Yermilova [Moscow: Gos. Izd-vo Detskoy Lit-ry, 1963]).

7. Georgiy P. Berdnikov, *Chekhov dramaturg* (Leningrad and Moscow: Gosudarstvennoye Izdatel'stvo "Iskusstvo," 1957), p. 200. The author is silent about the string in his other book, *A. P. Chekhov* in the series *Russkiye dramaturgi* (Moscow and Leningrad, 1950), too.

8. Aleksandr I. Revyakin, "*Vishnevyy sad*" *A. P. Chekhova* (Moscow: Uchebno-Pedagogicheskoye Izdatel'stvo, 1960), pp. 177 and 182, respectively.

9. Abram Derman, *O masterstve Chekhova* (Moscow: Sovetskiy Pisatel', 1959).

10. Korney I. Chukovskiy, *O Chekhove* (Moscow: Izdatel'stvo "Khudozhestvennaya Literatura," 1967), and Vladimir Yermilov, *A. P. Chekhov* (Moscow: Sovetskiy Pisatel', 1954).

11. Sergey Balukhatyy, *Chekhov dramaturg* (Leningrad: Gosudarstvennoye Izdatel'stvo "Khudozhestvennaya Literatura," 1936), pp. 243–44.

12. Aleksandr I. Roskin, *A. P. Chekhov: Stat'i i ocherki* (Moscow, 1959), and Vasiliy V. Golubkov, *Masterstvo A. P. Chekhova* (Moscow, 1958).

13. Maurice Valency, *The Breaking String* (New York: Oxford Univ. Press, 1966), pp. 284 and 287.

14. Ibid., pp. 289–90.

15. Pitcher, *The Chekhov Play*, p. 182.

16. D. S. Mirsky, *A History of Russian Literature*, ed. F. J. Whitfield (New York: Random House, 1926), p. 381.

17. Quoted from Revyakin, "*Vishnevyy sad*," p. 177.

18. Styan, *Chekhov in Performance*, p. 287.

19. Mirsky, *Russian Literature*, pp. 381–82.

20. From David Magarshack we learn that Chekhov had heard the sound as

a child, in a little hamlet in the Donets Basin, where he used to spend the summer: "It was there that he first heard the mysterious sound, which seemed to be coming from the sky, but which was caused by the fall of a bucket in some distant coal mine" (*Chekhov the Dramatist* [New York: Hill and Wang, 1960], p. 286).

21. Hingley, *Chekhov*, pp. 238–39. We might mention, too, the reference to the sound by Siegfried Melchinger (*Anton Chekhov*, in the series *World Dramatists* [New York: Ungar, 1972]): "its eeriness startles people, who then make it into a mystery. Therefore, Chekhov utilized, for his own ends, the possibility that such a sound can exist and have this effect" (p. 147)—an opinion he repeats later (p. 154). But the idea here, as worded, is not entirely clear.

22. In fact, Stanislavskiy often eagerly overdid such sound effects (out-of-place birdcalls, croaking frogs, chirping crickets, etc.), much to Chekhov's annoyance.

23. Nilsson, "Intonation and Rhythm," p. 179.

24. Fergusson, "The *Cherry Orchard.*"

25. Letter to Vladimir Nemirovich-Danchenko, August 22, 1903, in Anton Chekhov, *The Cherry Orchard*, trans. T. Guthrie and L. Kipnis (Minneapolis: The Univ. of Minnesota Press, 1965), p. 121. Cf. also *The Cherry Orchard* in *The Oxford Chekhov*, Vol. III, trans. and ed. R. Hingley (London: Oxford Univ. Press, 1971), p. 319. Valency states: "Chekhov's world, in general, is quiet, so quiet that when a string breaks in the sky, we hear it" (*Breaking String*, p. 301).

26. Yermilov, A. P. *Chekhov*, pp. 391, 393, and 395.

27. Sophie Lafitte, *Tchékhov* (Paris: Hachette, 1971), p. 268.

28. Pitcher, *The Chekhov Play*, p. 201.

29. Aimée Alexandre, *A la recherche de Tchékhov* (Paris: Editions Buchet/Chastel, 1971), p. 257.

30. Styan, *Chekhov in Performance*, pp. 287 and 288.

31. In Revyakin, "*Vishnevyy sad,*" p. 177. He also wanted the sound to be "more melancholy and soft" (*grustneye i myagche*). Revyakin's source is Stanislavskiy.

32. Magarshack, *Chekhov the Dramatist*, p. 286.

33. Wolf Düwel, *Anton Tschechow* (Halle [Sale]: Veb Verlag Sprache und Literatur, 1961), p. 172.

34. Cf. Johannes Bolte, ed., *Zeitschrift des Vereins für Volkskunde* 20 (1910), and n. 9: Motiv E761.5.2: Life Token: zither string breaks. Secondary reference in Bächtold-Stäubli, note 35, below. I am grateful to Dr. Andrew Cincura for his counsel in the area of folklore.

35. Hanns Bächtold-Stäubli, ed., *Handwörterbuch des deutschen Aberglaubens* (Berlin and Leipzig: W. de Gruyter & Co., 1935–36), VII, 889–90 (see *Saite*). The wedding omen is further explained elsewhere: "When during an orgy a chord on the instrumentalist's fiddle snaps, then there are either married couples on the dance floor or a dancing pair will soon become engaged" (Bächtold-Stäubli quotes Evald Tang Kristensen, *Gamle folks fortaellinger om det jyske almveliv*

126 CHEKHOV'S GREAT PLAYS

[Arhus: Fortfatterens forlag, 1900], p. 889). While the *Todesfall* omen has greater relevance for our purposes, it may still be marginally interesting to note that there are dancing couples in the ballroom in *The Cherry Orchard* and that several of them perhaps will be getting engaged (dancing the *Grand Rond* when Act III opens are Pishchik and Sharlotta, Trofimov and Mme. Ranevskaya, Anya and the post office clerk, Varya and the stationmaster, Dunyasha and others). No snapping string is heard at this point, of course; however, it has just been heard (near the close of Act II).

36. Cf. F. X. Pritz, *Überbleibsel aus dem hohen Altertum* (Linz, 1854), p. 86. Also *Sagan und Märchen aus dem Obersallis* (Basel: Verlag der Schweiz. Gesellschaft für Volkskunde, 1913), II, 176, n. 63. Secondary references in Bächtold-Stäubli, note 35, above.

37. Pritz, *Überbleibsel*. Cf. also Johann Georg von Hahn, *Griechische und albanesische Märchen* (München und Berlin: G. Müller, 1918), II, 18, n. 64; also Bolte, *Zeitschrift des Vereins für Volkskunde* 20 (1910) p. 70, n. 9. According to Bächtold-Stäubli, von Hahn's motif is similar to the one given by Edwin S. Hartland, *The Legend of Perseus*, Vol. II (London: D. Nutt, 1895), p. 11.

38. We might note here that translators (into English) have needlessly complicated the issue by attempting to identify the instrument. Lyricized by the creative imagination, the raucous, metallic bucket's clang of childhood recollection became the vibrating, melancholy tone of a breaking chord on a string instrument—*any* string instrument, since the word is *struna*. But we may find the translation commonly pointing to a harp (because the sound comes from the sky?), or to a violin (because Chekhov's father, an excellent musician, played the violin? or because the Jewish band that performs in Mme. Ranevskaya's home is dominated by violins?). Magarshack (*Chekhov the Dramatist*, p. 286) suggests a balalaika (because this instrument is most readily associated with Russia? or because one of the variants of the stage directions in Act II reads: "Someone is heard walking quietly along the road and quietly playing a balalaika"?—cf. *The Oxford Chekhov*, p. 324). One translator is even tempted to remove the string and leave just the instrument: "A distant sound that seems to come out of the sky, like a breaking harp (-string) slowly and sadly dying away . . ." (*Six Plays of Chekhov*, trans. Robert W. Corrigan [New York: Holt, Rinehart and Winston, 1962], p. 340). Nor have the guitar, the mandolin, and the zither been forgotten as possibilities. As for Chekhov's own understanding of the meaning of a snapping string, we might recall the sentence in "Rudin," chapter 10, when one character describes another in pessimistic tones: "His string has been stretched too far—and it has snapped."

39. J. E. Cirlot, *A Dictionary of Symbols* (New York: Philosophical Library, 1962), pp. 235–36. Note how many references there are in the play to the sun that has set, or, conversely, to the moon that is rising.

40. *Aeneid* 4.462–63: "and on the roofs in doleful song the solitary owl oft complained and spun out his long notes in mournful strain." (Translation mine)

41. Cirlot, *Dictionary of Symbols*, p. 141.

42. *Iliad* 10. 274–77: and "and on the right by the wayside Pallas Athene sent down a heron to them; they could not see it through the dark of night, but they could hear its cry. And hearing it Odysseus harkened at the bird-sign, and prayed to Athene." (Translation mine)

43. In this connection, the episode of the stranger suggests a counterpoint with the unwritten portion of the play following the curtain fall. The stranger who asks for help and is given a gold piece parallels the strangers (the new society) who "ask" for the cherry orchard and are "given" it. As if enacting Lopakhin's blunt, speculative words in Act I: "You must tear down the old buildings . . . , cut down the old cherry orchard . . . [so as to let in the strangers who will pay] ten rubles per acre a year," the strangers will come after the second snapping of the string to deal a death blow to the previous style of life.

44. Styan suggests that at the end of Act II Chekhov is "familiarizing us with the sound . . . , so that [at the very end] it will not then disrupt the experience of the whole by its strangeness, but tie this movement with that" (*Chekhov in Performance*, p. 287).

45. Somehow the pattern of sunrise and sunset (moonrise) throughout the play fits the optical scheme, if only because, in the dialogue and stage directions together, there are at least eight literal references to such astronomical movements, not to speak of those used figuratively.

46. Nilsson, "Intonation and Rhythm," p. 172.

47. Letter to V. I. Nemirovich-Danchenko, November 2, 1903, in *The Oxford Chekhov*, p. 328.

48. Letter to K. S. Stanislavskiy, February 5, 1903, in ibid., p. 318. See also the Guthrie and Kipnis edition of *The Cherry Orchard*, p. 118. Pitcher calls this "a Turgenevan atmosphere of white dresses" (*The Chekhov Play*, p. 161). Chekhov's insistence on white stands out dramatically by comparison with the infrequency of other colors mentioned in the play. None is a "life" color. Varya is dressed in black; a figure in the ballroom wears a gray top hat; Mme. Ranevskaya's other room is violet (a tone of mourning and death, thus counterbalancing her other room, which is white); and the sky is a cold clear blue—enough to set the white cherry blossoms into pronounced relief. None of these opposing colors acquires the ubiquitous personality that white acquires throughout the work. White is a precious color: like the life of the older generation, it is so easily soiled (like the blossoms, which will so easily fall with the "frost"). It does not fit the laborer, and if the tramplike stranger wears a white cap, it is perforce "shabby," just as, conversely, Dunyasha's hands are "white, as white as a lady's."

49. S. I. Ozhegov, *Slovar' russkogo yazyka*, izd. 7-e stereotipnoye (Moscow: Sov. Entsiklop., 1968).

50. Ironically, the yellow ball becomes white the last time he aims his imaginary shot. Is it not so that if the white ball is pocketed the game is over?

51. For this reason, the Oxford edition, which translates the billiard game's

"yellow" references by "red," in accordance with how the sport is played "in English-speaking countries" (*The Oxford Chekhov*, p. 335), is in error.

52. Letter to V. I. Nemirovich-Danchenko, November 2, 1903, in ibid., p. 328. Need one also recall that a yellow house (*zheltyy dom*) means a madhouse, or that prostitutes in Russia used to carry yellow cards, or that the color is associated with oppressiveness (cf. the yellow parlor in Mme. Bovary's home in Tostes, or the yellow hotel room Svidrigaylov rents before his suicide)?

53. As examples of the loss of control over the physical world, we might single out the following: in Act I, a bouquet, a chair, and a saucer fall, and Gayev gets something in his eye; in Act II, Dunyasha develops a headache, Mme. Ranevskaya fumbles in her bag, and gold pieces scatter from a dropped purse; in Act III, a billiard cue is broken, Pishchik thinks he has lost his money from his pocket, Lopakhin is hit accidentally on the head, later he trips, a telegram falls, and Trofimov falls down the stairs; and in Act IV, Trofimov loses his rubbers, a hat box is crushed, Varya cannot find something in her luggage, and a thermometer is broken. Each can say, with Yepikhodov, "A misfortune befalls me every day."

54. See Pitcher, *The Chekhov Play*, p. 209.

55. Letter to O. L. Knipper, September 25, 1903, in *The Oxford Chekhov*, p. 320.

56. Letter to O. L. Knipper, March 18, 1904, in ibid., p. 330.

МОСКОВСКІЙ ХУДОЖЕСТВЕННЫЙ ТЕАТРЪ

"The emblem of the Seagull on our curtain symbolizes for us the beginning of our creative life, our love for Chekhov, his enormous role in the MAT."

—Vladimir Nemirovich-Danchenko

The photograph of the logo of the MAT was made from Nikolay Efros, *Moskovskiy khudozhestvennyy teatr* (1898–1923) (Moscow-Petersburg: Gosizdat, 1924).

The Nemirovich-Danchenko quotation may be found in Ivanova, Ye., ed., *P'yesy A. P. Chekova v Moskovskom Khudozhestvennom Teatre* (Moscow: Iskusstvo, 1961), p. 13.

PART II

CHEKHOV AND THE
MOSCOW ART THEATER

BY MICHAEL HEIM

When in Act I of *The Seagull*, Treplev, the aspiring young playwright, calls for "new forms" in the theater, does Chekhov identify with him? Only in the sense that Treplev is formulating an important problem: Chekhov meant to bring the state of the Russian theater to the attention of his audience. After formulating the problem, however, he pulls back. He does not in the least identify with Treplev's solution to the problem. The abstract monodrama Nina performs and the exotic production Treplev has dreamed up for it are parodies of new forms—sometimes sympathetic, sometimes biting; they are not an attempt on Chekhov's part to tell playwrights what to do. Chekhov had a more modest view of his profession. The author's job was not to provide answers—no one knows all the answers—it was to provide questions. Answers, if there were any, would come from a readership primed by an author to think in a new way.

For a striking example of how this author-reader relationship actually bore fruit, let us examine the relationship between the author of *The Seagull* and the directors and cast of the Moscow Art Theater, the work's first informed, committed readership. Responding sensitively to the theatrical thematics running through the play, they created a theatrical form adequate to its new dramatic form. Today, long after the fact, the theatrical message is obvious: the modern theatergoer recognizes Treplev's play as an immature but sincere attempt at renewing the theater and Arkadina's hysterical histrionics as a reflection of her acting technique, her stage behavior. But even this, the most literal level of the play, was far from obvious to the audience attending the first performance of the play in October 1896 at the Aleksandrinskiy Theater in St. Petersburg.

Opening night was a benefit performance for a fat, mustachioed comic actress popular for her slapstick roles. Although there was no part for her in the play, her faithful audience filled the theater expecting to be entertained—if not the way she entertained them, then at least with broad theatrical effects. (*Pashenka*, the play immediately preceding *The Seagull*, had been applauded wildly by the same kind of audience. It told the story of a café singer who marries into an aristocratic family, then escapes back to her former life and shoots herself when her husband comes after her.) Looking forward to an evening of either farce or melodrama, they made vociferous fun of Masha's snuff, Treplev's bandage, and the stuffed seagull, and could only have been bitterly disappointed when Treplev's suicide took place offstage. Chekhov forced himself to sit through two acts, but finally he fled—first the theater, then St. Petersburg. As a result, news of the play's success at the following performances, attended by a more sophisticated audience, was slow in reaching him. When it finally came, he admitted that first, he had overreacted (the day after the première he wrote, "I will *never* again write or put on plays"), and second, the Nina (Vera Kommissarzhevskaya) had been superb.

Two years later, in the winter of 1898, the Moscow Art Theater included *The Seagull* in its inaugural season. By then the play was making the rounds of the provinces and enjoying considerable success, but Chekhov was still reticent enough about a Moscow production to rebuff the Moscow Art Theater's first request for the play. The project was the brainchild of Vladimir Nemirovich-Danchenko, one of the two founders of the Theater and a longtime admirer of Chekhov's. "I am willing to guarantee, he wrote to Chekhov, "that in a skillful production, free of banality and absolutely faithful, the hidden dramas and tragedies will engage the whole audience."[1] Nemirovich-Danchenko's partner, the better-known Konstantin Stanislavskiy, also needed to be persuaded. After his first reading of the play, he pronounced it tedious and unstageworthy, and he persisted in his position until well into the rehearsal period. In the end, however, Nemirovich-Danchenko, the Moscow Art Theater's literary manager, managed to bring both parties around to his point of view. He was soon vindicated. The production caused such a furor that it saved the floundering Theater from financial ruin. In return, the Theater provided Chekhov with a viable showcase for his plays and a regular audience that not only appreciated them but thirsted for them.

Although written several years before the Moscow Art Theater came into existence, *The Seagull* anticipated that Theater's main innovation: its emphasis on ensemble playing or, in negative terms, the abolition of the star system. Chekhov illustrates the vacuity of the star mentality in the persons of Arkadina—who, a star of the second magnitude and slightly past her prime at that, revels in the tributes of provincial students—and Shamrayev, the estate manager, who pesters her with anecdotes of the stars of his generation. He also comes close to suggesting an alternative when Dorin points out optimistically that although the Russian theater may have fewer stars than before, "the average actor has come a long way." But far more important than the lines is the structure underlying them. For Chekhov had written a play that needs no stars, a play that in fact could not be fully appreciated without the kind of principles the Moscow Art Theater stood for.

Who is the "star" of *The Seagull?* At first glance, it is Nina. She is, after all, the title character and the character who undergoes the greatest amount of development during the play. But what about Treplev? In any good melodrama a character who shoots himself is the main character. (Such was the case in *Pashenka,* and such is the case in Chekhov's earlier play, *Ivanov,* which was nothing if not a tour de force for the actor in the title role.) If we place Nina and Treplev on the same level, we cannot leave Arkadina and Trigorin far behind. They are not only essential to the action in their own right; they are to a large extent established, old-guard, passé versions of them.

Each of these artistically oriented couples has a less intense analogous couple. Masha and Medvedenko lead the sort of boring, humdrum existence Treplev might well have forced on Nina. The analogy goes further. Nina has taken her life into her own hands by escaping into the world of the theater; Masha at least breaks away from her parents by marrying Medvedenko. Just as Chekhov refused to offer his audience pat solutions, so he refused to guarantee his characters success, even in their most high-minded undertakings. But when Nina rejects the seagull image in her final meeting with Treplev, when she calls herself an actress, the worst is clearly past. She knows what direction to take and may well develop into precisely the type of actress the Moscow Art Theater had set out to train. (Stanislavskiy and Nemirovich-Danchenko did a good deal of their initial recruiting in provincial theaters like the one Nina is going off to.) Masha's marriage to Medvedenko may not have brought her any relief, but like Nina she has not given up. Medvedenko has accepted a post in another district, and she hopes the change of atmosphere will help her to "tear Treplev out of her heart." And Medvedenko, boor that he is, has the sense to pack up and leave both her family (Shamrayev's petty despotism) and his (the quadruple tyranny of a mother, two sisters, and little brother). One of the main reasons for Treplev's suicide is that he is unable to make just such a move; he is unable to cut off ties with his family, his mother, and strike out on his own.

If Masha and Medvedenko parallel and—to a certain extent—parody Nina and Treplev, then by the same token Polina Andreyevna and Dorn parallel and parody Arkadina and Trigorin. Both women are possessive mistresses; both men are weak-willed lovers of long standing. Both Arkadina and Polina Andreyevna are jealous of Nina, and both are capable of hysterical outbreaks. But while Arkadina gets what she wants (Trigorin goes away with her), Polina Andreyevna does not (Dorn refuses to let her come and live with him).

Structurally, this layered effect gives the play increased depth of characterization. Dramatically, it means that no one character may stand out without upsetting the balance. More than any theater in Russia at the time, the Moscow Art Theater was attuned to maintaining that balance. Identifying with both Nina's quest and Chekhov's talent, it adopted a stylized seagull as its emblem.

After attending several of the early rehearsals for the play, Chekhov moved south for his health. Rehearsals for a December opening had begun in August (rehearsals for the Aleksandrinskiy Theater production lasted no more than ten days), and Stanislavskiy and Nemirovich-Danchenko prepared the actors in tandem. Enthusiastic as he was about the reports he received, Chekhov had promised another play then gaining popularity in the provinces, Uncle Vanya, to the Malyy Theater in Moscow, and could not pass it on to the Art Theater. But the Malyy was a government-supported theater and was therefore obliged to submit the script to a government-supported committee. When the committee members found a bit too much of themselves in the portrait of Professor Serebryakov, they took umbrage and demanded extensive changes. Outraged, Chekhov withdrew the play, and before long it was in rehearsal at the Moscow Art Theater.

At about this time, the spring of 1899, Chekhov made his first pilgrimage to Moscow since well before the Art Theater had opened its doors. As a tribute, the company gave a private performance of *The Seagull* for him. No one was very happy about the outcome, least of all Chekhov. "I saw *Seagull* without any sets," he wrote to Maxim Gor'kiy. "I can't judge the play with equanimity, because the seagull herself gave such an abominable performance—she blubbered loudly throughout—and Trigorin (the writer) walked around the stage and spoke like a paralytic. He is not supposed to have 'a will of his own,' but the way the actor conveyed it was nauseating to behold" (May 9, 1899). Though harsh on the surface, Chekhov's criticism shows a kind of indirect respect for the company. All he had admired in the Petersburg production was the work of a single actress; in the Moscow production he denigrated the work of two actors, thereby giving tacit approval to the rest. One factor, however, greatly complicated the situation: the Trigorin Chekhov so railed against in the letter was played by Stanislavskiy.

Stanislavskiy was primarily a showman. He regarded literature as more or less an accessory to the theater; for him, a play was an excuse to go into production. The initial uneasiness he felt with Chekhov the author lingered on throughout their years of collaboration. At worst, he would simply state that Chekhov was never any good at interpreting his works. At best, he would brand Chekhov's suggestions as cryptic, but adopt them. During the Moscow Art Theater's first season Stanislavskiy played Trigorin as a dandy, a lady-killer; the text clearly indicates his main character trait to be passivity. When Chekhov advised him to wear tattered shoes and checkered pants, he was merely taking a leaf out of Stanislavskiy's own book: using props to help get at a character, moving from externals to internals. Women fall in love with Trigorin despite his looks, not because of them. Stanislavskiy was taken in by what Arkadina and Nina say about him; he did not go beneath the surface. Likewise, he accepted Treplev's play as a work of genius undermined only by Nina's performance. "How talented this Treplev is with his Chekhov-like soul and true understanding of art," he wrote in his autobiography, *My Life in Art*.[2] Later, in *Uncle Vanya*, he missed the irony in Astrov's courtship of Yelena, and Chekhov felt it necessary to give him another "cryptic" message: "Uncle Vanya is the one who snivels; Astrov whistles." As an actor, Stanislavskiy was more attuned to individual roles than to the general structure of the play, and was therefore inclined to take them at face value. The result was often an appreciable loss of subtlety.

Another problem Chekhov continually faced with the Moscow Art Theater—and again it is associated with Stanislavskiy rather than with Nemirovich-Danchenko—was that of excessive effects, both aural and visual. These, too, have their origin in Stanislavskiy's acting techniques. They were meant to contribute as much to the actor's mood as the spectator's. With its first production—Aleksey Tolstoy's *Tsar' Fedor*, a period piece from the time of the boyars—the Moscow Art Theater gained a reputation for naturalistic detail, and at times the search for historical accuracy in sets and costumes reached fantastic proportions. Perhaps the plethora of sound effects in the Theater's Chekhov productions stems from a certain overcompensation for the lack of exotic scenic effects. Chekhov's plays all take place in the Russia of their day and required no special research. In any case, even Stanislavskiy could joke about it— many years later, at least. Here is how he dealt with the issue in *My Life in Art*: " 'It's so nice and quiet,' the hero of my play will remark, Chekhov said to someone in a voice loud enough for me to hear. 'Isn't it wonderful: no birds, no dogs, no cuckoos, no owls, no clocks, no sleigh bells, no crickets.' "[3] Crickets, in fact, came to be almost as much a trademark of the Moscow Art Theater as the seagull.

Also problematical was the related question of lengthy pauses and general pacing. Special effects usually occurred during pauses, and the two together significantly increased performance time: Ol'ga Knipper, Chekhov's future wife and a key member of the company, gives the following account of Chekhov's reaction to the pacing of the private *Seagull* performance: "Chekhov, gentle, considerate Chekhov, walked up to the stage, watch in hand, pale and earnest, and said in no uncertain terms that everything was fine, but 'may I ask you to end my play with the third act. I refuse to allow you to do Act IV. . . .' There were many things he did not agree with—the pacing most of all—and assured us all we were not playing it as he had written it."[4] Commentators of Chekhov's plays make much of the significance of the pauses. The standard—and perfectly valid—argument is that since the dialogues hint at what the characters mean rather than state it outright, since the characters may not even be quite sure what they mean themselves, strategically placed stretches of silence give everyone on both sides of the footlights the time and atmosphere to appreciate what is going on beneath the surface. But Chekhov plainly indicated where he meant the pauses to take place, and though he did not specify how long they were to last, he was appalled at Stanslavskiy's tendency to drag them out.[5]

A conductor is entitled to his own interpretation of a score; a director is entitled to his own interpretation of a play. The question is, at what point does leeway become license? With *Three Sisters* Chekhov began writing expressly for the Moscow Art Theater, and by rights the amount of leeway the theater allowed itself should have diminished. After all, author and theater were partners; they were engaged in a common cause. Yet throughout the staging of *Three Sisters* the problems that had arisen in *The Seagull* and *Uncle Vanya* continued to arise. Though still sequestered in the south, Chekhov received regular progress reports from members of the company and transmitted his reactions partly by mail and partly by special courier—Ol'ga Knipper. Since he felt the play stood or fell with the third act (which takes place during the fire in town, in the room Ol'ga and Irina have been sharing), the problems it posed are especially pertinent.

According to reports from Ol'ga Knipper from early 1901, for example, there was a great deal of noise and bustle on stage, and a fire alarm would blow with increasing frequency and insistency as the act progressed. Chekhov objected strenuously: the noise was supposed to come from town, from far off, and the intervals at which the alarms were to be rung were clearly indicated in the script. Curiously enough, Stanislavskiy viewed the issue from an entirely different point of view. "Chekhov was quite satisfied with us," he wrote about Chekhov's impressions of the first *Three Sisters* rehearsals he attended in Moscow.[6] "The only thing that bothered him was we were not ringing the military signals right. He kept worrying and complaining to us about it. We suggested he take over rehearsing the sound effects for the fire himself, and put all our equipment at his disposal. Chekhov was thrilled with the role of director, and went about it enthusiastically, giving us a long list of objects to have ready for the sound effects rehearsal." Clearly, the two men were talking at cross-purposes. The "lack of communication" Chekhov is famous for had its place offstage as well as on.

Again in Act III Chekhov rejected Stanislavskiy's idea of having Natasha slam doors and peer under the furniture for potential enemies as she crossed the stage. His stage directions have her walk a straight line without stopping, and he wanted them respected. He felt they made the scene more bloodcurdling. And they did not drag things out.

Later in the act, when Masha confesses her love for Vershinin to Ol'ga, Stanislavskiy had Ol'ga kiss Masha just before she exits, thereby indicating she has accepted Masha's infidelity and is bestowing her blessing on her. The context makes it clear, however, that such is not the case. Details like these seriously affected the entire tenor of the play.

Chekhov did not introduce any radical changes into his last two plays, the only two he wrote with the Moscow Art Theater and its audience in mind. The major themes and devices develop and deepen steadily from one play to the next. But one minor shift may well reflect the influence of the Moscow Art Theater and its emphasis on ensemble work. As titles, both *The Seagull* and *Uncle Vanya* are misleading. They focus attention on a single character where several share the spotlight equally. By giving his next play the title *Three Sisters*, Chekhov emphasized the family aspect (already present, in a sense, in the "uncle" of the previous title) and called attention to the importance of the interaction among characters, the forte of the Moscow Art Theater. In *The Cherry Orchard* he went a step further and shifted the title away from the characters onto their most vital concern. The ensemble had taken over entirely.

But *The Cherry Orchard* also gave rise to a new conflict. Every theater group gathering to read *The Cherry Orchard* for the first time reopens the debate as to whether to treat the play as a comedy or a tragedy. The reason the debate never ends is that Chekhov wrote the point of contention into the play. Ambiguity is the very cornerstone of the action. Just when things seem to have reached an unbearable impasse, Yepikhodov will bump into a chair, Trofimov will lose his rubbers, Lopakhin will moo. The disparity between the way the characters envision their lives and the way they actually live them (Ranevskaya's dreams of childhood innocence and her sordid present, Yasha's dreams of Paris and his Russian past, Sharlotta's inner life and her clownlike façade, and all the misadventures of all the mismatched lovers) moves the audience's emotions back and forth, from one extreme to another. That movement must be constantly visible onstage. To Chekhov's dismay, it was entirely lacking in the Moscow Art Theater production. The problem was not poor ensemble work; it was Stanislavskiy's basic conception of the play. Stanislavskiy was content to read it as a tragedy, pure and simple.

By pacing the production slowly, Stanislavskiy fulfilled his ideal of a tragic *Cherry Orchard* but distorted Chekhov's intention. A fast tempo would have shown how ineffectual the characters are—it would have implied the action need not have ended as it does; the slow tempo showed how hopeless the situation was—it implied there was no way out. This latter interpretation is notably tendentious, and Chekhov, here as elsewhere, was more concerned with pinpointing problems and bringing them before the public than prophesying the doom of a social class or way of life. In desperation he consented to several cuts in Act II, including a beautiful and poignant exchange between Sharlotta and Firs, but still the play went on too long. He was very upset by critical remarks from Moscow and relayed them immediately to his wife. "They say that Stanislavskiy [who played the part of Gayev] is awful in the fourth act and that he drags terribly. It's horrible. An act meant to last twelve minutes at most goes on for forty minutes in your production. One thing is certain: Stanislavskiy has ruined my play" (March 29, 1904). And at the very end of his life Chekhov said to a friend, "Can that possibly be my *Cherry Orchard?* . . . They're making me a crybaby and a boring writer both." [7] When he objects to being turned into a crybaby, he is rejecting the ideological stance that follows from the play's tragic tempo; when he objects to being turned into a bore, he is rejecting the aesthetic principle that a tedious reality must be tedious in art, onstage.

The conclusion is inescapable: Chekhov the dramatist was far in advance of the theater of his day, even the Moscow Art Theater. What the Art Theater did give Chekhov was, on the one hand, a group of young, vibrant actors untainted by the acting clichés of their time and willing to sacrifice stardom to the cause of a strong ensemble, and on the other, an audience whose initial good taste developed and grew along with the Theater. What it failed to give him was a guiding literary intelligence with the Art Theater to see the plays through production. Nemirovich-Danchenko came close to this ideal, and Chekhov much appreciated his efforts. But Stanislavskiy's stronger personality and greater visibility often gave him the upper hand in the partnership. [8]

From the beginning the commercial success of the plays as performed by the Moscow Art Theater militated against change, and when the theater traveled abroad—shortly after Chekhov's death to Berlin and later to Paris and New York—it introduced more than one generation of directors, actors, and translators to their first "authentic" contact with Chekhov, and set the tone for years to come. Until recently, departures from the Moscow Art Theater Chekhov canon were few and far between. Now that the situation has changed, the issue of "new forms" arises again. If Chekhov and the theater are to be served well, those new forms must rest securely on a sensitive reading of the text, free of preconceived notions and capable of providing structural unity.[9]

NOTES

1. This letter first appeared in the *Yezhegodnik Moskovskogo khudozhestvennogo teatra.* 1944 (Moscow: Muzey MKhAT, 1946). The Chekhov letters quoted below come from Anton Chekhov, *Polnoye sobraniye sochineniy*, pp. 18–20 (Moscow: Goslitizdat, 1949–51).

2. *My Life in Art* (Boston: Little, Brown, 1924), p. 355. The English-language edition of *My Life in Art* is highly inadequate. The translation often obscures or distorts the text (I have amended it freely there), and many passages are missing completely (see note 6, below, for an example). Moreover, newly published documentary material make a critical edition imperative.

3. *My Life in Art*, p. 420. Yevtikhiy Karpov, the director of the original Petersburg *Seagull*, once dropped in on a production of *The Cherry Orchard* playing in Yalta and claiming the patronage of both the Moscow Art Theater and Chekhov himself. Chekhov vigorously denied all participation, and in Karpov's words, "the only thing meant by 'modeled after the Moscow Art Theater production' was that there was an assistant director standing backstage throughout the play constantly whistling, cawing, cuckooing, chirping, croaking, and peeping—in other words, drowning out the actors' lines with his bird and frog imitations" ("Dve posledniye vstrechi s A. P. Chekhovym," in *Chekhov i teatr* [Moscow: Iskusstvo, 1961], p. 372).

4. Ol'ga Knipper-Chekhova, "Ob A. P. Chekhove," *Vospominaniya i stat'i. Perepiska*, (Moscow: Iskusstvo, 1972), I, 49.

5. Translators have generally been remiss in indicating Chekhov's pauses. Most English translations fails to reproduce them accurately.

6. This passage, absent from the English translation of *My Life in Art*, comes from the standard edition of the Russian original (*Moya zhizn' v iskusstve* [Leningrad: Academia, 1928], pp. 407–8).

7. "Dve vstrechi," p. 373.

8. For many years Stanislavskiy and Nemirovich-Danchenko presented a

united front to the world, but a recently published exchange of letters (in *Isto-richeskiy arkhiv* [1962], II, 3–58) shows they were constantly at loggerheads. The letters are summarized in Nina Gourfinkel, "Repenser Stanislavski," *Revue d'Histoire du Théâtre*, 2 (1971), pp. 103–28.

9. Readers interested in pursuing the relationship between Chekhov and the Moscow Art Theater will profit greatly from Simon Karlinsky's *Letters of Anton Chekhov* (New York: Harper and Row, 1973), reissued in paperback as *Anton Chekhov's Life and Thought* (Berkeley, Los Angeles: Univ. of California Press, 1976) (Moscow: Iskusstvo, 1955). The views Karlinsky expresses in his commentaries and notes serve as the point of departure for the present study. The standard work in Russian is M. N. Stroyeva's *Chekhov i Khudozhestvenyy teatr* (Moscow: Iskusstvo, 1955).

HUNTSMEN, BIRDS, FORESTS, AND THREE SISTERS

BY SIMON KARLINSKY

In describing the domestic arrangements of her parents at Yasnaya Polyana, Tolstoy's daughter Aleksandra emphasized the major role that dogs
and horses played in their day-to-day existence.[1] Few people who live in
the twentieth century find themselves in such close proximity to such
large numbers of these two domesticated species of animals. Those who
have read Pushkin's "Count Nulin," Gogol''s *Dead Souls*, Turgenev's
Sportsman's Sketches, Tolstoy's *War and Peace* and *Anna Karenina*, and
almost anything by Aksakov will know that the pursuit on horseback of
foxes, wolves, and hares, with the aid of large packs of hunting hounds,
was the favorite pastime of nineteenth-century Russian gentry. The hunting of small game with a dog and rifle was widely practiced by all strata
of the Russian population. On the staff of most rural estates were kennel
masters, kennel hands, and special professional huntsmen (*yegerya*),
whose job it was to keep the estate kitchens supplied with edible game of
every imaginable sort.

From the *Testament* of Prince Vladimir Monomakh, written at the
beginning of the twelfth century to Tolstoy's great novels of the 1860s
and 1870s, hunting was depicted in Russian literature as a noble and
poetic passion, a major component of the good life, and the most direct
way of achieving communion with nature and with the Russian common
people. In Turgenev's *Sportsman's Sketches* (more correctly, *Diary of a
Hunter*) and in Sergey Aksakov's *Diary of Bird Hunting in Orenburg
Province*, the hunter wandering about the countryside in pursuit of wa-
terfowl and of the birds of the forest and the fields is shown as a warm,
responsive person who is in tune with the creatures of the wild and with

the natural beauty of his country. Aksakov's approach to wild birds and animals—his love and admiration of them, combined with a determination to exterminate as many of them as possible—did not seem paradoxical to his contemporaries. It took an early-twentieth-century critic, Yuliy Aykhenval'd, a great admirer of the author of *Family Chronicle*, to realize that "the meek murderer Aksakov fell passionately in love with nature and devoted his life to bringing death into it."[2]

Perhaps the most powerful instances of poetic idealization of hunting in Russian literature are to be found in the novels of Tolstoy. Olenin in *The Cossacks* imagines that he has grasped the meaning of life and the essence of his own humanity while hunting boar and pheasant in the Caucasus. In *Anna Karenina*, Konstantin Levin's rapport with his wonderfully humanized bird dog, Laska, combined with his haymowing and other agrarian activities, serves to characterize him as a decent man, whose natural, sincerely felt mode of life is contrasted with the artificial worlds of bureaucracy and high society in which the lives of other major characters of the novel are spent. The accidental encounter of Levin on the train with Alexey Aleksandrovich Karenin, as described in their conversation at Stiva Oblonskiy's dinner party, is most telling in this respect. Levin had traveled to the Tver' province in order to kill a she-bear that had been discovered there, the she-bear whose skin Oblonskiy later finds him measuring in a Moscow hotel room. Karenin, who in most ways is Levin's intellectual and moral opposite within the scheme of the novel, was on a fact-finding errand, connected with an investigation of the status of national minorities. There is little doubt that Tolstoy regards Levin's bear-hunting trip as a meaningful and admirable activity and wishes to contrast it to Karenin's travels, which he sees as a pointless bureaucratic exercise. And, of course, the overwhelmingly vivid scenes in *War and Peace* (when Natasha literally squeals in ecstasy and delight upon seeing a pack of hounds tear a jackrabbit to bits and when her brother Nicholas plaintively asks God what sin he had committed that God is allowing a hunted wolf to escape) belong among the most unforgettable depictions of hunting in world literature.

There was, then, in Russian literature of the nineteenth century, a widespread tradition of depicting the hunt and hunters both reverently and poetically. It is against the background of this tradition that we can best appreciate the audacity and originality with which the hunting theme was treated in a story that appeared in June 1881 in the Moscow humor magazine *The Alarm Clock*. The title of the story was "St. Peter's Day," and it was signed by a name that meant nothing to anyone outside the narrow little world of Moscow humor magazines: Antosha Chekhonte. The story deals with the opening of the hunting season, which began legally on the feast day of St. Peter, June 29. Instead of the civilized, humane, or heroic hunters of the literary tradition, we are shown a nasty bunch of ill-tempered, squabbling people who shoot every living creature in sight, including meadowlarks, starlings, and domestic pigeons. When no birds can be found, the hunters kill a ground squirrel by throwing rocks at it. The deep understanding of wild animals and their ways, which is usually ascribed to hunters, is belied in "St. Peter's Day" when the ground squirrel is cut open and one of the hunters declares that it lacks a heart and other internal organs and that its insides consist entirely of intestines. Nor is there any of the expected poetic rapport between the hunters and their hounds: *these* hunters beat and mistreat their dogs and throw pebbles at them. The most distinguished member of the hunting party, a retired general, tears out the throat of a wounded quail "with his own fangs." The representatives of the human and canine younger generation, the schoolboy Vanya and the puppy Tshchetnyy (the name means "in vain"), who have been taken along to teach them about the sport, have clearly not had an edifying experience during the outing. At the end of the day, the puppy is scared witless, and the boy is hideously sick from his first exposure to hard liquor.

Exactly one year after the appearance of "St. Peter's Day," Antosha Chekhonte produced another similar story, "The Twenty Ninth of June," which he published in a different humor magazine. The subject is again the opening day of the hunting season. The group of hunters in this story is not as indiscriminately destructive as the ones in "St. Peter's Day," but only because they are too busy gossiping and telling each other dirty stories to do much shooting. At the beginning of the story, these absurd people are ironically contrasted with the true and natural bird hunters, the hawks, owls, and kites whose hunting is clearly seen as more real and meaningful than that of the humans.

Also in 1882, Antosha Chekhonte published a journalistic piece about the popular sport of baiting wolves and foxes with hounds in an enclosed area at the Khodynka Field outside Moscow. In "Impressions of Wolf

Baiting" (*Na volchey sadke*), the joys of capturing and killing wolves, so memorably described by Aksakov and Tolstoy, are shown from the opposite perspective.[3] The happily howling audience, which includes elegantly dressed upper-class women and small children who had been brought by their parents for an educational experience, fails to understand that it is witnessing a sordid massacre of anguished, terrified animals. The author's sympathy is entirely on the side of the tormented wolves and foxes, and the reader ends up feeling disgust for the inhumanity of the promoters and the spectators of this ugly sport.[4]

In August 1883, Antosha Chekhonte offered to the humor magazine, *The Dragonfly* (one of his regular outlets at the time), still another story about hunting, "He Understood." The protagonist of the story is an impoverished, runty little peasant named Pavel Khromoy ("Paul the Lame"), who is out hunting with an absurd homemade shooting weapon and an emaciated, limping mongrel for a bird dog. Caught *in flagrante* when he shoots a starling out of season in the local landowner's forest, thus combining poaching with a hunting season violation, Pavel explains to the landowner that his compulsion for shooting inedible birds (mostly starlings and jackdaws) is a form of alcoholism. The landowner, revolted by the senseless extermination of birds, softens when alcoholism is mentioned, for he knows it from experience and realizes how irresistible alcoholism can be. He lets Pavel go without punishment.

The editors of *The Dragonfly* thought the story not humorous enough and rejected it. The author then submitted it to the leading Russian hunting journal, *Nature and Hunting*. The editors of *Nature and Hunting* saw the story as a "pretty little toy or a piece of pastry."[5] They agreed to print it provided it could be had for free. We know that the literary activities of the story's author during the period of his medical studies were strictly a money-making proposition. However, an exception was made for "He Understood," and it appeared in *Nature and Hunting*, signed, not with a pen name, but with the author's real name, Anton Chekhov.

In his often hastily written productions of 1881–83, Antosha Chekhonte had not yet learned to write like Anton Chekhov. In terms of their literary art, "St. Peter's Day," "The Twenty Ninth of June," "Impressions of Wolf Baiting," and "He Understood" cannot be meaningfully compared with the mature, masterful writings of Aksakov, Turgenev, and

Tolstoy on the same subject. Nor is it surprising that these four early pieces were lost in the torrent of the young Chekhov's other early satirical stories and humorous sketches. Neither the critics nor the readers noticed that Chekhov was quietly questioning and challenging the millennia-old assumption about the beauty and nobility of killing wild animals for sport and laying bare the primeval murderous instinct that often underlies the hunting impulse.

The attitude of the mature Chekhov toward the sport of hunting was for the most part negative, though not always consistent.[6] His interest in man's relationship to wild animals, however, and in man's effect on their habitat remained constant for the rest of his life. This interest was expressed not only in Chekhov's typical attention to the natural environment in which his characters dwell, but also in his continuous reading of books and articles by biologists, explorers, and physical scientists (most notably, Charles Darwin, Nikolay Przhevalskiy, Aleksandr Voyeykov, and Herbert Spencer). By the years 1887–89, these concerns had enabled Chekhov to formulate a set of views about the interaction between humanity and other forms of organic life on this planet and about man's potential for damage to the environment that seem most unusual for his time and are also strikingly reminiscent of the ecological views that have become current during the recent decades, especially in the West.

Chekhov's novella The Steppe (1888) may be read as an account of a journey through the steppe regions of southern Russia, or as a journey through various social strata of that time or as a journey through several stages of a little boy's mood and mind. But read on still another level, The Steppe is a journey through a series of ecosystems. The last term did not exist in Chekhov's time but it can still be justifiably used because in his account of the various relays of the characters' travels through the steppe, Chekhov is careful to note and point out the interrelationships of the local plant life, birds, and animals with the available sources of water and the weather conditions. Even such a recent preoccupation as the danger of releasing harmful chemicals into the natural environment is present in The Steppe, where it is associated with the character of the cart driver Vasya.

Chekhov had little sympathy for the Rousseauist concept of natural man that so attracted Tolstoy. Vasya represents Chekhov's own idea of a natural man, and he makes for an interesting contrast with Tolstoy's Platon Karatayev from *War and Peace*. Whereas Karatayev was imbued with a native Christian goodness, Vasya is almost animal-like, with a preternaturally sharp sense of vision that enables him to discern the motionless creatures that lurk in the steppe and with whom he identifies much more closely than with his fellow humans. Vasya's sense of identity with the animals of the wild is almost Buddhist. He is hurt when his colleague Dymov cruelly whips a harmless grass snake to death; he greets a passing fox as if it were a relative; and he has equally warm feelings toward the minnow he catches and eats alive, to the disgust of the other drivers. Surely it is not by accident that it is Vasya of all the drivers who had his face disfigured by phosphorus poisoning that resulted from his onetime employment at a match factory.

In the story "The Reed Flute" (*Svirel'*), written one year before *The Steppe* and in the play *The Wood Demon*, written one year after it, Chekhov outlined a view of ecological interaction between man and his natural environment that was so far removed from the literary or scientific thought of his time that it was either shrugged off by his contemporaries or went unnoticed. Whereas the famed writer Sergey Aksakov merely pointed out in his *Diary of Bird Hunting* the reduction in the number of migratory birds with every passing year, but refused to connect this reduction with excessive hunting, the increase of human population or any other observable factor,[7] Chekhov's aged and illiterate village shepherd Luka Bednyy ("Luke the Poor") in "The Reed Flute" quite perceptively relates the disappearance of the once abundant birds and fish to the lowering of the water level in the local rivers and streams, to the indiscriminate destruction of forests, and to the decline in the health and strength of the human population. Luka conveys his insights to an audience consisting of one single person and attributes the situation to God's warning to mankind that the end of the world is at hand.

In *The Wood Demon*, Chekhov passed Luka's discoveries on to a man trained in medical and biological sciences and capable of drawing appropriate scientific conclusions, the hero of the play, the landowner, physician and forester Mikhail Lvovich Khrushchev. Artistically, *The Wood Demon* may well be Chekhov's weakest play. But it is also the most polemically pointed of his plays and the one that most concretely embodies his innermost ideas about life, society, and nature. As a rule, Chekhov avoided depicting what the Russian critical tradition likes to call "the positive hero." Khrushchev is the only instance of such a character in a play by Chekhov. Because he is so unarguably right during much of the play, Chekhov tried, not entirely successfully, to humanize him by making him something of a prude. Rather uncharacteristically, Khrushchev believes and spreads the gossip about Yelena's affair with Voynitskiy and he treats Yelena, the only other character who understands and appreciates his conservationist efforts, rudely and callously. If the resultant characterization is not really convincing, it is because advocacy of ideas was simply not Chekhov's forte and was alien to his artistic method.

The other characters of *The Wood Demon* regard as some sort of peculiar eccentricity Khrushchev's concern about the destruction of forests and its effect on the rivers, the animal life, and the climate, as well as his denunciations of labels and stereotypes and of the congealed slogans of the reform epoch of the 1860s. This was also how Chekhov's contemporaries viewed this aspect of the play when it was first published and performed, including even his close friends, such as Grigorovich, Suvorin, and Pleshcheyev.[8] Chekhov himself soon grew dissatisfied with *The Wood Demon*. He eventually reworked it into *Uncle Vanya*, an immeasurably superior play artistically. In *Uncle Vanya*, the ecological insights that were first articulated by the shepherd Luka in "The Reed Flute" and then given a rationalistic and scientific cast by Khrushchev in *The Wood Demon*, were deepened and at the same time compressed. But here they were assigned to a rather disreputable character, Doctor Astrov, which may have minimized their impact.

It should be emphasized that Chekhov's thinking in these three works is not merely conservationist, but ecological in the recent sense of the term.[9] Various forms of nature conservation, such as game protection laws and forestry regulations, were known and practiced in Russia long before Chekhov's time.[10] Ecology as a scientific discipline devoted to the study of the interaction of living organisms with their environment had its origin in the work of the German biologist Ernst Haeckel in the 1860s[11] (although the term itself had already been used in its modern meaning by Henry David Thoreau in a letter written in 1858).[12] It was only in the second half of the twentieth century that the concept of ecology began to merge with what was earlier meant by nature conservation. Yet this merger had already taken place in the three works by Chekhov on ecological themes, which were written in the 1880s and 1890s. Chekhov wrote of the mutual interaction of forests, bodies of water, climate, animals, and human populations in ways that are simply not found in the Russian literature of his time. In *The Steppe*, and even more pointedly in his masterful later story, "In the Ravine," Chekhov also takes up the subject of industrial pollution, another theme that was largely disregarded by the people of his time.

The question arises: What may have been the sources of his ideas in this entire sphere? The American geographer Ian Murray Matley in a suggestive article he published in *Russian Review* in 1972 named the historian Sergey Solov'yev and the climatologist and traveler Aleksandr Voyeykov as the contemporaries whose views might possibly have stimulated Chekhov's environmentalist concerns in *The Wood Demon* and *Uncle Vanya*. [13] The choice of Voyeykov's name was particularly felicitous because, unknown to Professor Matley, Chekhov indeed knew and valued Voyeykov's book *Climates of the Earth* (1884) [14] and wrote of it with enthusiasm to Alexey Suvorin in his letter of March 22, 1890. Chekhov might also have read Voyeykov's essay, "The Influence of Forests on the Climate," which was published in 1878 in *Nature and Hunting*, the same journal where Chekhov's "He Remembered" appeared. [15]

Both Voyeykov's book and his essay contain much information about the interaction of forests and climate that was bound to be of interest to Chekhov. But Voyeykov's writings do not touch on the situation of birds and animals; nor does he say anything about the effect of human activity on the environment. Still, Ian Murray Matley's article raises the basic question of the necessity of studying scientific literature in order to get to the origins of Chekhov's literary art. Critical and philosophical writings, to which the purview of literary scholarship is usually restricted, are not sufficient in Chekhov's case. For a deeper grasp of his themes and his style, scholars will have to turn to the writings of biologists, climatologists, explorers, and geographers whose works Chekhov constantly read and studied and who made a major contribution to his literary formation.

If one searches in the nineteenth century for expressions of concern about man's impact on the natural environment similar to Chekhov's, one will find it most frequently articulated in the literature of the country where this impact was most clearly visible at the time: the United States of America. This concern was initially voiced not by scientists or foresters, but by writers and painters, whose artistic vision and intuition told them that the natural beauty of the North American continent was suffering irreparable damage. James Fenimore Cooper wrote about this in his novels *The Pioneers* (1823) and *The Prairie* (1827). The artists John James Audubon (in his essay "The Ohio," 1834)[16] and Thomas Cole (in "Essay on American Scenery," 1836) wrote about the forests of America "fast disappearing under the axe" in terms remarkably similar to what Chekhov's Khrushchev and Astrov had to say about the forests of Russia. The poet William Cullen Bryant toured the Great Lakes region in 1846 and sadly noted that the wild and lonely woods of that area would soon be chopped down to give way to cottages and boardinghouses,[17] thus unwittingly anticipating the tone and the theme of *The Cherry Orchard*.

In 1852 came the publication of Thoreau's *Walden*, the book that was crucial in changing the American public attitude toward nature and wilderness from indifference and hostility to appreciation and concern. Finally, in 1864, George Perkins Marsh, known to his contemporaries primarily as diplomat and philologist, published a remarkably prophetic book, *Man and Nature*, described in more recent times as "the first book to attack the American myth of superabundance and the inexhaustibility of the earth" and "the fountainhead of the modern conservation movement."[18]

Among these American writings on the subject that was so close to his heart, Chekhov may have known the novels of Cooper. Both *The Pioneers* and *The Prairie* were translated into Russian soon after their publication,[19] and like the rest of Cooper's novels, they remained the favorite reading of Russian schoolchildren for the rest of the nineteenth century. (Chekhov's story "The Boys," 1887, is a humorous and affectionate satire of Russian children's craze for the romance of the prairies, Indians, and pathfinders, which arose due to the popularity of Cooper and of his Anglo-Irish imitator Thomas Mayne Reid, the latter long forgotten in the English-speaking countries, but perennially popular with the Russians.)

Chekhov was very definitely familiar with Thoreau's *Walden*, which he read when it was serialized in Suvorin's newspaper, *New Times*, in 1887. In a letter to Vladimir Korolenko of October 17, 1887, Chekhov conveyed his impression of Thoreau's book: "He's got ideas and a certain freshness and originality about him, but he's hard to read. The architectonics and construction are impossible." Thoreau's somewhat Rousseauist views on the corrupting influence of civilization and technology could

hardly have appealed to Chekhov, who saw the new scientific and tech-
nological developments of his time as beneficiary and promising. But
Thoreau's appreciation of the woods and of the solitude around Walden
Pond is sure to have struck a responsive chord in Chekhov.[20]

It is George Perkins Marsh's *Man and Nature*, however, with its syn-
thesis of the earlier thinking on man's effect on the forests and rivers, the
extermination of wildlife and erosion of the soil, that comes closest to
what Chekhov had to say in "The Reed Flute," *The Wood Demon*, and
Uncle Vanya. *Man and Nature* was translated into Russian in 1866,
during a period of reforms and political turmoil.[21] The theme of the
book was too remote from Russian issues of the time and the appearance
of the Russian translation went virtually unnoticed.[22] Although there is
no evidence that Chekhov was familiar with Marsh's book (which he
would undoubtedly have liked enormously), there exists another book,
far more popular and widely known at the time, through which Marsh's
conservationist ideas might have reached Chekhov. This book is *La Terre*
by Élisée Reclus.

Reclus, the French geographer and noted theoretician of anarchism,
was struck by Marsh's notion that "we are even now breaking up the floor
and doors and window frames of our dwelling for fuel to warm our bodies
and to seethe our pottage."[23] The concluding chapters of the second
volume of *La Terre*, published in France in 1869 and in Russian translation in 1883, are a simplified retelling of some of the basic theses of
Man and Nature. Chekhov mentioned *La Terre* in the list of books he
had intended to donate to the Taganrog municipal library (adding "Not
purchased" in the margin), which was appended to his letter to Pavel
Iordanov (the mayor of Taganrog) of November 24, 1898. However, the
initial publication of the Russian translation of the second volume came
during Chekhov's university years, a time when he followed the new
developments in the sciences with particular avidity. It appears highly
probable, therefore, that he read the second volume of *La Terre* shortly
after its appearance in Russia in 1883, that is, prior to writing "The Reed
Flute" and *The Steppe*. This would explain the similarity between the
ecological thinking of Chekhov and the last two sections of the final
chapter of *La Terre*,[24] with their citations and paraphrases from Marsh's
book. Sonya's speech in the first act of *Uncle Vanya* about the flourishing
of the arts and sciences and the chivalrous attitude of men to women in

those countries where the forests had not been cut down seems also to have been suggested to Chekhov by Reclus. This idea, found in the concluding pages of the second volume and illustrated by the brutalization of the inhabitants of Spain and Italy after their forests were destroyed in the Middle Ages, seems to belong to Reclus himself, rather than to Marsh.[25]

Although it is important to know of the stimuli Chekhov may have received from reading Voyeykov, Thoreau, or Marsh as paraphrased by Reclus, we must not underestimate his own artistic sensibility as well as his commitment as a physician and a biologist. The combination of this sensibility and this commitment enabled Chekhov both to express his ecological thinking in a number of important literary productions and to derive from it a series of personal symbols that dominate much of his writing for the theater from *The Wood Demon* on. It is of course generally known that *The Wood Demon* was the progenitor of *Uncle Vanya*. But in a wider sense, this most personal of Chekhov's plays is also, despite its undeniable artistic and formal shortcomings, ancestral in one way or another to every single one of the great plays of Chekhov's maturity.

The text of *The Wood Demon* is permeated by two sets of contrasting bird symbols, which in the original Russian depend on the grammatical gender of the respective bird names, with the species whose names are feminine symbolizing the female characters and the masculine bird names applied to men. Yelena and Sonya are likened to caged captive birds (the Russian word for "bird" being feminine in gender) at several crucial points. Yelena's temporary escape from her husband is compared to a bird's regaining its freedom. Professor Serebryakov is compared to a horned owl, and Khrushchev promises at the end of the play that he will grow the wings of a free eagle (the environmentalist in touch with nature contrasted with a cabinet scholar bogged down in sterile theorizing). This avian imagery was eliminated in *Uncle Vanya*, but the even more significant image of wantonly destroyed forests is given greater prominence, both on the realistic and on the symbolic levels of the play. The pointlessly destroyed seagull, introduced with Treplev's line, "I was base enough to kill this gull today," becomes the central symbol of the first play of Chekhov's maturity as a playwright, standing both for the subsequent fate of Nina and for the human propensity for destructive behavior that can manifest itself in personal relationships as well as in man's dealings with nature. Similarly, the cherry trees that could not be saved from destruction set the tone and illustrate the predicament of the human characters in *The Cherry Orchard.*

Chekhov's most pervasive, comprehensive, and consistent application of the imagery and symbolism derived from his conservationist ethic is found in the play that many consider his masterpiece, *Three Sisters.* At the core of the play are three sets of unobtrusive and yet essential symbols: birds, which represent freedom and escape; trees, which stand for the good and meaningful life the good characters want to achieve and the bad ones to destroy; and the huntsman, who callously exterminates living beings.

In Act I, Irina, intoxicated with her youth and happiness, imagines a wide blue sky and big white birds over herself, whereupon Chebutykin calls her "My white bird." In Act II, Tuzenbakh cites migratory birds, such as cranes, as proof that the meaning of life is to go on living. Then Vershinin speaks of the imprisoned French minister who saw in birds visible through his prison window the embodiment of freedom but who no longer noticed them after he was released. In Act IV, Masha, feeling trapped in her marriage to Kulygin, envies the migratory birds and wishes she could fly away as they do. The old doctor Chebutykin compares himself to an aged migratory bird grown too old to fly and unable to join Irina and Tuzenbakh in their escape to a meaningful life.[26] Irina says that after she had accepted Tuzenbakh's proposal, she felt as if she had grown wings. But Tuzenbakh is prevented from achieving his escape by Captain Solenyy, the huntsman. In one of his first lines in Act I, Solenyy jokes about shooting Dr. Chebutykin out of boredom. In the last act, he declares his intention to shoot down Tuzenbakh as if he were a woodcock,[27] which he then proceeds to do.

Tree imagery is used in *Three Sisters* in an equally unobtrusive manner, and it is perhaps even more telling. In Act I, Vershinin establishes his credentials as a decent, sensitive man by speaking appreciatively about the local forest and the river, which he sees as contributing to a wholesome climate, and by mentioning his love for the "dear, modest birch trees." Solenyy, nature's opponent, tries to ridicule this speech with his unsuccessful joke about the location of the railroad station. At the beginning of Act IV, the likable officer Rodet bids farewell, not only to his human friends, but also to the trees. The even more likable Baron Tuzenbakh, before going off to the duel that will end his life, speaks of his newly found appreciation of firs, maples, and birches, which, he feels, are looking at him with curiosity and expectation. He then says: "What beautiful trees and, actually, what a beautiful life must there be next to them." He goes on to compare himself prophetically to a dried-up tree that still sways with the live trees in the wind.

After Tuzenbakh's departure, the tree theme is taken over by another ecologically destructive character, Natasha. Natasha's role in the play is that of a usurper. In Act I, she gains control of the brother of the three sisters. In Act II, she is in control over their mode of life. By Act III, Natasha is the mistress of the Prozorov house, having driven Ol'ga and Irina into a small garret room and trying to throw Anfisa out. In Act IV, the three sisters have been evicted out of their father's house. Ol'ga lives at her school; Irina is ready to leave for the brick factory; and Masha says: "I will not go into the house. I can no longer enter it." At the end of the play Natasha intends to consolidate her victory by chopping down the beautiful trees: "Well then, tomorrow I shall be alone. *She sighs*. I will order them first of all to chop down this avenue of firs, and then this maple tree here. . . . It is so ugly in the evening." After destroying the magnificent trees that meant so much to the departing Vershinin and the exterminated Tuzenbakh, Natasha plans to replace free nature with a tame variant of it that is acceptable to her: "And here I will order them to plant little flowers, lots of little flowers and they'll smell. . . ."[28]

From Antosha Chekhonte's early immature story "St. Peter's Day" to Anton Chekhov's last great masterpieces—"In the Ravine," *Uncle Vanya*, and *Three Sisters*—there is a continuous expression of longing for a decent, natural, and unpolluted life, a life that mankind cannot achieve if it continues to exterminate other living beings, destroy forests, and abuse the planet that we all share. Like many other basic Chekhovian themes, this longing was ignored by his contemporaries. Today it strikes us as genuinely visionary and deeply prophetic.

NOTES

1. A. L. Tolstaya, *Otets* (*My Father*) (New York: Izd-vo im. Chekhova, 1953), I, 7.

2. Yu. Aykhenval'd, *Siluety russkikh pisateley* (*Silhouettes of Russian Writers*), series 1 (Moscow: Izd-vo Nauchnogo Slova, 1906), pp. 126–27.

3. Cf. S. T. Aksakov, *Zapiski ob uzhen'ye ryby* (*Fishing Diary*) in *Sobraniye sochineniy* (*Collected Works*) (Moscow: Izd-vo A. A. Kartseva, 1900), the sections "Shchastlivyy sluchay" ("A Fortunate Incident"), V, 265–66 and "Gon'ba lis i volkov" ("The Chase of Foxes and Wolves"), pp. 254–57; and L. N. Tolstoy, *War and Peace* (any edition), vol. 2, Book 4, sections V and VI.

4. Chekhov's "Impressions of Wolf Baiting" makes for an interesting comparison with the description of the same event by A. E. Korsh in his article "The Baiting of January 6, 1882" in the February, 1882 issue of *Nature and Hunting* (*Priroda i okhota*). The spectacle that aroused the young Chekhov's indignation is described by Korsh with evident pleasure and appreciation. In response to people who consider the custom of wolf baiting a cruel and inhuman sport, Korsh wrote: "Humanitarianism is a fine thing, but like everything else it should be applied sensibly and in moderation."

Almost every issue of *Nature and Hunting* contained accounts of the hunting, baiting and poisoning of wolves and foxes. The general tone of these accounts indicates that wolves and foxes were regarded as harmful pests, subject to total extermination. Against this background, Chekhov's attitude to wolves, in "Impressions of Wolf Baiting" and his later story "Whitebrow" strikes one as unprecedented.

5. Letter from the editors of *Nature and Hunting* to Chekhov, October 23, 1883. Cited from A. P. Chekhov, *Sobraniye sochineniy* (*Collected works*) (Moscow: Gos. Izd-vo Knudozhestvennoy literatury, 1960), II, 560.

6. In Chekhov's story "The Huntsman," 1885, hunting is represented as a form of art and huntsman-hero appears as a figure of a misunderstood artist. In his letter of November 8 or 9, 1893 to Ivan Gorbunov-Posadov Chekhov cites a passage about the wounded stag from Shakespeare's *As You Like It* and in his letter of December 17, 1892 to Aleksey Suvorin he makes the following comment on this passage: "If you happen to see Leskov, tell him that Shakespeare in *As You Like It*, Act II, Scene 1, has some good words concerning hunting. Shakespeare himself used to go hunting, but you can see from this scene what a poor opinion he had of hunting and of murdering animals in general."

Chekhov's letter to Suvorin of April 8, 1892 contains an ironical, self-mocking account of how Chekhov had to finish off a woodcock ineptly wounded by Isaak Levitan. On May 9, 1889, Chekhov wrote to Maksim Gor'kiy in reply to Gor'kiy's offer to present him with a hunting rifle: "I used to enjoy hunting small game, but it doesn't attract me any more." However, in a letter of April 13, 1904 to Boris Lazarevskiy who was leaving for the Far East, Chekhov suggested that Lazarevskiy hunt Siberian tigers. (Unless otherwise indicated, Chekhov's letters are quoted from *Anton Chekhov's Life and Thought*, ed. Simon Karlinsky (Berkeley and Los Angeles: University of California, 1976).

In *The Island of Sakhalin*, Chekhov stated his opposition to the proposed introduction of hunting as a regular occupation among the exiled settlers: "One should not permit a former murderer to kill animals on a regular basis and to commit those brutal actions which are unavoidable during almost any hunt, such as stabbing to death a wounded stag, finishing off a still-living partridge by biting through its throat, etc." (A. P. Chekhov, *Sobraniye sochineniy* (Moscow: Gos. Izd-vo Knudozhestvennoy literatury, 1963), X, 301–2. The translation from the Russian is my own).

7. S. T. Aksakov, *Sobraniye sochineniy* (Moscow: Izd-vo A. A. Kartseva, 1897), VI, 27.

8. In his letter to Chekhov of March 24, 1889, Aleksey Pleshcheyev wrote that the views and the actions of Khrushchev in *The Wood Demon* strike him as unmotivated and self-contradictory: "And what sort of an idealist is he? [. . .] He loves the forest, but he treats humans in a far from human way." (Cited from L. S. Pustil'nik's article "Chekhov i Pleshcheev" in the Chekhov issue of *Literaturnoye nasledstvo*, 68 (*Literary Heritage*) (Moscow: Izd-vo Akademii Nauk SSSR, 1960), p. 304.

Dmitriy Grigorovich, who encouraged the young Chekhov and thought very highly of his work, believed that *The Wood Demon* was an unsuccessful imitation of Dostoeyevskiy: "this is something or other half-way between *The Possessed* and the Karamazovs." (A. P. Chekhov, *Polnoye sobraniye sochineniy i pisem* (*Complete Collected Works and Letters*) (Moscow: "Nauka," 1976), Pis'ma (*Letters*) III, 455.

Aleksey Suvorin's opinion of *The Wood Demon*, as stated in his letter to the actor Pavel Svobodin, shows that Suvorin failed to notice the significance of the ecological and conservationist theme in the play (ibid., p. 470).

9. One of the first to note this was the Soviet scholar Aleksandr Chudakov in his superb book *Poetika Chekhova* (*Chekhov's Poetics*) (Moscow: "Nauka," 1971). In my own introduction to an American edition of Chekhov's letters with commentary, written before I had a chance to see Chudakov's book, I pointed out the similarity of Chekhov's views in this sphere to contemporary ecological thinking (*Letters of Anton Chekhov*, translated from the Russian by Michael Henry Heim in collaboration with Simon Karlinsky. Commentary and Introduction by Simon Karlinsky (New York: Harper and Row, 1973), pp. 28–29. This volume was subsequently published in a revised paperback version as *Anton Chekhov's Life and Thought*).

10. See the *Great Soviet Encyclopedia*, 1955, XXXI, 477, for various laws introduced in Russia in the seventeenth and eighteenth centuries that dealt with the protection of endangered species and set up forest preserves.

11. A good account of the origin of the term "ecology" is to be found in the collection *Ocherki po istorii ekologii* (*Studies in the History of Ecology*), "Nauka," Moscow, 1970. Despite the introduction of the discipline of ecology by Haeckel in the 1860's, the exact meaning of the term remained unclear for many decades. Thus the Russian 1904 edition of the Brockhaus-Efron Encyclopedia defines ecology as the study of animals' dwellings, such as burrows and nests.

12. Paul H. Oehser, letter to the editor in *Science*, 129, No. 3355, p. 992.

13. Ian M. Matley, "Chekhov and Geography," *The Russian Review*, 31, No. 4, 1972.

14. A. I. Voyeykov, *Klimaty zemnogo shara* (*Climates of the Earth*), St. Petersburg, 1884. Reprinted in the Soviet edition of Voyeykov's selected writings (A. I. Voyeykov, *Izbrannyye sochineniya* (Moscow-Leningrad: Izd-vo Akademii Nauk SSSR, 1948, I.

15. A. I. Voyeykov, "O vliyanii lesov na klimat" ("The Influence of Forests on Climate"), *Priroda i okhota*, 1878, No. 4, pp. 1–23. Reprinted in *Izbrannyye sochineniya* (1952), III, 42–58. Chekhov stated his opinion of *Nature and Hunting* and described his great interest in this magazine in his letter to his brother Ivan written early in 1883 (*Pis'ma*, "Nauka," [1974], I, 90).

16. John James Audubon, "The Ohio," cited from his book *Delineations of American Scenery and Character* (New York: G. A. Baker and Co., 1926), p. 1–5.

17. The essays of Thomas Cole and William Cullen Bryant are cited from Roderick Nash, *Wilderness and the American Mind* (New Haven and London: Yale University Press, 1976), p. 97.

18. See David Lowenthal's introduction to the centennial edition of George Perkins Marsh, *Man and Nature*, (Cambridge: Harvard University Press, 1965).

19. *The Pioneers* was published in Russian (as "The Settlers") in 1832. *The Prairie* appeared (as "The American Steppes") in 1829.

20. The following passage from Chekhov's letter to Suvorin of May 28, 1892 reads as if it might have been inspired by *Walden*: "I bought three mouse traps and catch twenty-five mice a day and take them off to the woods. I feel wonderful in the woods. It's terribly stupid of landowners to live among parks and fruit orchards rather than in the woods. There is a feeling of divine presence in the woods, to say nothing of the practical advantages. . . ."

21. A Russian translation of Marsh's *Man and Nature* by N. Nevedomskiy, St. Petersburg, 1886, is listed in the *Catalogue of Russian Books at the Library of St. Petersburg University of* 1897, I, 470. This information was communicated to me by Douglas Weiner of Columbia University, whose help is hereby gratefully acknowledged.

22. The Russian edition of the Brockhaus-Efron Encyclopedia, 1896, lists G. P. Marsh only as a statesman and philologist. *Man and Nature* is listed among his other books, with no indication of its special significance. There is no mention of the Russian translation of the book.

23. On the connection between Marsh and Reclus, see David Lowenthal's introduction cited in note 18 above.

24. Élisée Reclus, *La Terre* (Paris: Hachette, 1869), II, 736–57.

25. Cf. Section X of the last chapter of the second volume of *La Terre* and Sonya's speech to Yelena in which she describes Dr. Astrov's activities at the end of Act One of *Uncle Vanya*.

26. A comparison of people to either a captive or a freed bird is frequently found in Chekhov's stories as well as plays. To give just two examples, the two lovers at the end of "The Lady with the Dog" are likened to two captured migratory birds; and the dying hero of "The Archbishop" believes he is as free as a flying bird, able to fly wherever it pleases.

27. The parallel between Tuzenbakh and the woodcock might have its origins in Chekhov's painful experience of having to finish off the woodcock which his friend, the painter Levitan, had wounded. A description of this incident, found in Chekhov's letter to Suvorin of April 8, 1892, concludes: "I had to obey Levitan and kill it. And while two idiots went home and sat down to dinner, there was one less beautiful, enamored creature in the world."

28. Quotations from the text of *Three Sisters* are cited in my own translation.

CHEKHOV'S DRAMA, MAETERLINCK, AND THE RUSSIAN SYMBOLISTS

BY LAURENCE SENELICK

"This is something decadent!"

No sooner has Nina Zarechnaya paused to take breath in her soliloquy in Konstantin Treplev's playlet than his mother Arkadina breaks in with her taxonomic explanation. This reception of *The Seagull*'s play within a play by its onstage audience was not unlike the common response to Vsevolod Meyerkhol'd's productions of symbolist drama in St. Petersburg some ten years later. In standard turn-of-the-century parlance, "decadent" and "symbolist" were synonymous terms. But the ordinary theatergoer would not have applied either one to Chekhov's major plays, which appeared simultaneously with the aesthetic revolutions occurring in Russian literature. Those plays have so often and so casually been relegated to the category of realism (though with the qualifier "poetic" attached) that it is worth recalling that certain of his more sophisticated contemporaries did strive to enroll his drama under the banner of symbolism. Some of the ideologues of the avant-garde—Andrey Belyy, Leonid Andreyev—hailed the Chekhovian theater as a continuation of the metaphysical drama initiated by Maeterlinck. On the eve of revolution, many symbolists sought to proclaim his plays expressions of transcendental values, of mankind sub specie aeternitatis.

Chekhov himself would have repudiated any allegation of programmatic symbolism, for he was loath to be pigeonholed. His attitude toward the Russian decadents was satirical when it was not downright hostile. He is reputed to have said, "they're swindlers, not decadents! They try to palm off rotten goods—religion, mysticism and all kinds of devilishness. . . . They've concocted it all to delude the public. Don't you believe them!"[1] And, like the common reader, he poked fun at Valeriy Bryusov's lyric sentence, "Cover up your pale legs," as he declared that any line of Lermontov's "The Sail" was worth all of Bryusov and his "tripe."[2] This ostensible philistinism derived in part from Chekhov's distrust of over-blown sentiment, mystagoguery, and flowery verbiage. The only poet of the new movement of whom he approved was Konstantin Bal'mont, pri-marily because of Bal'mont's sunny optimism and attractive personality. As to mysticism in the theater, Chekhov regarded the later work of Ibsen and his portentous mythopoeia as undramatic and tiresome. Therefore, it is surprising to find that he was so enthusiastic a promoter of Maeter-linck, whose early dramas would appear to be the model for Treplev's play of cosmic conflicts.

The influence of Maeterlinck on the Russian stage was short-lived; by 1907, Aleksandr Blok could note that many found him flat and tedious and irrelevant to Russian progress in art.[3] His most lasting residual effect was Leopol'd Sulerzhitskiy's production of *The Blue Bird* in Munich secessionist style at the Moscow Art Theater, a production that was cop-ied in Paris, London, and even Hollywood, and had considerable impact on the conservative realm of children's theater. Chekhov had been among the first to welcome Maeterlinck, whom he must have read in French, for the first Russian translation did not appear until 1899. As early as 1895, Chekhov was writing to Suvorin, advising him to stage Maeterlinck's plays at his Petersburg theater: "If I were your producer, in two years I would turn it into a decadent playhouse or try my hand at doing so. The theatre might perhaps look strange, but still it would have a personality" (November 2, 1895).[4] This suggestion was made a week before Chekhov finished writing *The Seagull*, but before one leaps to the conclusion that a copy of Maeterlinck's plays was at Chekhov's elbow as he wrote of Nina and Treplev, one should recall that the same letter, far from doctrinaire, also recommended Zola's *Thérèse Raquin*. Chekhov's advice to young playwrights invariably stresses the need to make charac-ters and situations effective on the stage, and he seems to have been impressed most by Maeterlinck's theatrical novelty. In a letter of 1897, describing *Les Aveugles, L'Intruse,* and *Aglavaine et Sélysette* as "strange, wonderful plays [which] would make an enormous impression, and if I had a theatre, I would definitely put on 'les Aveugles,' " he instanced as an important asset of the play "a splendid scene-plan with the sea and a lighthouse in the distance" (July 12, 1897).[5] In other words, Chekhov was not espousing Maeterlinck's aesthetic so much as his ability to provide the theater with effective material. It is noteworthy that Chekhov did not recommend for production another drama of the supernatural, Bjørnstjerne Bjørnson's *Beyond Human Power*, although he found it moving and intelligent; he counseled Suvorin, "It won't do for the stage, because there's no way to play it, no action, no living characters, no dramatic interest" (June 20, 1896).[6]

This statement is all the more noteworthy because it almost duplicates Nina's comment on Treplev's play: "It isn't easy to act in your play. There are no living people in it. . . . There isn't much action in your play, nothing but lines and speeches [literally, *chitka*, a reading]" (Act I). Nina's taste is, of course, suspect, for her role model in life is the *routinière* Arkadina, and Nina is also a great admirer of Trigorin's facile craftsmanship; but from a theatrical viewpoint she is dead right. Chekhov apparently based Treplev's experiment in new forms on Maeterlinck's spooky one-acts, but at the same time denuded it of Maeterlinck's intellectual commitment and knack for effective stage situations. There is an echo of Maeterlinck's notorious repetitiveness: "Cold, cold, cold. Empty, empty, empty. Horrible, horrible, horrible," and the Belgian's ambience of desolation and dolor. But the allegory is much cruder than anything in Maeterlinck's writing, and Treplev's fustian and his lurid use of sulfur and red flares, correctly cited by Arkadina as "stage effects," are more reminiscent of Chekhov's parodies of the sensational melodramas staged by Mikhail Lentovskiy in Moscow in the 1880s.[7]

Maeterlinck's influence on Chekhov's playwriting, then, is not to be sought so much in Treplev's freakish interlude as in the body of *The Seagull* itself. Unlike the estates of *Ivanov* or *The Wood Demon*, Arkadina's estate is set on the shore of a "spell-binding lake," and Act I takes place in a wild part of the park, damp and lonely, at sun down of an oppressive evening. It is a landscape out of Böcklin or Munch, rather than Levitan. Moreover, the characters are not the usual rural gentry, but bohemian misfits in this enchanted domain: Sorin, the sybaritic ex-bureaucrat, longing for cabs and telephones; Arkadina, stifled by "country boredom," yearning for her hotel room and the plaudits of the crowd; even the estate overseer, an incompetent, retired military man obsessed by theater. This isolation of disoriented persons in an unfamiliar, almost menacing environment, redolent of mystery, is a common symbolist device. Maeterlinck maroons his sightless in just such a remote forest, and his medieval characters go astray in just such overgrown parks. *The Seagull's* fourth act, with its cluttered and confined sitting room, itself disoriented by becoming Treplev's study and Sorin's sickroom, resembles the abstract chambers of Maeterlinck's *L'Intruse* and *Intérieur:* the wind whistling without, the shred of abandoned stage curtain flapping, as Medvedenko relates, "bare, unsightly, like a skeleton" with an unseen figure weeping behind it, the tapping watchman—all recall those intimations of mortality that encroach on Maeterlinck's sequestered figures. And as in Maeterlinck, the doors and windows take on special meaning, as apertures to another world. Treplev's uneasiness causes him to throw open a window that Arkadina insists be closed; later he opens the glass door, thus allowing the past, in the form of a muffled Nina, to enter, an encounter that impels him to suicide.[8]

This is, however, symbolist stagecraft and, at least in *The Seagull,* Chekhov was not seconding Maeterlinck's fatalistic view of human passivity. (Indeed, Treplev's *mysterium* about a Universal Soul in conflict with eternal Evil becomes trivialized in Act IV when Doctor Dorn equates it with losing oneself in a crowd in the streets of Genoa.) Abnegation of responsibility on grounds of human impotence was not sympathetic to Chekhov's way of thinking, although this strain of symbolist philosophy recurs with great emphasis in the plays of Fedor Sologub and, to some degree, those of Andreyev, Bryusov, and Blok.

This fatalism in symbolist drama is a natural consequence of the Bergsonian metaphysics of time of which symbolism partakes. Those things most immersed in time, or rather, "duration," man's subjective notion of time, are the most mutable. Human life evolves within time. That which is lifeless is relatively unchanging, mechanical, automatic. Life, says Bergson, is an "evolution in time and complexity in space. . . . Each living being is a closed system of phenomena incapable of interfering with other systems. . . . [The living being is characterized by] a continual change of aspect, the irreversibility of the order of phenomena, the perfect individuality of a perfectly contained series."[9] For Bergson, the depiction of a living being trying to stop time through mechanical solipsism was comic; for the symbolists, however, as for Goethe in *Faust,* it becomes horrifying. Driven by a desire to capture the moment, to stop time in its course, man grows incapable of joining the eternal flow. Haunted by the limited scope of his lifetime, bounded at either end by the involuntary acts of birth and death, he is obsessed with the concerns of the moment.

In most symbolist drama, therefore, Death is an overwhelming presence dominating and vitiating the characters, and acts as the central if unseen antagonist. Maeterlinck's earliest plays were nothing more than presentiments of death intuited by various, barely differentiated human creatures. A later, crude impersonation is Someone in Gray, the stony figure of fate in Andreyev's *The Life of Man*, who measures the span of a lifetime by a candle flame. Chekhov was less simplistic; the awareness of death is not the factor responsible for his characters' passivity. If regarded at all, it is thought of as an escape, the consummation devoutly to be wished by *naïves* like Sonya and Ol'ga, the flight from responsibility taken by neurasthenics like Ivanov and Treplev. For Chekhov, time is not so much duration as repetition, a scaled-down version of Nietzsche's "eternal recurrence." What is horrific is not that man must die and be thus rendered futile, but rather that he is condemned to lose himself in the routines of measured time. In this respect, Chekhov subscribes to Maeterlinck's well-known statement in *Le Trésor des humbles*, asserting "the impossibility of superior life within the confines of the humble and inevitable reality of daily life."[10] For Maeterlinck, this constituted tragedy; but Chekhov, though fully alert to the dire effects of submersion in everyday trivia, was uncertain as to the meaning of "superior life." Those of his characters who fantasize most about the time to come—Treplev, Vershinin, Trofimov—are, logically, the most feckless and inefficient in this world, and Chekhov hardly regards ineffectual high-mindedness as a good thing.

This point was missed by Yuliy Aykhenval'd, who called these passive idealists

> aristocrats of the spirit, in each of whom a noble legacy of the Prince of Denmark is concealed in mourning weeds for their "grieving and fateful thought," they move slowly through life and, concerned with their inner world, they take no notice of its motley and business-like clamor. The will, turned toward internal affairs, quietly oscillates within them; but, in return, inquiring thought and refined, tender feelings do not fall silent, do not doze off within them. For this reason they cannot be activists (*deyateli*), but in

any case they have ceased to be even agents (*del'tsy*) or doers. They incarnate in themselves the characteristic and best quality of mankind—the ability to theorize, to thirst spiritually.[11]

For a long time, this was the accepted view of those who were put off by or blind to Chekhov's comic objectivity and who sought a "positive hero" in his plays. The Astrovs and the Lopakhins and even the Natashas are doers, but flawed and occasionally repugnant personalities; the prerevolutionary intelligentsia, seeking a protagonist to identify with, would see its own passivity reflected in Chekhov's dreamers.

Consequently, there is some irony in the fact that this supposedly passive nature of Chekhov's characters was found most offensive by the leading cadre of mystical decadents, the Merezhkovskiy-Gippius circle, which objected to what it read as Chekhov's hopelessness. For Merezhkovskiy, "Chekhov's heroes have no life [*zhizn'*], they have only living [*byt'*]—living without incident or with only one incident—death, the end of existence."[12] His own high idealism was affronted by what he saw as Chekhov's earthbound positivism, his rejection of Christian values, and his "spiritual bumming." He was "horrified at the vulgarity" of *Uncle Vanya*[13] and confessed "I have come to hate the Art Theatre and Chekhov too."[14] Zinaida Gippius returned to this charge many times. She castigated the pessimism of *Three Sisters*: "A cold wind is fanned from the abyss, but Chekhov himself knows nothing, only gets depressed and bored. His strength, his love, true love, for life stiffen in the clutches of the devil who is most glad to win back such a choice tidbit for his beloved Death."[15] And Chekhov's technique was also at fault in this:

> He discovered the microscope, he founds atoms and shows them to us. This is not subtlety; Chekhov is not the poet of subtleties, but the poet of minutiae. . . . Where there is death, stagnation and despair in Chekhov, there is no creativity or truth. It is unfortunate that the grey and the white, the most miniscule atoms of dust and diamonds are so mixed in him, life and death so horribly, trivially and fleshily intermingled.[16]

Or, to put it less rhetorically, Chekhov was too much the naturalist ever to transcend to the spiritual plane of symbolism.

If Merezhkovskiy and Gippius were appalled by Chekhov's apparent lack of faith, their young protégé Valeriy Bryusov dismissed the plays out of hand as workmanlike replicas of reality with no central idea or anything in particular to say. "Chekhov's dramas are written as the last word in realistic art, no less skillfully than Hauptmann's true-to-life dramas. Just as you may scan with curiosity the album of an amateur photographer who has travelled with his kodak to localities you yourself have not visited, so you may not be bored looking at the pictures drawn by Chekhov and the characters he puts in them." [17] In his lecture on the "Theatre of the Future," delivered in 1907, Bryusov omitted Chekhov from the repertory of meaningful drama intended to survive.

This first wave of Russian symbolists rejected Chekhov's dramas and failed to recognize his affinities precisely because Chekhov made use of symbolist techniques without adopting the ideological superstructure that went with them. Whatever admixture of Maeterlinck may be present in *The Seagull*, it went undetected by the critics, for neither of its original productions—the semifiasco at the Aleksandrinskiy and the runaway success at the Moscow Art—highlighted this aspect of the play. Nor were its successors, *Uncle Vanya* and *Three Sisters*, taken to be anything but masterful depictions of contemporary Russian life and the plight of the hypersensitive. In appraising *Vanya*, however, the proponent of stage naturalism, Sergey Glagol', was struck by the constant fluctuation between comedy and drama, which left the audience bewildered and uneasy. Quoting Gerhard Hauptmann's remark about his own play *Die versunkene Glocke*, "It is hard to explain, it must be felt," Glagol' indicated that *Vanya* was devoid of everything normally considered dramatic at the same time it held the attention. The only explanation he could offer was that the drama's inner action was covert and greater than what could be seen and heard, or, in other words, the play "has a symbolic character." [18] This *aperçu* was shrewd; rather than concentrating on a single symbolic element, such as a seagull, the critic had perceived that the entire play worked on two separate planes. But regrettably, he did not pursue his analysis further, for the notion of two co-existing levels of meaning is a fertile one in examining Chekhovian drama.

As to *Three Sisters*, most critics were alive to the symbolic weight of "To Moscow, To Moscow" and the extension of Ol'ga, Masha, and Irina to encompass the entire Russian intelligentsia, but matters were not carried beyond that simple point. Even Innokentiy Annenskiy's rhapsodic re-creation of the play, "A Drama of Mood," was more intent on distilling an impression than extracting a symbology.

The première of *The Cherry Orchard* in 1904 gave fresh impetus to the interpretation of Chekhov as a symbolist: first, because that play is his most thoroughly integrated and cohesive in terms of patterns of imagery and symbolic resonance. That the orchard was to be taken emblematically and not as a reproduction of an actually impoverished estate was manifest to some who knew the realities of rural life. As Ivan Bunin pointed out,

> nowhere in Russia were there orchards comprised *exclusively* of cherries; only *sections* of the orchards on these estates (though sometimes very vast sections) grew cherries, and nowhere . . . could these sections be *directly beside* the main house, nor was there anything wonderful about the cherry trees, which are unattractive, as everyone knows, gnarled with puny leaves, puny blossoms when in bloom (quite unlike those that blossom so profusely and lushly right under the very windows of the main house at the Art Theatre).[19]

The setting, then, and central image, however evocative it might be for the audience, was another imaginary landscape.

Second, by 1904 the symbolist movement in Russian theater had gained a foothold, through the propagation of Maeterlinck's writings in translation, the propaganda for a Dionysian and congregational theater by Vyacheslav Ivanov and his followers, and the profusion of symbolist poetry in Russian. Chekhov's death that same year enabled theorists to speculate without fear of contradiction from their subject, and even those with no vested interest were quick to comment on *The Cherry Orchard*'s special quality. For instance, the liberal critic M. Nevedomskiy, in an essay entitled "Symbolism in Chekhov's Last Play," found it typical of the current state of literature and "*symbolic* in two senses: both in regard to those symbolic devices depicting reality, to which the artist has recourse in it, and in the sense of a symbol of that transitional state through which all modern art is going."[20] Intrigued by what seemed to him a sharpness of contour in character drawing, Nevedomskiy described the dual nature of the characters as "both living persons, painted with the color of vivid reality, and at the same time schemata of that reality, as it were, its foregone conclusions."[21]

The first writer of any critical genius to subject this duality to intense scrutiny was Andrey Belyy, who, beginning with an obituary on Chekhov, attempted to locate precisely where Chekhov stood between his own contemporaries and the younger generation of literary experimenters. In Belyy's view, Chekhov's symbolism was potential rather than actual, a stored-up dynamite capable of exploding the compromises that vitiated Russian literature (the metaphor of detonation was popular around the time of the 1905 revolution). Chekhov was never a symbolist in the sense of Bryusov, but created works that were fertile soil in which Russian symbolism might take root. The central passage in his longest essay on Chekhov (1907) is worth quoting fully:

> Chekhov disposed all the multifarious purely realistic devices around his central symbolic focus; that is why we find in him echoes of Maeterlinckianism (always rather cheap) and Hamsun's moodiness. But in Chekhov the unity of symbol and actual image is a distant background; between this background and ourselves he delineates a series of perspectives, all serving as a diapason of inner experiences underlying the images, until a Chebutykin pops up in the foreground. . . .
>
> Everything that Maeterlinck told us, we surmise involuntarily in Chekhov's writing. Here Maeterlinck gave us only a clue to our ability to penetrate through words into the remote zones of Chekhovian intimacy. And we understand once more the gentle sorrow of the Chekhovian smile. Chekhov silently bore this smile to the grave and said nothing more; perhaps he could not say, because he himself did not know, what his realism is turning into, and how far he had led the realism of Russian literature.[22]

Unlike Bryusov whose vision is of the world as already formed symbols and who conveys his artistic vision by communicating them per se, Chekhov begins with a realistic image that is then metamorphosed into a symbol. Belyy, who was fond of ambiguity, preferred that approach and admired Chekhov's ability to conventionalize reality.

> Even if he sketches his characters with many strokes, each of them is synthetic: imperceptibly he leads us into the sphere of the conventionalized and we, all unawares, fill in his strokes with details on our own. . . . Every phrase lives its own life, but all the phrases are subject to the musical rhythm. The dialogue of *Three Sisters* and *Cherry Orchard*—yes, it is musical! But often we fail to hear it, because his heroes do not betray the silence, and whisper their everyday words about "Balzac was married in Berdichev."[23]

This musicality, which Meyerkhol'd also found to be an important factor in the Chekhovian ethos and over which much ink has been spilled since, is in fact another trait that Chekhov shares with Maeterlinck, and not a cheap one. It is part of symbolism's legacy from its often unacknowledged wicked uncle, Richard Wagner, whom Nietzsche called "music's melancholiac." "Mood music" may be a trivial way to refer to Wagner's experiments in syncretism at Bayreuth, but his aim was to overwhelm and infiltrate nonrationally an enthralled auditorium with a complex medley of emotional significance. His influence had long seeped into the art theaters of Europe, and even Stanislavskiy had music composed to underscore the mood of his productions. The abstract nature of music makes it the ideal medium for atmosphere and presentiment, and it is closely imitated by Maeterlinck's incantatory dialogue, linkages of word and phrase that imply more than they state. Chekhov too, although producing the effect of conversation recorded from real life, is so highly selective in his dialogues' vocabulary and the recurrence of phrases, the ebb and flow of arias, duets, and ensembles, as to justify the term "lyric" or "fugal" applied to them. *Uncle Vanya*, for example, is permeated with terms for suffocation and stifling; *Three Sisters* keeps striking, as its keynote, *nadoyela*, "I'm fed up," in many different sharps and flats. But, as Belyy suggests, this is not so much symbolic as impressionistic, the laying on of strokes that mean little individually but form a pattern, a whole greater than the parts, when the auditor/viewer steps back to hear/see the effect at a distance.

Three years earlier than Belyy's essay on Chekhov, Aykhenval'd has also grasped that *The Cherry Orchard*'s music was composed of commonplace phrases.

> Psychological inconsequentialities create the music of subtle sensation. It is worth giving ear a while to these slow and pensive speeches, and you will realize that people who converse so idiosyncratically with one another are, in fact, very attentive to one another. Each one hears the other's silence. Each one wordlessly, subtly understands the other. Voicelessly soul converses with soul. Amidst it all there is a certain wireless contact, and during the pauses unheard words are enunciated distinctly on light wings across the stage.[24]

To put it more simply, Chekhov's characters do not fail to communicate, but communicate all too thoroughly on planes other than the verbal. The famous Chekhovian pause, if abused by Stanislavskiy and the Art Theater, was not so much a naturalistic token of inarticulateness as a symbolist device to evoke the world beyond. The symbolist universe had been neatly formulated by Novalis: "There is a sequence of ideal events running parallel to reality which seldom coincide."[25] A symbol may produce a double image of the ideal superimposed onto reality, but a more effective means of tapping into the coexistent sphere is through hiatuses in reality. The pause then becomes the moment when the familiar falls away to reveal what Vyacheslav Ivanov might have called the *realiora*, "the more real."

Belyy, in his earlier brief piece on *The Cherry Orchard* (1904), elaborated this notion to provide his most ingenious interpretation of Chekhov as symbolist. Symbolism, according to Belyy, was a natural evolutionary stage for the realistic artist, who becomes dissatisfied with superficial delineation of phenomena and proceeds to reproduce "the texture of an instant," an isolated moment. Life is like an intricate network of lace, and each moment investigated a loop in that lace, that outlines something beyond itself. "The lace of life, composed of discrete loops, becomes a series of doors in parallel corridors, leading to something else."[26] Unconsciously the realistic artist with his emphasis on detail finds himself engaged in something that is suffused with the supernatural. Owing to the more refined sensibilities of modern man, life's lacery has grown more transparent, and as we tread a path of glass, we become terrified to see the void beneath us. Chekhov the realist/symbolist works in precisely this way; as his characters engage in trivia, "we behold the spiritual poverty transpicuous within them,"[27] we decode the secret cipher in the minutiae of their lives. Zinaida Gippius had regarded these minutiae as a dead end, but Belyy viewed them as escape hatches. Unlike Maeterlinck, Chekhov never infuses his characters with his own mystical philosophy, for he has no mystical philosophy; his symbols are all the more profound for reverberating against the background of the phenomenal.

According to Belyy, *The Cherry Orchard* is a less polished play than *Three Sisters*, because it is a more powerful sample of symbolism; its unevenness results from the abrupt shifts between reality and the abstract, which produce a sensation of terror.

> How terrifying are the moments when Fate soundlessly sneaks up on the weaklings. Everywhere there is the alarming leitmotiv of thunder, everywhere the impending storm-cloud of terror. And yet, it would seem there's good reason to be terrified; after all, there's talk of selling the estate. But terrible are the masks behind which the terror is concealed, eyes goggling in the apertures. How terrible is the governess cavorting around the ruined

family, or the valet Yasha, carping about the champagne, or the oafish bookkeeper, and the tramp from the forest![28]

If Belyy's analysis seems overdrawn, particularly for a play Chekhov insisted was "almost a farce," it is because he emphasizes the grotesque members of the cast, whose presence does in fact keep the play from settling down into drama or tragedy. And the tramp from the forest happens to arrive in Act II just after the portentous moment of the snapped string.

> *Everyone sits down, absorbed in thought. The only sound is* FIRS, *softly muttering. Suddenly a distant sound is heard, as if from the sky, the sound of a snapped string, dying away mournfully.*
>
> LYUBOV' ANDREYEVNA: What's that?
> LOPAKHIN: I don't know. Somewhere far off in a mineshaft a bucket dropped. But somewhere very far off.
> GAYEV: Or perhaps it was some kind of bird . . . such as a heron.
> TROFIMOV: Or an owl . . .
> LYUBOV' ANDREYEVNA *shivers:* Unpleasant anyway.
>
> *Pause.*[29]

Carefully situated in a specific social milieu as these characters are, they are also akin to Maeterlinck's sightless or the family in *L'Intruse* dimly trying to surmise the nature of the potent force that hovers just out of the picture. The intrusion of the tramp, chanting his snatches of Nadson and Nekrasov, is terrifying because it is a rude awakening, a return to the mundane after a glimpse into the abyss. The thought-filled pause, then the uncanny sound, and the ensuing pause it produces weave one of Belyy's loops of lace through which we ascend into the *au-delà.*

If Belyy and Samuel Beckett had been contemporaries, the Russian might have quoted the Irishman's essay on Proust, to speak of "the perilous zones in the life of the individual, dangerous, precarious, painful, mysterious and fertile, when for a moment the boredom of living is replaced by the suffering of being."[30] Beckett, himself a collateral descendant of Maeterlinck, writes plays whose characters desperately try to overlay the terrors of existence with the condoling routines and habits of day-to-day life. A contemporary Belyy might point to Chekhov's Sonya and Vanya burrowing in bookkeeping to stave off their pain or Ranevskaya forgetting impending disaster in an idiotic party, as Beckettian figures grounded in a palpable reality. What are Ranevskaya and her tele-grams from Paris but Winnie fumbling in her hangbag for her toothbrush while up to her waist in rubble? What is isolated Sharlotta Ivanovna and her roadside cucumber but Gogo solaced by a carrot while waiting for Godot?

Waiting is, of course, a Maeterlinckian action, a metaphor for life, with Death as the belated caller. Chekhov's characters too hover in ex-pectation, awaiting happiness or catastrophe, and as they wait, they while away the time with numbing routine. The aforementioned party in *The Cherry Orchard*, held on the day of the auction, is the *locus classicus* of this strategy, and Belyy expatiates on it as a "crystallization of Chekhov's devices":

> In the foreground room a domestic drama is taking place, while at the back, candle-lit, the masks of terror are dancing rapturously: there's the postal clerk waltzing with some girl—or is he a scarecrow? Perhaps he is a mask fastened to a walking-stick or a uniform hung on a clothes-tree. What about the stationmaster? Where are they from, what are they for? It is all an incarna-tion of fatal chaos. There they dance and simper as the domestic calamity comes to pass.
>
> A detail is touched in with a certain brushstroke never seen before. Reality splits in twain: it is and it is not, it is the mask of another, and people are mannequins, phonographs are profundities—terrible, terrible . . .[31]

Belyy had obviously been influenced by the Moscow Art production, which was at pains to emphasize the frowsiness of the party guests; but significantly, the same scene was seized upon by the young director Mey-erkhol'd in his attack on that production. Writing to Chekhov (May 8, 1904), he insisted "the play is abstract like a symphony by Chaykovskiy . . . in [the party scene] there is something Maeterlinckian, terrifying,"[32] and he amplified these remarks in his essay "The Natural-istic Theatre and the Theatre of Mood" (1906) in which he stressed the musicality needed to realize Maeterlinckian drama. "This nightmarish dance of puppets in a farce" is how he described the third act, going on to characterize the contrapuntal sense of imminent doom as "a fateful beginning in Chekhov's new mystical drama."[33]

This party scene, singled out by propagandists for symbolism as the most suggestive and revealing, takes place in physical production on three levels: the scenes occurring on the forestage, the forced and heedless

gaiety of the ball in the background, and the offstage auction whose outcome looms over the onstage events. Without leaving the sphere of the
mundane, we have Novalis's parallel series of events. Characters are
thrust forward from the indistinct background and then return to it. New,
barely identified figures like the postal clerk and the stationmaster surge
forward, unaware of the protagonists' affairs, their actions making ironic
comment. The stationmaster, for instance, begins to recite A. K. Tolstoy's orotund poem, "Greshnitsa" ("The Fallen Woman"), about a cour-
tesan's conversion by the Christus at an orgy in Judea. The opening lines,
"The people seeth: joy, laughter flash, / The lute is twanged, the cymbals
clash, / Verdure and flow'rs are strewn about, / And 'midst the columns
in th'arcade / In heavy folds the rich brocade / With riband patterns is
picked out,"[34] make a sardonic statement about the frumps gathered on
this dismal occasion. They also reveal the subsequent interview between
Trofimov, who scolds her for having a lover, and Ranevskaya, a self-
confessed *greshnitsa* in Act II, who twits him for not having a mistress,
to be a parodic confrontation between a Christ in eyeglasses and a Mag-
dalene in a ballgown. Sharlotta, doing her magic tricks, is described in
the stage directions as a nameless *"figure in a grey tophat and checked
trousers"* that waves its arms and jumps up and down, an unexplained
phantasm erupting out of nowhere, just as Anya pops up behind an out-
stretched rug as the climax of a conjuring trick. The act culminates in
the counterpoint of Ranevskaya's weeping and Lopakhin's laughing, as
the musicians play more loudly at his command.

Irony and musical juxtaposition there is in abundance. But is there the
mystical symbolism that Belyy and Meyerkhol'd found? Certainly, Valeriy Bryusov was unimpressed by it all. Act III, which he admitted had a
"special success," "is all built on hackneyed effects, long used in the most
popular dramas. A ball is going on in the house while the mood of the
leading characters is depressed and dispirited: a contrast which Dumas
had already flaunted, and his imitators after him."[35] He was right. The
party as a playground for contrasts in mood was a staple of romantic
playwriting. The best-known examples occur in Scribe's *Gustave III ou
Le Bal masqué* and the fourth act of Dumas *fils' La Dame aux camélias*
(a play Chekhov knew well), remembered because of their transposition
into Verdi's *Ballo in maschera* and *La Traviata* (which title might be

translated as *Greshnitsa*). But Russian dramatic tradition is even richer in such situations. Griboyedov's *Woe from Wit* had interwoven the hectic tempo of Chatskiy's despair with the inanity of a soirée in high society; Pushkin's *Feast in Plaguetime*, based on an English model, mordantly contrasted libertinism and fatality; and Lermontov's *Masquerade*, the consummate specimen, made a costume ball the setting for deceit, betrayal, passion, and murder, as the masks grew ever more sinister and diabolical. Chekhov's innovation, his consonance with Maeterlinck's tragedy of everyday life, was to reduce the romantic elements to the humdrum: the party in *Cherry Orchard* is a sorry collection of provincial nobodies, upstart servants and a *kletzmer* orchestra, making the gaiety seem even more hollow and the pervasion of the grotesque more deadly.

At the time, it was claimed that Russian symbolist dramatists had followed his example, while making the convention more abstract and generalized. Vladimir Botsyanovskiy, writing in 1910, cited Chekhov's "men in a shell" as the prototypes for the impotent heroes of symbolist drama, and Blok's *Little Showbooth* and Andreyev's *Life of Man* as epigones of the party secene in *The Cherry Orchard*. The sketchily characterized background figures in Chekhov become fully depersonalized as the forces of worldly vulgarity in the "Man's Ball" scenes of Andreyev's play, while Pierrot's fairground hamming in Blok's "lyrical drama" is a poeticized rendition of Sharlotta's stunts.[36]

Not Blok nor Andreyev, nor, for that matter, Meyerkhol'd who directed those plays, admitted to such an influence, and their own interpretations of Chekhov denied that he had successful followers. There were some ill-advised attempts to copy Chekhov's dramatic subject matter, as in Gor'kiy's *Summer Folk* and *Children of the Sun*, and his atmosphere, as in Boris Zaytsev's *The Lanin Estate*, but they were awkward and unachieved. Meyerkhol'd considered Chekhov's plays to be mired in their times, "durable only for one decade," stamped with the intense lethargy of the 1890s and defunct "along with the general apathy which the year 1905 takes to its grave."[37] Blok insisted in his essay "On Drama" that "dramatic technique is fortuitous in Chekhov," who worked from intuition, and his "mysterious gift has not passed on to anyone else, and his innumerable imitators have given us nothing of value."[38] Chekhov's disciples, in Blok's opinion, concentrated on the same everyday details, but their attempts at lyricism and inertia paralyzed the drama; better models of dramatic innovation could be provided by Mikhail Kuzmin and Leonid Andreyev.

Andreyev, who was a symbolist more by volition than by vocation, elaborated his own distinctive explanation of Chekhov's uniqueness in the theater. He had begun by regarding Chekhov as a realist; in his 1901 critique of *Three Sisters*, he had held that it was "not an invention, not a fantasy, but a fact, a happening, something every bit as real as stock-options at the Savings Bank."[39] But this statement was made when Andreyev was still a card-carrying member of Gor'kiy's *Znaniye* group and closely identified with naturalism. By 1914, when he had passed through his own, rather overwrought phase of symbolist playwriting and when symbolism had become an outmoded fashion, Andreyev in his "Second Letter on the Theatre," deemed Chekhov the "most logical of panpsychologists," that is, the best exponent of the increasing psychologicality of modern life. Chekhov animated not only his characters but the weather, the furniture, all the things in his plays, animated them in the word's etymological sense of imbuing them with a soul; or, more correctly, a portion of the vast soul that encompasses the visible and invisible worlds alike. Similarly, Chekhov animated time, so that his pauses are filled with the unspoken thoughts and sensations of the characters.

> Whether a servant-girl plays a balalaika at the gate, transmitting to the stage the barely audible, almost guessed-at tune "Little Siskin" (*Ivanov*), or a cricket chirps, as in *Uncle Vanya*, or dogs bark as in *The Cherry Orchard*, or tambourines rattle, shouts from a fire float by, Natasha wanders through the dark rooms with a candle, Yepikhodov eats an apple—everything contributes to one end, panpsychism, everything comes across not as things from reality or true-to-life sound and its utterance, but as the protagonists' thought and sensation broadcast everywhere. How odd, for instance, that at the end of *Three Sisters*, all the protagonists of the drama are *thinking and feeling to the rhythm of the military march*, which, seemingly by chance, is played in the street by the departing soldiers; and the turmoil in their souls is expressed yet again not by bare, spontaneous remarks, but also by the apparently fortuitous figure of a girl with a harp and her absurd, inappropriate ballad "Once I loved, once I suffered."[40]

Andreyev noted that Chekhov's dialogue, for all its vaunted realism, was in fact quite unlike normal speech patterns. The speeches in his plays do not so much begin and end as pick up and continue what has gone before; there are no true pauses or reticences, for the dialogue is merely "transferred from persons to things, from things to persons again, and from persons to time, to silence or clamor, to a cricket or shouting at a fire. Everything lives, has a soul and a voice; oh, how removed this theatre was from that insufferable naturalism which has been imputed to it and which takes cognizance only of *things*; who needs it?"[41]

There is wry irony in the fact that Andreyev, perhaps the least committed of the Russian symbolists, should be the one most insistent on Chekhov's estrangement from naturalism. It is as if Chekhov were being anatomized by one of his own characters, Treplev, especially since the notion of "panpsychism" sounds vaguely like Treplev's universal soul. Andreyev's emphasis on the animation of things goes beyond Maeterlinck, however, because there is no suggestion that the animation corresponds to a higher sphere or that the sounds, whether they issue from a cricket or a marching band, are illimitable reverberations of another world. Chekhov the artist is the demiurge here, responsible for instilling the soul in things. In this respect, he approaches Mallarmé's ideal of poetry as an act of creation and the poet as the all-encompassing, all-suffusing mind that pervades and surpasses its subject. The Mallarméan mind of the symbolist artist is not narrative but allusive, not expository but significative: it does not elucidate the meanings within things, but confers meaning upon them. Andreyev's panpsychism, then, makes the loftiest claims for Chekhov's artistry and puts him squarely in the mainstream of twentieth-century artistic consciousness. Seen in this light, the plays must be taken, not as reproductions of an external reality, but fragments of Chekhov's life-giving imagination, parceled out into recognizable and accessible images, dynamic particles held in collusion by his creative omniscience. However extreme this interpretation may seem—the last original view of Chekhov's playwriting before the Revolution caused audiences to judge his dramas as irrelevant vestiges of an obsolete society, affectionate pastels of discarded values—it may serve in defining that elusive, inimitable quality called Chekhovian.

NOTES

1. Aleksandr Serebrov, *Vremya i lyudi* (Moscow, 1960).

2. Ivan Bunin, *O Chekhove* (New York: Chekhov Publishing House, 1955), p. 209.

3. Aleksandr Blok, "O drame," in *Sobraniye sochineniy v shesti tomakh* (Moscow: Pravda, Ogonek, 1971), V, 149. First published in *Zolotoye runo*, 7–9 (1907).

4. A. P. Chekhov, *Polnoye sobraniye sochineniy i pisem v tridtsati tomakh* (Moscow: Nauka, 1978), *Pis'ma*, V, 89. In fact, the first Russian production of Maeterlinck's plays was given when Mikhail Lentovskiy's Troupe presented *Intérieur* under the sensational title *Secrets of the Soul*, December 10, 1895.

5. A. P. Chekhov, *Sobraniye sochineniy v dvenadtsati tomakh* (Moscow: Khudozhestvennaya literatura, 1964) XII, 162–63. For more on Chekhov's relation to Maeterlinck, see T. K. Shakh-Azizova, *Chekhov i zapadnoyevropeyskaya drama yego vremeni* (Moscow: Nauka, 1966).

6. Ibid., p. 97.

7. See Laurence Senelick, "The Lake-shore of Bohemia: *The Seagull*'s Theatrical Context," *Educational Theatre Journal* (May 1977), pp. 199–213. For the possible relationship of Treplev's play to Andrey Belyy's *mysterium*, *He That Is Come*, see Zoya Yurieff, "Prishedshy: A. Belyy and A. Chekhov," in *Andrey Belyy, a Cultural Review*, ed. G. Janechek (Lexington, Ky: Univ. of Kentucky Press, 1978), pp. 44–55.

8. One recent article has suggested in some detail that the lotto game is a deliberate imitation of Maeterlinckian stasis. See W. Gareth Jones, "*The Seagull*'s Second Symbolist Play-within-the-Play," *Slavonic and Eastern European Review*, 53 No. 30 (January 1975).

9. Henri Bergson, *Laughter, An Essay on the Meaning of the Comic*, trans. C. Brereton and F. Rothwell (New York: Macmillan, 1911), pp. 88–89.

10. Maurice Maeterlinck, *The Treasure of the Humble*, trans. Alfred Sutro (London: G. Allen, 1897).

11. Yuly Aykhenval'd, "Sovremennoye iskusstvo," *Russkaya mysl'* (1904) kn. 2, p. 258.

12. Dmitriy Merezhkovskiy, *Anton Pavlovich Chekhov, yego zhizn' i sochineniya* (Moscow, 1907), p. 192.

13. Valeriy Bryusov, *Dnevniki 1891–1910*, quoted in Yu. K. Gerasimov, "V. Ya. Bryusov i uslovnyy teatr," *Teatr i dramaturgiya. Trudy Leningradskogo gosudarstvennogo instituta teatra, muzyki i kinematografii* (1967), II, 255.

14. Letter to P. Pertsov, December 1901, quoted in ibid., p. 256.

15. Anton Krayniy (pseud. of Zinaida Gippius), "O poshlosti," *Literaturnyy dnevnik* (1899–1907) (St. Petersburg: M. V. Pirozhkov, 1908), pp. 221–22.

16. "Chto i kak," in ibid., pp. 231, 238.

17. From Bryusov's unfinished article on *The Cherry Orchard* (1904), ordered

by Zinaida Gippius, and first published in G. Yu. Brodskaya, "Bryusov i teatr," *Literaturnoye nasledstvo*, 85 (1976), p. 195.

18. Sergey Glagol', "Probleski novykh veyaniy v iskusstve i moskovskiye teatry," in S. Glagol' and James Lynch (pseud. of L. Andreyev), *Pod vpechatleniyem Khudozhestvennogo Teatra* (Moscow: Zhizn', 1902), p. 162.

19. Bunin, pp. 215–16.

20. M. Nevedomskiy, "Simvolizm v posledney drame A. P. Chekhova," *Mir bozhiy*, 8, otd. 2 (1904), p. 18.

21. Ibid., p. 19.

22. Andrey Belyy (Boris Bugayev), *Arabeski* (1911) (München: Wilhelm Fink, 1969), pp. 397–99.

23. Ibid.

24. Aykhenval'd, p. 261.

25. Translated from the French; quoted in Una Taylor, *Maurice Maeterlinck, a Critical Study* (London: Martin Secker, 1914), p. 19.

26. "Vishnevyy sad," in Belyy, p. 401.

27. Ibid., p. 403.

28. Ibid., p. 404.

29. *The Cherry Orchard*, trans. Laurence Senelick (Arlington Heights, Ill.: AHM Press/Crofts Classics, 1977), p. 31.

30. Samuel Beckett, *Proust* (London: Chatto and Windus, 1931), p. 8. Another Irishman is apposite here: James Joyce's famous definition of "epiphany" as "a sudden spiritual manifestation, whether in the vulgarity of speech or of gesture or in a memorable phase of the mind itself," seems to fit Chekhov's dramatic technique. *Portrait of the Artist as a Young Man*, in *The Portable Joyce*, ed. Harry Levin (New York: The Viking Press, 1947), p. 469.

31. Belyy, p. 401.

32. Vsevolod Meyerkhol'd, *Perepiska* (Moscow: Iskusstvo, 1976), p. 45.

33. Vsevolod Meyerkhol'd, "Teatr (K istorii tekhnike)," in *Teatr. Kniga o novom teatre* (St. Peterburg: Shipovnik, 1908), pp. 143–45.

34. *The Cherry Orchard*, p. 42, n. 24.

> Narod kipit, vesel'ye, khokhot,
> Zvon lyutney i kimvalov grokhot,
> Krugom i zelen', i tsvety,
> I mezh stolbov, u vkhoda doma,
> Parchi tyazheloy perelomy
> Tes'moy uzornoy podnyaty . . .

A K. Tolstoy, *Sobraniye sochineniy v chetyrekh tomakh* (Moscow: Ogonek, Pravda, 1969), I, 477.

35. Brodskaya, p. 195.

36. V. Botsyanovskiy, "Chekhov i simvolisty," *Teatr i iskusstvo*, 3 (1910), p. 56.

37. V. Meyerkhol'd, "Russkie dramaturgi," *Stat'i, pis'ma, rechi, besedy* (Moscow: Iskusstvo, 1968), I.

38. Blok, p. 155.

39. Leonid Andreyev, "Tri sestry," in *Polnoye sobraniye sochineniy* (St. Petersburg: A. F. Marks, 1913), VI, 322.

40. Leonid Andreyev, *Pis'ma o teatre* (1911–14) (Letchworth, Herts: P Prideaux Press, 1974), p. 28.

41. Ibid., p. 29.

CHEKHOV: A VIEW OF THE BASIC IRONIC STRUCTURES

BY RICHARD D. RISSO

Dramatic irony is knowledge of a disparity between what a character does and anticipates and what actually occurs, what Kenneth Cameron and Theodore Hoffman refer to as a "comparison between two states of knowledge" (knowledge possessed by the audience as compared with knowledge possessed by an onstage character).[1]

Central to all of Chekhov's work is the depiction of an action in which human beings are consciously caught between the petty routines of daily existence and their visionary aspirations for a happier more meaningful life. Therefore, Ol'ga's sentiment at the close of *The Three Sisters*—"it seems as though a little more we shall know what we are living for, why we are suffering. . . . If we only knew—if we only knew!"—reveals an attitude more darkly echoed by Madame Ranevskaya in *The Cherry Orchard*. "What truth?" asks Madame Ranevskaya in response to Trofimov's charge that she face the truth of her situation regarding the auction of her estate, "I seem to have lost my sight. I see nothing." Similarly, Voynitskiy, in *Uncle Vanya*, in a moment of self-pity for what he realizes has been a wasted life, asks Doctor Astrov, "What am I to do? What am I to do?" Astrov replies, "Nothing!" and we are reminded of Doctor Dorn's more gently expressed but equally hopeless response to Masha in *The Seagull* following Masha's confession of love for Treplev—"But what can I do, my child? What? What?"

Although Chekhov, like Doctors Dorn and Astrov, has no simple solutions, no remedies beyond tea, vodka, and valerian drops to relieve his characters of their sufferings, his sympathetic understanding and deep compassion is evident through the plays, communicated to us, as Robert

Brustein observes, in moods that alternate between "wistful pathos and flashes of ironic humor."[2]

The Seagull, like all of Chekhov's work, defies analysis along conventional lines. There is no linear action or traditional plot development with a beginning, middle, and end, and there is no clear objective that propels a forward action. Yet, there is enormous energy and emotional intensity in Chekhov's plays that derive from the playwright's examination of character inner action. In The Seagull, certain simple distinctions may be made in defining the basic desires of the major characters: Treplev wants identity; Nina wants a successful stage career; and Polina wants to openly reveal her love for Dorn. Ironically, we recognize, as the characters themselves cannot, that the needs of each character remain unfulfilled because they are directed toward other characters who are themselves in pursuit of satisfying similar needs. We have, then, in The Seagull, a series of unresolvable situations that are both pathetic, and because of their similarity, ironically comic. Thus, Polina loves Dorn and Medvedenko loves Masha; Masha, however, loves Treplev, who loves Nina, who loves Trigorin, who is emotionally dependent on Madame Arkadina, who loves herself. The opening scene in the play between Masha and Medvedenko offers an appropriate model of the parallel situations described above.

Medvedenko arrives at the Sorin estate to meet with Masha. Masha responds to his daily declarations of love with complete indifference: "Your love touches me," she says, "but I can't reciprocate it—that's all." In mutual disappointment, their frustrations are directed toward a topic of conversation in which one tries to outdo the other in describing their individual hardships, and the scene ends as it began with a sense of estrangement that is both mildly pathetic and comically ironic. A similar situation exists between the play's two central figures, Treplev and Arkadina. Treplev's struggle with Arkadina is a struggle for acceptance, identity, love. Every attempt to fulfill these needs is met with failure and increasing estrangement. Arkadina is too egocentric, too preoccupied with her own needs to look beyond to the needs of her son, and, as a consequence, Treplev's struggles are doomed to failure. It is ironic, however, that both characters are driven by the same essential need to survive. And despite Treplev's criticisms of his mother as one who is jealous, superstitious, melodramatic, and stingy, Treplev himself possesses similar qualities. His jealousy of Trigorin is apparent as is his own superstitious nature, evidenced in his pulling of the flower petals performed to the childlike ritual of "She loves me, she loves me not." Treplev's stinginess cannot be argued either for or against, since he has nothing anyone particularly wants, including love. His tendencies toward self-dramatization are apparent in the play Treplev has written in which he cries out to his mother through the voice of Nina, the actress, "I am alone." Here, Chekhov uses the play-within-a-play device to ironically underscore Treplev's estrangement. Treplev's feigned suicide attempt is a second indication of his melodramatic nature, for in view of his expert markmanship (a fact previously established in his scene with Nina in which he carries on to the stage the body of the seagull he has just shot), we are led to believe that Treplev's action was not an attempt at suicide so much as it was an attempt to gain his mother's sympathetic attention. There are no parallels to be drawn between the Medvedenko/Masha and Treplev/Arkadina relationships except in the general sense that each of the four characters is involved in the struggles and failures to accomplish his similar objectives.

With the exceptions of Arkadina and Trigorin, whose objectives are to maintain their established artistic and literary careers, all the characters reflect the same frustration, born of needs left unfulfilled. We pity these characters, and our sympathies are combined with an ironic understanding that despite the events that have occurred during the two years that transpire during the course of the play, the essential conditions of the characters' lives remain unaltered. Masha remains "rooted" in her love for Treplev; Nina continues to pursue her dream for a glamorous stage career; and Medvedenko returns to his home at the end of the play in the same manner as he appeared at the beginning—alone and on foot.

John Gassner, commenting on Uncle Vanya, observes that "Life in this tragedy rusts away."[3] However, although the play concentrates on the wasted life of the central character, Voynitskiy, there are comic accents in the play which ironically contrast with the play's dominant moods of despair, frustration, and mental and physical exhaustion. These comic accents are supplied through the brief but frequent appearances of Marina, the old nurse, and Telegin, the former landowner reduced to poverty. When, for example, Voynitskiy (Uncle Vanya), speaks despairingly of his many self-sacrifices, Telegin provides a near parody to Vanya's suffering in his own account of personal self-sacrifice. "My wife ran away from me with the man she loved the day after our wedding, on the grounds of my unprepossessing appearance. But I have never been false to my vows. I love her to this day and I am faithful to her. I help her as far as I can, and I gave all I had for the education of her children by the man she loved." By means of parody, Telegin's speech conditions our sympathies for Vanya and for others in the play who speak of their wasted lives with such exaggerated despair. Although Chekhov has created Telegin as a completely realized and credible individual of physical, social, and psychological dimensions, it does seem clear, in the half-dozen appearances he makes throughout the play, that Telegin serves an essential function in providing comic balance to Vanya's dark frustrations. Comic accent in moments of intense seriousness is also provided by the old nurse, Marina. In a moment of frustration, Vanya responds abruptly to Yelena's casual observation on the climate of the day with, "A fine day to hang oneself." In comic contrast to Vanya's disgruntled reply, we hear the complaisant Telegin quietly tuning his guitar in the background while Marina calls a hen in a tone that mocks Vanya's gloominess—"Chook, chook, chook." A similar example of the ironic use of comedy in moments of intense seriousness occurs at the close of Act III when Vanya, infuriated by Serebryakov's proposal to sell the estate, hurries offstage with Serebryakov in close pursuit. A pistol shot is heard offstage, accompanied by a shriek of alarm from Yelena. In a parody of melodramatic effects, Chekhov leads us to believe that the enraged Vanya has murdered Serebryakov; but our nervous expectations are momentarily deflated by Marina's comic dismissal of the whole situation, "Ough! Botheration take them!" Heightening his parody on melodramatic form as well as on Vanya's impassioned state, Chekhov has Serebryakov reappear onstage with Vanya, pistol in hand, following in close pursuit. There is a brief onstage tussle as Yelena vainly attempts to take the pistol from Vanya's hand. Vanya frees himself from Yelena's grasp and fires a second time at Serebryakov at near point-blank range. Vanya misses the shot, and one of Chekhov's most melodramatic moments is brought to a deafening climax. Vanya's shot misses, but Chekhov is clearly on target in creating one of the most ironically hilarious moments in theater. An additional ironically comic effect in this scene is provided by the old nurse who continues to "knit a stocking" undisturbed by the violent activity that surrounds her. It is essentially through Chekhov's minor characters (Telegin and Marina) that our sympathies for the distraught Vanya become tempered and brought into balance by ironic laughter.

Although Chekhov cannot avoid the temptation of including at least one pistol shot in *The Three Sisters*, the play contains none of the melodramatic seriousness or broad humor of *Uncle Vanya*. The central action traces the now familiar struggles and failures of the central characters' desires to gain happier, more meaningful lives, and the intrinsic irony of the play is revealed in the disparity between what the characters hope to achieve and what, in fact, is achieved. Chekhov quickly suggests this disparity in the opening scene of the play in which Ol'ga, speaking to her sisters, Masha and Irina, expresses her passionate longing to be back home again in Moscow. Meanwhile, Tuzenbakh, in an unrelated conversation with Chebutykin, replies as if in mocking response to Ol'ga's speech, "Of course, it's nonsense"; and, to Ol'ga's cry a few lines further in the scene "Yes! To Moscow, and quickly," the sense of mockery is repeated indirectly by the laughter of Chebutykin and Tuzenbakh, who are heard laughing, presumably at a private joke.

Ol'ga, Masha, and Irina are intelligent, refined, and passionate people. They have been educated to extol the virtues of work, and, paradoxically, they have been encouraged by parental attitude to refrain from making any real effort. "We are the children of parents who despised work," cries Irina; and Masha informs us of how difficult it was, after their father's death, to "get accustomed to the idea that we hadn't any orderlies to wait on us." Ironically, the three sisters havs been educated to laud the virtues of work and to despise the actual practice. Therefore, when Irina states that "A man ought to work, to toil in the sweat of his brow, whoever he may be, and all the meaning of his life, his happiness, his ecstasies lie in that alone," we recall Ol'ga's earlier remarks on the subject:

> Being all day in school and then at my lessons till the evening gives me a perpetual headache and thoughts as gloomy as though I were old. And really these four years that I have been at the high school I have felt my strength and my youth oozing away from me every day. And only one yearning grows stronger and stronger. . . .

Our sense of ironic contrast is compounded by our realization that the sisters' dream of returning to Moscow becomes more and more remote as the petty and vulgar reality from which they strive to escape (a reality exemplified by Natalya and Protopopov) intrudes upon their lives with increasing dominance.

The Three Sisters concludes on an optimistic note for a better life, if not for the characters themselves, at least "for the people who come after us." But this optimism for the future is qualified by their continuing uncertainty as to the meaning of their suffering. For Chebutykin, the need for meaning doesn't matter, and Vershinin realizes that "We have no happiness and never do have, we only long for it." Irina will "teach in a school somewhere and give her life to people who need it," but her intentions to pursue a teaching career like her decision to marry Tuzen- bakh convey a hopeful yet futile struggle to alter the hopeless tedium of her existence.

The play concludes neither optimisticaly nor pessimistically with re- gard to the sisters' hopeful expectations. It is, rather, an ironic conclusion in which hope for a more meaningful and happier life is tempered by our understanding that the future may carry no better or worse promise than the present situation from which they strive so desperately to escape.

Chekhov's fondness for the ironic discrepancies between what a char- acter says and what a character does is again a device that is readily apparent in *The Cherry Orchard*.

Gayev's opinion of himself as a highly principled man, dedicated to the pursuit of "useful work" and "the ideal of public good and social consciousness," is in ironic contrast to the ineffectual, wasteful, and to- tally irresponsible man we know him to be. Moreover, the comic irony is compounded by the fact that he addresses his self-serving speech to the family bookcase and in the presence of Lopakhin who, more than any other character in the play, exemplifies those qualities that Gayev ascribes to himself.

A second example of ironic discrepancy is evident in the Madame Ranevskaya/Trofimov confrontation in Act III. We sympathize through- out the play with Lyubov''s apparent inability to expiate the past and to take responsible action in an attempt to save the family estate. Trofimov is correct (though not original) in observing that Lyubov' "must face the truth" regarding the loss of the cherry orchard at public auction. Ironi- cally, however, he fails to "face the truth" about himself. He is, as Lyu- bov' states, "good for nothing," for despite his passionate idealism for a better world achieved through "extraordinary and unceasing labor," he refrains from ever working himself. Trofimov and Lyubov' share a similar inability to "face the truth" about themselves; although, ironically, they reveal the truth about themselves through their critical observations of each other. The comic irony is exaggerated to farcical proportion following Trofimov's departure from the scene, when he tumbles down a flight of stairs while laughter is heard from the guests assembled offstage. There is pity for Lyubov''s inability to expiate the past, and there is humor in Trofimov's inability to expiate himself from his visionary conceptualizations for a brighter future. Neither character can or will engage in the present realities; and their common dilemma, viewed sympathetically (Lyubov') and humorously (Trofimov), is conveyed through the visual symbol of the dance that carries them both from the stage.

Examples of ironic contrast have been limited thus far to those contrasts which occur in situations of character inner action. There is, however, a dimension of comic disparity in *The Cherry Orchard* that is not directly related to character inner action but to the three separate time frames (movements) that Chekhov employs to accentuate the play's rhythmic dynamics. The time frames are: (1) The sense of time that Lopakhin urgently measures in terms of days, hours, and minutes. In the opening lines of the play, for example, we learn from Lopakhin that Madame Ranevskaya's train is two hours late; and later, in the same act, Lopakhin informs Luybov' that the cherry orchard will be sold on August 22. In the final act, prior to Lyubov''s departure, Lopakhin advises everyone to "Take note, ladies and gentlemen, the train goes in forty-seven minutes; so you ought to start for the station in twenty minutes. You must hurry up!" (2) The second time frame is occupied principally by Lyubov' and Gayev and is in direct contrast to the accelerated time frame governed by Lopakhin. The movement of the second time frame is static. It is time idly spent by Lyubov' and Gayev in their "nursery" (Acts I and IV); in a drawing room of the estate (Act III); or among the ruins of the neighboring churchyard (Act II). These environments accentuate further the sense of regression that is in distinct contrast to the forward, accelerated pace established by Lopakhin. The two contrasting movements are not in conflict; they exist separately to establish a rhythmic dynamic equivalent to musical counterpoint. There is, therefore, no sense of confrontation of opposing values or discord between Lyubov' (symbol of the dying upper classes) and Lopakhin (symbol of the harsh, practical world that will displace the upper class). The passing of the Ranevskaya way of life is felt more as a natural passing that, as Pishchik reminds us, we should "Never mind . . . be happy. God will succor you . . . no matter . . . everything in this world must have an end."

A way of life, then, has simply been displaced by another way of life. It is a natural displacement, and, therefore it is neither good nor bad, sad nor pleasant. Because of its naturalness, the displacement occurs as effortlessly and as imperceptibly as the change of seasons that occur during the course of the play from late spring (May) to early fall (October). (3) The natural seasonal changes constitute the play's third time frame (movement) that contrasts, ironically, with the two movements previously mentioned.

Madame Ranevskaya makes no attempt to save the cherry orchard, and there is no real sense of despair prior to her final departure. We are assured by Madame Ranevskaya's daughter, Anya, that Lyubov' will be taken care of, and, ironically, we learn also that Gayev is to be employed (at least temporarily) with a bank.

The futile struggles of Chekhov's characters to attain happier, more meaningful lives, so characteristic of the principal characters in *The Seagull, Uncle Vanya,* and *The Three Sisters,* are not apparent in *The Cherry Orchard.* Chekhov seems to have honed this final play to an even finer degree of dramatic action; and what surfaces, perhaps even stronger, is the deep compassion and humor that characterize all his work.

NOTES

1. Kenneth M. Cameron and Theodore J. C. Hoffman, *The Theatrical Response* (London: Macmillan, 1969), pp. 242–43.

2. Robert Brustein, *The Theatre of Revolt: An Approach to the Modern Drama* (London: Methuen, 1962), p. 139.

3. John Gassner, *Masters of the Drama* (New York: Random House, 1954), p. 516.

A FINE DAY TO HANG ONESELF:
ON CHEKHOV'S PLAYS

BY SONIA KOVITZ

I

Nothing ever happens the way you want it to. I didn't want to be
a headmistress, and yet I became one. It means we are not to be
in Moscow. . . .

—Ol'ga in *The Three Sisters* [1]

Finally you come to a halt, when you realize that you won't have what
you want. Or when you get what you want, then you no longer want it:
Masha with Kulygin, Yelena with Serebryakov, Andrey with Natasha. Or
you no longer know what to want. Astrov is bothered because, as he tells
his old nurse, "there is nothing I want, nothing I need, no one I love."
Astrov has stepped backward. Uncle Vanya steps forward and kicks the
wall he sees before him. "If man will strike, strike through the mask!
How can the prisoner reach outside except by thrusting through the
wall?" [2] Before firing an (inaccurate) shot at Serebryakov, Uncle Vanya
screams while barring his path:

> You have ruined my life! I haven't lived! Thanks to you, I have destroyed,
> annihilated, the best years of my life. You are my worst enemy!

But Uncle Vanya discovers that it is his own foot that hurts when he
kicks the obstacle. Treplev, "cold as if I were living in a dungeon," sa-
lutes the wall in true romantic style by shooting himself. The three sisters
(or at least two of them, Irina and Ol'ga) want desperately to believe in
something beautiful on the other side of the wall, in Moscow. Masha,
like Ranevskaya ("oh my sins . . ."), has collided with the wall in full

force and goes on loving anyway. It is the same stone wall that Dostoy-evskiy's underground man beats upon, and the same that Ippolit (in *The Idiot*) shakes his fist at; he is dying, and he stares out the window at a brick wall. The wall is reality. If this meaningless word means anything, it is whatever you shake your fist at when you can't go any farther; it is what blocks your path. In Chekhov's "Ward No. 6," Andrey Yefimych spends his first night as an inmate imprisoned in the same insane asylum that he had been visiting as a doctor for twenty years:

> Andrey Yefimych walked to the window and looked out at the field. It was growing dark, and on the horizon at the right rose a cold livid moon. Not far from the hospital fence, some two hundred yards, stood a tall white building surrounded by a stone wall. It was the prison.
> "So this is reality," thought Andrey Yefimych, and he became terrified.[3]

Tolstoy's Ivan Il'ich facing the back of his sofa: "And every moment he felt that despite all his efforts he was drawing nearer and nearer to what terrified him."[4] "It seems as if just a little more and we shall know why we live, why we suffer," says Ol'ga.

We think we are moving somewhere, toward the fulfillment of our dreams, and when we arrive at the destination (Moscow), we will finally begin to live. But instead we find ourselves rushing headlong into a stone wall, a black bag—the stifling provinces, meaningless work, frustrated love, loneliness, illness, death.

> IRINA: There is nothing, nothing, no satisfaction of any kind, and time is passing, and I feel that I'm moving away from the real, beautiful life, moving farther and farther into some sort of abyss. I am in despair, and why I am alive, why I haven't killed myself before now, I don't know. . . .

Chekhov's plays are about the life journey that sets out for the golden towers of Moscow and arrives instead at the heart of darkness: "idleness, kvas, goose with cabbage, after-dinner naps, base parasitism." The immovable wall of reality, in opening to reveal the abyss, turns into a mirror. By frustrating our desires and forcing us to a halt, it plunges us into the hell of our own nature.

II

Midway in our life's journey, I went astray
from the straight road and woke to find myself

alone in a dark wood.

—Dante, *The Inferno*[5]

"You know," says Doctor Astrov, "when you walk through a forest on a dark night, if you see a small light gleaming in the distance, you don't notice your fatigue, the darkness, the thorny branches lashing your face . . . but for me there is no small light in the distance." Astrov's name—from the Greek *astron*, star—says that he is the small gleaming light. But it is a long, hard road to discover that the light is within, which is why you cannot see it in the distance. In the fantasy novel A *Voyage to Arcturus*, the hero arrives finally at the tower of his destination on his search for Muspel (God, spirit, the source of life):

> He pulled his body up, and stood expectantly on the stone-floored roof, looking round for his first glimpse of Muspel.
> *There was nothing.*
> He was standing upon the top of a tower. . . . Darkness was all around him. He sat down on the stone parapet, with a sinking heart; a heavy foreboding possessed him.
> Suddenly, without seeing or hearing anything, he had the distinct impression that the darkness around him, on all four sides, was *grinning*. . . . As soon as that happened, he understood that he was wholly surrounded by Crystalman's [the devil's] world, and that Muspel consisted of himself and the stone tower on which he was sitting. . . . The truth forced itself on him in all its cold, brutal reality. . . . Muspel was fighting for its life—against all that is most shameful and frightful—against sin masquerading as eternal beauty, against baseness masquerading as Nature, against the Devil masquerading as God. . . .
> Now he understood everything. The moral combat was . . . a grim death struggle in which what is worse than death—namely, spiritual death—inevitably awaited the vanquished. . . . By what means could he hold back from this horrible war![6]

But there are many ways to hold back. Where Astrov loses heart because he can see no light in the distance, Vershinin consoles himself by imagining one. "Life is hard," he says. "It presents itself to many of us as desolate and hopeless, and yet, one must admit that it keeps getting easier and easier, and the day is not far off when it will be wholly bright." Both men are aware of the stakes in the grim death struggle, but each holds a view of the course of the battle that excuses himself from participating.

Here is the guilt of complicity, whether dressed in cynicism or hopeful rhetoric.

> ASTROV: In the whole district there were only two decent, cultured men: you and I. But after some ten years of this contemptible, barbarian existence we have been encompassed by it—it has poisoned our blood with its putrid fumes and we have become just such vulgarians as all the rest.
>
> VERSHININ: At the present time there are only three of your sort in this town, but in generations to come there will be more and more, a time will come when everything will change to your way, people will live like you. . . .

To enter moral combat puts the naked self on the line. Most of Chekhov's characters hide within a mask or shell of ingenious evasions. Vershinin slides either forward or backward in time: "When my little girls were standing in the doorway in their underwear, the street red with the blaze . . . I thought that something of the sort must have happened many years ago, when the enemy made a sudden raid." Astrov, pained by the devastation of the forests, asserts with passion:

> Man is endowed with reason and creative powers, so that he may increase what has been given to him. . . . When I hear the rustling of young trees which I have planted with my own hands, I realize that the climate is somewhat in my power.

But in his own life Astrov will recognize no such power. To Uncle Vanya's weeping, "to begin a new life . . . tell me how to begin," he replies sharply: "Oh, come now! What sort of new life can there be! Our situation—yours and mine—is hopeless."

III

> *For thousands of years the earth has borne no living creature. And now in vain this poor moon lights her lamp.*
> —From Treplev's play

Treplev's suicide, closing the fourth act of *The Seagull*, is also the dramatic conclusion to his own play interrupted in Act I. The dissolution of his life overturns the triumphant outcome predicted by the great world soul. "In the cruel persistent struggle with the devil, the principle of the forces of matter, I am destined to be victorious; then matter and spirit shall merge in glorious harmony." Suicide is the spirit's admission of defeat. Where Arkadina and Trigorin slowly, obliviously expire within the airless shell of their egoism, the youthful Treplev succumbs outright, in a state of raw exposure, to the pure pain of being alive. If Satan (as Yahweh's dynamic agency in the Job story) is "the misery of the world which alone drives man inward,"[7] then Treplev gives up and falls to the wayside long before God can reveal himself.

Treplev's fate of incompletion is forecast by the imbalanced dualism of his play. To spirit Treplev gives the flesh of a woman; to the world soul, the form of the individual; to the beauty of youth, the wisdom of age. He resolves these fundamental oppositions in advance, in a single figure, rather than risk dramatizing their conflict. The male adversary, the devil, is denied live presence and an active role in the arena of the struggle. With unintentional irony, the "father of eternal matter" is reduced to the disembodied threat of blood-red eyes in the distance and the smell of sulfur. The scenario reveals Treplev's fear of the dark and problematic side of his own nature even while is is drawn to it—the daemonic chaos, the pain and struggle of embodiment, the terror of the union of opposites, and the act of creation. "He yearns for man. . . ." Although in his play Treplev considers the spirit's victory over "the forces of matter" to be predestined, in his own life he abdicates by projecting his soul's power onto Nina; he relies on her presence to bring him psychic wholeness and life. In Treplev himself the opposites never join. From states of idealistic but insubstantial exaltation he falls to the despairing heaviness of inert matter ("whatever I write is dry, hard, dark"). Disdainful of reality, solitary, "drifting in a chaos of images and dreams," Treplev is an eternal youth (*puer aeternus*):

> The one thing dreaded by such a type of man is to be bound to anything whatever. There is a terrific fear of being pinned down, of entering space and time completely, and of being the one human being that one is.[8]

In Simone Weil's account: "flight from real life with its limitations, and from time, the essential limitation; not to attempt anything that makes one aware that one isn't God."[9] In his dreams Treplev is a bringer of new forms. In his mother's drawing room before her actor and writer friends, "I felt their eyes measuring my insignificance—I could guess their thoughts and I suffered from humiliation." When Treplev suffers the deeper humiliation of losing Nina to Trigorin, he kills the seagull as

a threat of suicide. Treplev ends his life in a refusal to tolerate his out-
rageous fortune. The seagull—live bird, murdered creature, metaphor,
stuffed object—follows the same futile trajectory, only through no choice
of its own.

IV

*Why is it that when we have barely begun to live, we grow dull,
gray, uninteresting, lazy, indifferent, useless, unhappy? . . . An
overwhelmingly vulgar influence weighs on the children, the divine spark is extinguished in them, and they become the same
pitiful, identical corpses as their fathers and mothers. . . .*
                                        —Andrey in *The Three Sisters*

Whence comes the spiritual power without which life is intolerable? Romantic love has for some centuries now been promising salvation to those
who feel themselves succumbing *à la* Madame Bovary to the "putrid
fumes" of this "contemptible, barbarian existence." Using every possible
variation of frustrated love, Chekhov pushes his characters to the edge of
the infernal pit. He strips them of their dreams and watches to see what
they will do next. They sing, whistle, play the violin or the guitar, do
card tricks, philosophize, commit suicide, murder, or both (Uncle Vanya
at least tries). It is on this "fine day to hang oneself," on the outskirts of
hell, as love goes up in smoke, that some of them finally wonder about
the divine spark. Andrey's question is the more urgent, the more obscure
the line dividing the spiritually alive from the spiritually dead. Chekhov
knows that we know who is who, and yet, the irrepressible ironist, he
plays with our presumption of knowledge. In continually goading us to
question his characters' moral and spiritual integrity, Chekhov plunges
us into what Kierkegaard called "the cleansing baptism of irony."

As philosophers claim that no true philosophy is possible without doubt, so
by the same token one may claim that no authentic human life is possible
without irony. . . . He who does not understand irony . . . lacks the bath
of regeneration and rejuvenation. . . . He does not know the invigoration
which, should the atmosphere become too oppressive, comes from lifting
oneself up and plunging into the ocean of irony. . . . It requires courage
not to surrender oneself to the ingenious or compassionate counsels of despair that would induce a man to eliminate himself from the ranks of the

living; but it does not follow from this that every huckster who is fattened and nourished in self-confidence has more courage than the man who yielded to despair. . . . Hence if one must warn against irony as a seducer, one must also praise it as a guide. . . . Irony is like the negative way, not the truth but the way.[10]

The path that we, Chekhov's viewers, travel—if we will—is the same that his characters need to set out upon. We enter a realm of discomfiting incertitude and often mortifying self-scrutiny, for we cannot judge others without judging ourselves. "There is in every personal life so much that must be repudiated."[11] Andrey describing the vulgar inhabitants of his town is also describing himself: Does his pain and awareness distinguish his life from theirs, or not?

> They just eat, drink, sleep, and then die . . . others are born and they too eat, drink, sleep, and to keep from being stupefied by boredom, they relieve the monotony of life with their odious gossip, with vodka, cards, chicanery, and the wives deceive their husbands, while the husbands lie and pretend not to see or hear anything. . . .

Natasha, cuckolding Andrey with Protopopov, incarnates the "vulgar influence" (the pungent Russian term is *poshlost'*) at its most virulent. Yet are not Natasha's pretensions to virtue and sensitivity modeled upon the three sisters? Chekhov often shows the characters most imbued with the essence of *poshlost'* in the act of mimicking those most oppressed by it. At times the uncanny reflection prompts us to ask just who is influencing whom. Natasha, entering the drawing room at Irina's name-day party after everyone is seated, says, "You have so much company, I feel terribly embarrassed." Ol'ga heightens Natasha's discomfort by saying, ever the proper schoolmarm, that the green sash is "not right." Although Natasha's pink-and-green dress is in fact "not right," a more generous sensibility would put Natasha's feelings before propriety. Natasha fully avenges her humiliation; she even remembers to tell Irina that her sash doesn't suit her—"it's not good taste." When entering the circle of the gentry, members of the lower classes feel so uneasy about their status that they can hardly resist affecting a "cultured," self-righteous façade. But they are not always wholly to blame for the insubstantiality of the acquired manners. "Any rudeness, even the slightest, even a tactless word, upsets me," says Ol'ga as she capitulates to Natasha's ousting of the old servant Anfisa. "Work without poetry, without meaning," Irina complains of her job at the telegraph office, after just that morning being rude "for no reason whatever" to a lady whose son had died. Even as our sympathies remain with the sisters, our judgment of them has been shaken.

Ironic resemblances between the living and the dead come in a metaphysical variety as well as a cultural one. The likeness may be the disguise of a petty demon who is hounding a soul in obsequious mockery. The servant Yasha in *The Cherry Orchard* approaches his mistress Ranevskaya, reminding us of the devil in check trousers—sponger, flatterer, repeater of private thoughts—who visited Ivan Karamazov:

> Permit me to make a request, be so kind! If you go back to Paris again, do me the favor of taking me with you. It is positively impossible for me to stay here. *Looking around, then in a low voice.* There's no need to say it, you can see for yourself, it's an uncivilized country, the people have no morals, and the boredom!

Yasha yearns (like Smerdyakov) for Paris no less passionately than the sisters yearn for Moscow. The full chorus of outcries at an unbearable existence—Treplev's tantrums, Uncle Vanya's histrionics, Vershinin's speeches, Solenyy's Lermontovian poses, Yepikhodov's laments—turns into a grand polyphony, of suspicious origin.

> YEPIKHODOV: I am a cultivated man, I read all sorts of remarkable books, but I am in no way able to make out my own inclinations, what it is I really want, whether, strictly speaking, to live or to shoot myself; nevertheless, I always carry a revolver on me. Here it is. *Shows revolver.*

But *poshlost'*, writes Nabokov, "is especially vigorous and vicious when the sham is *not* obvious and when the values it mimics are considered, rightly or wrongly, to belong to the very highest level of art, thought or emotion."[12] Pushkin's Yevginiy Onegin, world-weary dandy, suffered from spleen—"nothing touched him, he noticed nothing," yet Tatyana finally wondered, "is he but a parody?"[13] "I cannot tire of marvelling at this void," Chaadayev wrote of Russia in 1829.[14] While some may have languished in elegant idleness, at least Gogol''s plump hero Chickhikov was seriously engaged, as he rushed about the provinces purchasing dead souls. "But a *poshlyak* even of Chichikov's colossal dimensions inevitably has somewhere in him a hole, a chink through which you see the worm, the little shriveled fool that lies all huddled up in the depth of the *posh-*

lust-painted vacuum." [15] By the end of the century, the postures were wearing thin. Rather than devise his own false front, Uncle Vanya chooses to deposit his longings for significance at the feet of Professor Serebryakov (his name from *serebro*—silver), "a being of a higher order." When the idol turns out to have feet of clay ("I dozed off just now and dreamt that my left leg didn't belong to me"), Vanya in his despair tries to shoot the old man. "I'm insane, I'm not responsible," he defends himself, to which Astrov replies, "that's a stale trick."

> Insights not only into man's secrets but into God's secrets are sold at such a bargain that it all begins to look rather suspicious. . . . We have forgotten that a result has no value if it has not actually been acquired. But woe to him who cannot tolerate the fact that irony seeks to balance the accounts! [16]

"My life is over," Uncle Vanya cries, while Serebryakov, not his idol but his alter ego, feels exactly the same: "every minute to be grieving for the past, watching the success of others, fearing death . . . I cannot! It's too much for me!" Each has worshiped a false appearance, and is left staring into the abyss when it falls. The devil traffics in the satisfactions of fake fullness, while the path to truth is by way of humiliation and emptying. Uncle Vanya slips out of the devil's grasp only at the moment of exposing to the air the shriveled fool within.

> *Covers his face with his hands.* I am ashamed! If you only knew how ashamed I am! No pain can be compared to this acute sense of shame. *Miserably.* It's unbearable!

Uncle Vanya has been set free, but all he feels is the pain. At the midway point of his journey (the nadir of the circle), all he sees is the nothingness. If he but knew, Uncle Vanya enters a "new life" at the moment in his shame and despair when he feels the furthest from it.

V

> It is only necessary to know that love is a direction and not a state of the soul. If one is unaware of this, one falls into despair at the first sign of affliction.
>   —Simone Weil [17]

In the final scene of *The Cherry Orchard*, the dying servant Firs mumbles to himself, forgotten inside the locked house:

> Life has passed, as if I'd never lived. I'll lie down awhile. . . . There's no
> strength left in you, nothing's left, nothing. . . . Ach, you . . . addlepate!
> *Lies motionless*

Addlepate (*nedotepa*) in Russian suggests someone who does not arrive
where he is supposed to. Born into servility, Firs is still a guilty accom-
plice in the *poshlost'* of his misspent life.

> They were arranging a marriage for me before your papa was born. . . .
> *Laughs.* I was already head footman when the Emancipation came. At that
> time I wouldn't consent to my freedom, I stayed with the masters. . . .

To leave behind the old and turn toward the new requires consent to
nakedness, to being divested of what once gave meaning. Most of Chekhov's characters expire as Firs does, still in footman's dress, locked in
the ornate vacuum, "as if I'd never lived."

> *A stillness falls, and nothing is heard but the thud of the ax on a tree far
> away in the orchard.*

The pain of freedom, as the live flesh of the old life is cut away, is that
the beauty and the evil cannot be separated and must fall together.

> Just think, Anya . . . all your ancestors were serf-owners, possessors of liv-
> ing souls. Don't you see that from every cherry tree, from every leaf and
> trunk, human beings are peering out at you? Don't you hear their voices?

"When I am alone, the silence frightens me," says Ranevskaya. The
nothingness that resonates in the breaking of the string at the end of *The
Cherry Orchard* is both finality and opening. "We have to be catholic,"
wrote Simone Weil, "that is to say, not bound by so much as a thread to
any created thing, unless it be to creation in its totality."[18] Says Trofimov, "All Russia is our orchard."

Chekhov arranges the destruction of each character's personal happiness for the same reason that God gives Job into Satan's power: to find
out who he is.

> Affliction is a marvel of divine technique. It is a simple and ingenious device
> which introduces into the soul of a finite creature the immensity of force,
> blind, brutal, and cold. . . .
> The man to whom such a thing happens has no part in the operation. He
> struggles like a butterfly pinned alive into an album. But through all the
> horror he can continue to want to love.[19]

"We shall live through a long, long chain of days and endless evenings," Sonya tells Uncle Vanya. "We shall patiently bear the trials fate sends us; we'll work for others, now and in our old age, without ever knowing rest." The act of allowing the obliterating truth to enter oneself wholly ("for the thing which I greatly feared is come upon me") opens another dimension of being. It is a dimension inaccessible to Ivan Il'ich in his black bag, as long as he pulls desperately in the opposite direction of what he fears. "We shall rest!" Sonya goes on. "We shall hear the angels, and see the heavens all sparkling like jewels; we shall see all earthly evil, all our sufferings, drowned in a mercy that will fill the whole world." Does Sonya see only a delusionary light in the distance? But her vision is neither imagined nor desired, but felt within. In the moment of embracing with love her own and Uncle Vanya's despair, she herself is the light.

> There is, or at least . . . there ought to be, in every human being a longing for [something] higher and more perfect. But this longing must not hollow out actuality; on the contrary, the content of life must become a true and meaningful moment in the higher actuality whose fullness the soul desires. Actuality in this way acquires its validity—not as a purgatory, for the soul is not to be purified in such a way that it flees blank, bare, and stark naked out of life—but as a history wherein consciousness successively outlives itself, though in such a way that happiness consists not in forgetting all this but becomes present in it. Actuality will therefore not be rejected and longing shall be a healthy love, not a cowardly effeminate ruse for sneaking oneself out of the world.[20]

NOTES

1. All quotations from the plays are from *Chekhov: The Major Plays*, trans. Ann Dunnigan (New York: Signet Classic, 1964).

2. Herman Melville, *Moby Dick* (New York: Signet Classic, 1961), p. 167.

3. Anton Chekhov, "Ward Six" in *Ward Six and Other Stories*, trans. Ann Dunnigan (New York: Signet Classic, 1965), p. 58.

4. Leo Tolstoy, "The Death of Ivan Ilych," in *Great Short Works of Leo Tolstoy*, trans. Louise and Aylmer Maude (New York: Harper and Row, 1967), p. 301.

5. Dante Alighieri, *The Inferno*, trans. John Ciardi (New York: New American Library, 1954), p. 28.

6. David Lindsay, A Voyage to Arcturus (New York: Ballantine Books, 1977), pp. 286–87.

7. M.-L. Von Franz, The Problem of the Puer Aeternus (New York: Spring Publications, Analytical Psychology Club of New York, 1970), p. 2. Cited in E. F. Edinger, Ego and Archtype (New York: Putnam's, 1972), p. 14.

8. Rivkah Schärf Kluger, Satan in the Old Testament (Evanston, Ill.: Northwestern Univ. Press, 1967), p. 132. Cited in Edinger, p. 93.

9. From the notebooks, cited by Simone Pétrement in Simone Weil: A Life, trans. Raymond Rosenthal (New York: Pantheon, 1976), p. 219.

10. Søren Kierkegaard, The Concept of Irony, trans. Lee M. Capel (Bloomington: Indiana Univ. Press, 1968), pp. 338–39.

11. Kierkegaard, p. 340.

12. Vladimir Nabokov, Nikolai Gogol (New York: New Directions, 1944), p. 68.

13. Aleksandr Pushkin, Yevgeniy Onegin (my translations). Nichto ne trogalo ego,/Ne zamechal on nichego, I, 38; Uzh ne parodiya li on?, VII, 24.

14. Peter Chaadayev, "Letter One," in Philosophical Letters and Apology of a Madman, trans. Mary-Barbara Zeldin (Knoxville: Univ. of Tennessee Press, 1969), p. 42.

15. Nabokov, pp. 71–72.

16. Kierkegaard, pp. 339–40.

17. Simone Weil, "The Love of God and Affliction," in Waiting for God, trans. Emma Craufurd (New York: Harper Colophon Books, 1973), p. 135.

18. Weil, "Last Thoughts" (Letter VI, May 26, 1942, to Father Perrin), in Waiting for God, p. 98.

19. Weil, "The Love of God and Affliction," p. 135.

20. Kierkegaard, pp. 340–41.

WOMEN IN
CHEKHOV'S PLAYS

BY NICHOLAS MORAVČEVICH

In the course of the last three decades, Chekhovian dramatic criticism in the West has gone through three distinct phases. The most notable critical studies that emerged in the 1950s and early 1960s concentrated mainly on countering the views that condoned the excesses of larmoyance and melancholy attributed to Chekhov throughout the first half of this century by a generation of critics whose attitude toward his work was strongly influenced by the vastly popular Moscow Art Theater interpretations of his great plays. With an eventual acceptance of a sunnier and more balanced view of Chekhov's creation during the late 1960s and early 1970s, Western critical interest in his drama shifted largely toward an analysis of the stylistic aspects of his technique and the tracing of thematic and structural ties that link his playwriting endeavor to that of the most prominent masters of the modern Western European theater. Finally, by the mid-1970s the swell of the women's liberation movement on both sides of the Atlantic provided for a new turn in Chekhovian scholarship by engendering several critical studies that endeavored to reexamine and reevaluate Chekhov's entire creative output from a fashionably novel and often vigorously argued feminist point of view. When measured by the significance of their often striking insights into the psychological interior of Chekhov's creative process, these works on the whole are no less valuable than those of their equally iconoclastic antisentimentalist predecessors. However, just as some of the earlier antitraditionalist critics who at times resorted to overstatement in the presentation of their intrinsically valid arguments eventually had to face the inevitable toning down of their more excessive claims at hands of their less embattled and more judicious followers (as David Magarshack, for example, had with his insistence on the fundamentally comic texture of the Chekhovian drama), some of the presently more vocal feminist critics (such as Virginia Llewelyn Smith, for example) might also in time discover that many of their sharpest sallies at Chekhov's alleged insensitivity toward women will gradually lose much of their currently potent partisan sting. In fact, one of the most worthwhile goals of this essay might be to provide an appropriate prologue for the emergence of such a calming trend that would eventually produce a more balanced assessment of the extent of Chekhov's skill in the portraiture of his feminine characters.

To do this justly, however, it should be noted at the outset that not all of the necessary objections against one-sidedness in the critical assessment of Chekhov's attitude toward women can be automatically placed at the feet of the currently prominent feminists, for as early as 1963 Sophie Laffitte argued that he was a misogynist;[1] and a year before her, Ilya Ehrenburg also observed that Chekhov, as far as his treatment of the feminine characters was concerned, could never had said as Flaubert did that "Madame Bovary, c'est moi!"[2] While the existence of such early criticism of Chekhov's artistic handling of feminine characterization clearly shows that on this subject he is a victim of the latest literary fashion, careful scrutiny of the evidence used to illustrate such views also shows that his alleged unfairness toward women does not seem to be equally apparent in all the spheres of his artistic endeavor. It is, for example, interesting to note that nearly all those who are inclined to object to Chekhov's ambivalent attitude toward the fairer sex base their arguments largely upon evidence derived from descriptive passages in his short stories, recorded details concerning his personal life and relationships, and various observations found in his numerous notebooks and correspondence. The image of women that emerges from his dramatic compositions, however, is clearly of a different kind. Beverly Hahn, for example, though quite critical of the handling of feminine sexuality in his stories, offers nothing but praise for the feminine characterization in the great plays of his maturity, and she is particularly impressed with his subtle and sensitive presentation of the social and psychological dilemmas of nonagressive, educated women from the ranks of the Russian intelligentsia.[3] Even Virginia Smith, for all her blanket condemnation of Chekhov's "disingenuousness" on the subject of women, admits that "all Chekhov's romantic heroines of the stage have an inherent advantage over their counterparts in his fiction: they have, when they are on the stage, a physical presence and cannot be shadowy or totally insipid."[4]

As grudging as it appears here, Ms. Smith's recognition of the exceptional vitality of Chekhov's dramatic heroines is nevertheless rather persuasive proof that women in the Chekhovian drama do not appear as peripheral "second sex" objects placed in the background of a male-dominated forestage. On the contrary, a less doctrinaire critic could very well argue that whatever Tolstoy, Turgenev, or Dostoyevskiy in the 1870s did for the realistic image of the Russian nineteenth-century woman in the realm of the novel, Chekhov in the 1890s matched with equal skill and empathy in the realm of drama. Prior to his emergence on the Russian literary scene, no Russian dramatist had given his feminine characters either such a plot centrality or such a consistently perceptive, sensitive, and sympathetic treatment. And in this light, Smith's suspicion that Chekhov's 1888 statement to Suvorin, "I don't like it when realistic novelists slander women,"[5] is clearly lacking in candor, in the context of his literary practice, appears particularly unfair. For the portraits of the feminine characters in his major plays offer sufficient proof that at least in his theatrical endeavor that is clearly not true.

What is true, however, is that Chekhov's ability to capture the most incisive psychological nuances in his represeniation of feminine characters in drama developed gradually over a considerable period of time. The feminine portraits that appear in his one-act farces (most of which are his own dramatizations of the previously published short stories) are on the whole conventional, and occasionally psychologically meager and monochrome, since they were intended to display a full measure of that blatant two-dimensionality that was preferred by the editors of the popular humorous journals in which Chekhov published his early prose work. And though the portraits of women in his early full-length plays, *Platonov*, *Ivanov*, and *The Wood Demon*, gradually get fuller and more lifelike, they too by and large continue to show his adherence to the conventional patterns in either plotting technique or characterization. All four women, for example, that appear in *Platonov* (Sasha, Sonya, Anya, and Mariya) are primarily delineated in terms of their amorous interest in Chekhov's surly and decadent hero, whose verbose encounters with each one of them in turn provide most of the play's plot development. The number of such lovelorn females in *Ivanov* is cut by half, but their plot function is still the same; both Anya and Sasha are head over heels in love with the morose, neurasthenic, and burned-out Ivanov, who himself is but an updated and slightly more subdued Platonov.

The female characters in *The Wood Demon*, on the other hand, are already noticeably richer in the diversity of their character traits, already psychologically more differentiated from one another, and more complex and challenging from an intellectual point of view. Not all of them, of course, are equally successful creations, but even those that are less vividly sketched are still quite engaging and memorable. Thus, for example, although Sonya (who yet has to undergo considerable modification before she reappears in *Uncle Vanya*) is introduced here rather implausibly as a beautiful but unpleasant and peppery bluestocking with a "weakness to suspect everyone's motives,"[6] she is still a very interesting foil for her main rival, the professor's wife, Yelena (conceptually much closer to her ultimate *Uncle Vanya* rendering), who is far more successfully portrayed as an aloof, coldly beautiful woman, profoundly bored by everything and everyone, including herself.

Starting with *The Seagull*, the feminine characters in the Chekhovian drama begin, not only to match their masculine counterparts in terms of complexity and plasticity of portraiture, but at times even to outdistance them in terms of aesthetic appeal and stage presence. Although a vast majority of them belong to the relatively small circles of the provincial intelligentsia and untitled rural gentry, their typological diversity is so great that they are often perceived as representative of a much broader cross-section of the Russian fin de siècle society than they really are.

Of the various archetypal categories into which they can be divided for the purposes of a psychologically accurate analysis, perhaps the most notable one (and of late the most scrutinized by the feminist critics as well) is that of a *jeune fille*. The most telling psychological characteristics of this type are, of course, easily summarized. The Chekovian *jeune fille* is above all a creature of straightforwardness, purity, sincerity, and youthful naı̈veté. She is trustful, delicate, intelligent, frequently pretty but in a certain demure, nonassertive way, always quite enthusiastic about people and ideas, childlike, and full of a certain ethereal, poetic frailty that inevitably clashes with her drab and prosaic surroundings. Every one of Chekhov's four mature plays contains such a character, and every one of them stands in such a prominent position within the respective play's plot that she is directly and profoundly affected by its unraveling. Virginia Smith defines this type of Chekhovian woman as a "female love object who is usually but not always the heroine in terms of the plot"[7] and concludes that her appeal "depends in the last analysis upon whether or not one finds the image of the childlike heroine too sentimental and idealistic to begin with."[8] Smith obviously does, for much of her subsequent discussion of the Chekhovian "romantic heroine" expands the idea implied here that his molding of this particular type was not based on a realistic observation and understanding of feminine behavior and psyche but on certain highly personal, ambivalent, secretly defensive, and escapist reveries on the subject of the nonthreatening ideal female. This clearly is not the case, for the traits that distinguish Chekhov's *jeune fille* are easily observable in life. Though it is indeed true that in creating this type Chekhov placed much emphasis on a certain translucent, almost noncorporeal charm of his heroines, on their pale, fragile countenance, their childlike freshness and innocence, and their utter defenselessness before the vulgarity of commonplace existence, it is also true that such traits and reactions are indeed characteristic of that particular period in the process of a young person's maturing when the boundless optimism of the childlike outlook on life begins to be tempered by the much more concrete and prosaic demands of commonplace existence. And since even Smith admits that "the freshness and optimism of a child's outlook in a young girl on the threshold of adult life, and the subsequent disintegration of this outlook, is a theme that recurs more than once in Chekhov's work,"[9] it is indeed very puzzling, then, why anyone would find such a type (and one whose predicament by general admission has been so superbly treated by Chekhov) to be too sentimental and idealized. Furthermore, Chekhov never presented any of his famous *jeunes filles* in drama without adding to the picture at least a trace of gentle *raisonneur*-like irony concerning the way they themselves perceive their condition and possible solutions to their problems, as even a most cursory examination of their responses to the plot conditions they face reveals quite clearly.

The youngest of the Chekhovian women of this particular type, and the most idealistic one in her attitude toward the future, is of course Anya from *The Cherry Orchard*, who is only seventeen. From the moment we encounter her as she returns with her mother from Paris (where, as she quickly tells us, she flew in a balloon!) until the family's final departure from their neglected and lost estate, her ebullient faith in the future continues unabated. Her mother's financial and personal problems, her uncle's utter inability to cope with the changing world, and the inevitable sale of the orchard that seals their dispossession seem to have little effect upon her; in her boundless youthful enthusiasm, fanned by Trofimov's populist rhetoric, she fervently believes that the ordeal through which they are muddling actually signifies the beginning of a bright new life. Yet it is obvious from what she says that the specific conditions of that life are neither too clear nor too important to her, and Chekhov's subtle irony concerning this comes across clearly when at the end of the play she announces to her mother, who is off to Paris again with the last of their money: "I'm going to study and pass my school examinations, and then I'll go to work and help you. Mama, we'll read all kinds of books together. . . . We shall read during the autumn evenings, we'll read through lots of books, and a new marvellous world will open before us. . . ." [10]

Of all the rest of Chekhov's *jeunes filles*, the psychologically closest to Anya (though three years older when the play begins and considerably more aware of her femininity) is Irina Prozorov from *The Three Sisters*. Her portrait, however, contains a far greater amount of detail and shading than Anya's, for in her case the entire process of change from a radiant and carefree late adolescence (the present that pleases her the most, for example, at her name-day party in the beginning of the play is a whistling top) to a tired and disillusioned womanhood takes place before our eyes, as a series of crises and misfortunes befalls both her personally and her family as a whole. Yet even here, for all the sympathy that Chekhov shows for her and her family's plight in the soul-killing ennui of a provincial town, he still remains sufficiently detached and objective to point out subtly to what extent her attempts to deal with the commonplace reality of life are ineffectual and unrealistic. Although at first she enthusiastically proposes that hard work is the ultimate cure for the problems of her class, after her first real encounter with it at the local telegraph office she obviously finds it far less enticing, and she says: "I am tired. No, I don't like the telegraph office, not one bit. . . . I must look for a different job, this one is beyond me. Everything I've wanted so much, all I've dreamed of, it isn't in the job I'm doing. It is work without poetry, without thought. . . ."[11] And finally three years later, as she realizes that their dream of Moscow will never come true, she explodes: "Oh, I'm so unhappy . . . I can't work, I won't work . . . I was a telegraph clerk, now I work in the City Council. And I hate and despise everything they give me to do."[12]

The portrait of Nina Zarechnaya in *The Seagull* is even richer in hue; in this instance, Chekhov not only produces an excellent sketch of a *jeune fille* in bloom and in the process of transition to adulthood and maturity (which is his great specialty) but also shows the period of her subsequent reaffirmation of the self in a gray and imperfect world that she finally accepts as the only reality there is. Therefore, at the end of the play, as she returns to the scene of her youthful dreams of fame and glory, she can tell the overwrought and still disoriented Treplev:

> I know now, Kostya, I've come to realize that in our work—it doesn't matter whether we play role on stage or whether we write—the important thing is neither the fame nor glamor nor what I used to dream about, but it's knowing how to endure. . . . I have faith, and it's not so painful to me. And when I think about my profession, then I'm no longer afraid of life.[13]

The last example of the Chekhovian *jeune fille* that should be noted, Sonya from *Uncle Vanya*, is perhaps less representative of certain major traits of this particular type of woman. She is not only older than her counterparts from other three plays when she first appears; she is also clearly shown to have neither their good looks nor their excess of youthful exuberance. But although her portrait is colored in more subdued hues, she too is gradually compelled to face the same conflict of daydreams with reality and eventually to abandon her illusions, nurtured for a long time by her shy love for Doctor Astrov, who remains altogether indifferent to it. Yet the fact that she is neither idealistically naïve nor a stranger to hard work (having spent years managing her country estate with Vanya) offers some plausible indication that she will be able to survive that blow and cope with reality by again immersing herself in work. This, in turn, suggests that she already shares certain characteristics with the type of a humble and toiling Chekhovian female (like Ol'ga from the *The Three Sisters*), who on the whole accepts life without illusions and finds solace in simply being useful.

Even more distant from the basic psychological characteristics of the *jeune fille* type than Sonya, but still not altogether separate from it, are the portraits of Masha Shamrayev from *The Seagull* and Irina's older sister, Masha, from *The Three Sisters*. Both of these unhappy and unfulfilled young women are in effect have-been *jeunes filles* who are compelled to share their lives with those whom the drab reality offered when they made their unhappy choices for the future. Thus, they are linked to the *jeune fille* type only through certain traces of their former selves in their present behavior and their visceral desire at least to slow down if not reverse their inevitable slide into the morass of the commonplace.

The second significant type in the gallery of Chekhov's feminine portraits is that of the dominant and assertive woman, who is usually, but not always, older and more experienced (particularly with men) than the *jeune fille*, and who frequently serves as a catalyst for the evolvement of the play's action. Diversity in individual portraiture within this particular category is much greater than within that already examined, for each one of the Chekhovian dominant women is, by virtue of her agility, much more in the center of action and therefore more highlighted and individualized than her *jeunes filles* counterparts, who are usually more passive, diffident, and more dependent upon the proper actions of others for the guarantee of their own well-being and tranquility. Yet all the Chekhovian dominant women have in common a certain strength of presence (which could be used for either positive or negative ends) and a certain propensity to hold firm to a particular course of action while disregarding the outcome. Though they are not of a distinct physical type, their strength on the whole tends to be enhanced by their physical appeal, and consequently they tend to be very much aware of the power of their femininity and the ways in which it can be used in defense of their self-interest.

Perhaps the most typical example of this type is the actress Arkadina from *The Seagull*. As a professionally very successful, beautiful, self-centered, and fashionable woman of about forty, she is from the beginning of the play's action faced with some formidable psychological challenges. On the one hand, she is torn between her love for, and her intense annoyance with, her twenty-year-old son from a previous marriage, Treplev, whose neurotic excesses provide for a constant Hamlet-Gertrude type conflict between them. On the other, she oscillates between her public pose of effortless superiority and her private desperate struggle for domination over her lover, a well-known and fashionable writer, Trigorin, who is younger than she, but being rather will-less has always needed her presence, vitality, approval, and almost maternal care. On Arkadina's estate, however, this begins to change. As Treplev annoys his mother with his decadent playwriting aspirations, Trigorin does even more with his unexpected interest in her son's girl friend, Nina, who eagerly responds to his attention, being totally mesmerized by his literary fame and her burning desire to become an actress herself. Two details from the play will suffice to show how superbly Arkadina guards her self-interest in this vortex of changing relationships and how obliquely Chekhov reveals her keen ability to control the unexpected and turn the scene in her favor. The first is from the beginning of the second act where Arkadina reads aloud to Dorn and Masha a passage from Maupassant's *Sur l'eau,* which depicts the ways in which writers are ensnared by French women. As she interjects that this is not so in Russia and adds, "To go no further, if you took Trigorin and me. . . ." [14] Sorin and Nina enter to join the group. After they are seated, Arkadina reopens the book to continue, and having silently read several lines to herself, quickly closes it, saying: "Well, the next isn't one bit interesting or even true." [15] However, what she here slyly omits to pursue because of Nina's presence is a very accurate depiction of her own and Trigorin's relationship, for Maupassant's passage says the following:

> Like water which, drop by drop, cuts through the hardest rock, praise tumbles down at every word on the susceptible heart of the man of letters. Then, as soon as she perceives that he is touched, moved, won over by this constant flattery, she isolates him, she severs bit by bit all his ties he may have elsewhere, and imperceptibly she gets him accustomed to come to her place, to make him pleased to be there, and to install his thoughts there. [16]

This unspoken passage is all the more poignant, since at the end of the third act, when Trigorin finally finds enough strength to beg her to let him experience the poetic love of a young girl that he has never known, she responds exactly as the quoted passage outlines. After a few complaints and tears, she falls on her knees before him with such a cascade of flattery of his person, and such a superlative litany of praise of his talent and accomplishments, that she has him in her power again in no time. Then at the end when he gives up and asks her to let him go away with her, she turns coy and responds—*"nonchalantly, as if nothing had taken place. If you want to, though you can stay on here. I'll go by* myself and you can meet me later on"[17]—knowing full well that no such thing would occur.

Most of Arkadina's enormous energy is self-directed. The retention of her lover is far more important for her than the rapport with her son, and as far as this main priority is concerned, she is very successful indeed, for she manages to reconquer her lover even after his affair with Nina. Though she may not be the best example of a mother, since her neglect of her son probably contributes to his eventual suicide, no indication exists anywhere that her portrait is the result of the author's specific antifeminine bias. To say that she is "subjected to the full force of the author's disapproval,"[18] as Virginia Smith does, is both arbitrary and unfair.

Even stronger in the singularity of her dedication to her petty, utilitarian goals is the provincial petite bourgeoise Natasha from *The Three Sisters*, who, under the guise of a diffident and insecure small-town bride, enters the Prozorovs' house to turn quickly into a demon of petty tyranny and possessiveness that gradually squeezes the sisters out of their home altogether. No one could possibly argue with the fact that she is easily the meanest of all the Chekhovian female characters in drama and possibly one of the most negative portraits of a mother in all of nineteenth-century literature as well. As such, she obviously fares so badly in comparison with the three sisters, who are shown as paragons of refinement, tact, and grace, that she is frequently dismissed as a caricature,[19] as a deliberate exaggeration symbolic of the author's innate abhorrence of provincial vulgarity. But the raw vitality, energy, and assertiveness behind her vulgar manners and selfish schemes are not artificial at all; they are the wellspring of her superior strength. The great truth about Natasha is that she is not deliberately mean or calculatingly devious and vulgar. Chekhov successfully shows that she simply exists quite naturally and comfortably as such. Andrey, for example, says appropriately that she resembles "a petty, blind animal, rough and hard-skinned," which "in any case . . . is not human";[20] Beverly Hahn further extends this characterization by pointing out that her mindlessness and crassness in the pursuit of personal advantage greatly enhance, rather than diminish, the lifelike quality of her destructive character.

> Chekhov realized . . . that because such people actually are persons—
> blind destructive persons not even conscious of their destructiveness—that
> they are as frightening as they are. We may be skeptical of the violence

Chekhov wants us to feel in Aksinya [from the story "In the Ravine"], thinking it too extreme; we can hardly doubt the reality of the more familiar kind
of violence which Natasha embodies.[21]

The next prominent female character in this category, Madame Ranevskaya from *The Cherry Orchard*, seems to possess plenty of that inner
vitality that the Prozorov sisters in their struggle with Natasha so lamen-
tably lack, as well as their refinement and breeding. Her aristocratic
mien, magnetic presence, gracious liveliness, and even her free-spending
attitude toward money—all these contribute to an image of a forthright
and energetic woman who knows her worth and manifests her inner
strength in an easy, elegant, and understated way. Born and brought up
in the comfortable world of the old landed gentry, she would probably
have lived a life of leisure and grace like many an earlier Turgenevian
heroine, had destiny not chosen to place her at the very end of that
vanishing way of life. So times have changed, but Ranevskaya and her
brother Gayev have not; and amid the sad reality of her family and class
decline, her vitality has taken a certain suicidal turn by being directed
away from any practical outlet. In direct contrast with her enormous
personal charm and grace, her natural energy is largely wasted, since as
soon as problems of survival arise, she simply refuses to focus her attention in the direction of any proper utilitarian solution. She has, for example, neither the interest nor the patience for such mundane subjects
as the lease of orchard parcels to the nearby town dwellers that Lopakhin
proposes as the soundest business scheme to avert the family's dispossession. Such a stand may not be very wise, but it shows clearly that she
intuitively prefers to fall and close an era in the style befitting her class
and tradition than to resort eagerly to those practical solutions that seem
to have about them an embarrassing feel of a *mauvais ton*. And still, her
vitality and quickness of mind are not at all paralyzed when it comes to
purely personal relationships and judgments, for she quickly and directly
tells Trofimov that all his theories about being above love (which he
announces to her daughter) are pure nonsense, and she quite practically
advises him to finish his studies first, if he ever wants her consent to
marry Anya.

The last female character of note that basically belongs to this group
of Chekhov's female portraits, Yelena Andreyevna from *Uncle Vanya*, is
easily the most unusual one as far as the source of her vibrancy, magnetism, and dominance over others is concerned. Externally, she is an

archetypal image of striking womanly loveliness, and that instantly gives far greater significance both to her presence and to her actions than they would otherwise have. Although by marrying the old professor Serebryakov despite a huge age difference between them she had consciously opted for a sedate life of a respected matron, her breathtaking beauty still radiates so much magnetism and allure that most of her energy and time during this sojourn in the country is spent on fending off the attention and pursuit of Vanya and Astrov, both of whom are thoroughly under the spell of her physical charm. To Vanya, her presence seems to offer the last chance to reclaim at least a small segment of his largely wasted life; to Astrov, an equally unique chance to awaken his innate fascination with beauty that the drabness of the country life has almost completely extinguished in him. Yelena's inner strength, however, is best manifested through her stubborn struggle not to allow the devastating effects of her beauty upon others also to change her own view of herself. She is, of course, unhappy in her life with the old professor, whom she in her inexperience married, mistaking her fascination for him as a scholar and a social celebrity for love. But she is also determined to accept her life as it is, since she knows that her nature is more that of a spectator than a participant in the maelstrom of life; and her great, though ascetically self-denying, strength is in knowing the truth about herself and in resisting the temptation to test it. Therefore, while musing about Astrov, whose attention she clearly enjoys, she rejects the idea of an involvement with him, saying, "My conscience would never let me rest . . . ,"[22] and she remains true to that resolution through all his subsequent entreaties to reconsider.

The third notable type of the Chekhovian female is that of a humble and understated toiler who bears life's everyday burdens with stoic resignation and patience while battling the anxiety about the future and the ennui of the present with hard work and care about others. And though such characters are often shown to be on the verge of utter exhaustion from all the burdens that are upon them, they are nonetheless the only ones that keep the unstable Chekhovian families caught in the vortex of transition from collapsing instantly altogether.

Ol'ga Prozorov from *The Three Sisters* is the best example of such a portrait. Being the eldest in the parentless vacuum of the family's dreary provincial existence, she has gradually become a surrogate mother to her siblings; and that responsibility has somehow robbed her of her own life so thoroughly that she, though only twenty-eight, even speaks of her personal hopes in an implied past tense. Her "gentleness and reserve give her an air of assurance, but she is in an intangible way prematurely aged."[23] Her work at the local school is tiring and full of drudgery. It gives her headaches of which she complains frequently, but she never questions the value of the job itself or considers changing it, as her younger sister Irina does as soon as it is clear to her that the labor at the local telegraph office lacks "poetry." On the contrary, Ol'ga very stoically endures all the personal disappointments of a fine young woman who quite imperceptibly finds herself at the very edge of spinsterhood, squeezed out of her home by a shrill and vulgar arriviste, disappointed profoundly in her hopes for her brother, and cheated by life itself of the all-redeeming dream of Moscow where, as all three sisters firmly believe, such things simply could not happen. So, to the very end of the play, Ol'ga continues to "look into the distance for comfort and justification in the joys of others."[24] Her closing lines—"If only we knew!"[25]—seem to reiterate her stoic faith that an explanation of the reason for all their suffering is both possible and forthcoming.

Functionally very similar to Ol'ga but sketched on a more prosaic plane is Varya from *The Cherry Orchard*, who alone quixotically struggles to stave off the family's financial ruin by locking up the storage rooms, pinching pennies, feeding the servants mostly with dried peas, and objecting mournfully to each instance of Ranevskaya's mindless irresponsibility in the handling of money. Though even her relationship with Lopakhin is negatively affected by her housekeeping mania, to the very end of the play she continues to supervise, inspect, and skimp on everything within her reach, admitting to Ranevskaya: "I just can't go through life without things to do, Mamochka. I must be doing something or other every single minute."[26] And as her secret hope of marrying Lopakhin finally flies out of the window amid the hubbub of the family's ultimate departure, in her quiet desperation she opts for the only thing she knows how to do: she is off to the neighboring estate of the Ragulins to look after their place as a housekeeper.

The only additional type that can be discerned among the remainder of the Chekhovian female portraits in drama is that of the elderly female servant, a type for which Chekhov seems to have had considerable sentimental attachment. Slow in motion and response and rather useless for most of their masters' service needs, these superannuated, kindly women are usually presented as guardians of the domestic everyday routine. As such, they provide a background of living scenery that gives any Chekhovian locale its special stamp of lifelike authenticity.

The first of these shuffling crones, the nurse Marina from *Uncle Vanya*, still seems to be occasionally involved in some useful household activity. In addition to keeping the samovar going and taking care of the chickens, she is actually the only one in the entire house who knows how to calm down the cranky old professor during one of his interminable gout attacks. Her counterpart, the old nurse Anfisa from *The Three Sisters*, however, is already more of an ornament from the past than a functioning domestic servant. Like an old cat by the stove, she drowsily idles her time away in between token attempts to be useful and the traditional helpings of tea, until the fury of Natasha finally packs her off together with the sisters. Ironically, at the end of the play, she seems to be the only one to have found some peace and happiness. Taken by Ol'ga to live at her school-provided apartment, at the end of the play Anfisa praises the Lord for finally letting her have her own room and bed, which, as she tells it with emphasis, are all "paid for by the government."[27]

The four remaining Chekhovian female portraits of lesser significance do not properly belong to any of the above outlined types, though each one may have some common characteristics with one or another. Polina Andreyevna from *The Seagull*, for example, is a mature woman, but not of a dominant sort, since her most telling trait is her uncontrollable jealousy of the sanguine Doctor Dorn, with whom she has a long-standing clandestine affair. Voynitskiy's mother, Mariya, from *Uncle Vanya*, is likewise related to other elderly Chekhovian ladies, except that her unshakable trust in the old professor and her singular interest in the study of polemical critical pamphlets place her easily in a subcategory of her own. The governess Sharlotta Ivanovna, from *The Cherry Orchard*, is largely defined through the magician's tricks she successfully conjures for the amusement of the assembled company while the estate is on the auction block, and the housemaid Dunyasha, from the same play, is drawn as wholly immersed in her giddy affectation of frailty and refinement that comes out as a parody of her masters.

Since this exhausts our review of the feminine characters in Chekhov's drama, what general conclusion could then be drawn about the extent of their verisimilitude to life, and thereby about the degree of Chekhov's success and fairness in their portraiture as well? The evidence presented here overwhelmingly suggests that as a playwright Chekhov probably displayed far less masculine tendentiousness in the treatment of the two sexes than any other prominent dramatist of his time. Whatever doubts may have been raised so far concerning his approach to female portraiture in the realm of the short story, the fact is that no hard evidence exists in the area of his female characterization for any justifiable suspicion of his misogyny in the realm of drama. Nor are there any clues that his view of the opposite sex was narrow and conventional; even when his female characters in drama are divided into broad categories according to their behavior and function, the plurality of the resultant types—and the even greater one of distinct variants within each of these groups—clearly suggest that Chekhov the dramatist was actually such a keen, fair, and sympathetic observer of the feminine scene, manner, and psyche that he should rightly be now in more danger of being labeled a "feminophile" than a "feminophobe." Although it is true that there is not a single "good natured, happy and unrepentant hussy"[28] in all of his mature plays, it is equally true that there is not a single jolly, boisterous, and devil-may-care rascal of note in them either. Having depicted brilliantly in his drama the world in transition, Chekhov obviously could not populate it with happy and well-adjusted people. That does not mean that his world, though usually shown in the process of disintegration, is wholly devoid of joy and exuberance. As Maurice Valency observed, "it is true that his plays are full of weeping women, and many of his men weep also, but these lachrymose natures are singularly volatile and they laugh as readily as they weep."[29] What is significant, however, is that in the crucible of that dreaded but inevitable Chekhovian change in which so many human hopes are abandoned, so many dreams extinguished and illusions shed, the Chekhovian female characters are as complexly developed and involved as are their masculine counterparts. The centrality of position, and even the very amount of dialogue that Chekhov gives women in his mature drama, are in themselves sufficient indication that his interest in them was genuine and profound. Much of it stemmed from his early naturalist affinity for depicting life as it is (which was probably stimulated by his medical studies), and from his later humanistic awareness of the tremendous waste of talent of many educated and able women from the middle and upper classes, condemned by custom and masculine egotism to lives of trivial domesticity. However, both Chekhov's humanistic concern for the emotional and social plight of women, and his gain of a certain sense of inwardness in depicting their psychology accurately, developed very gradually—which is probably the reason that the treatment of women in his dramatic endeavor, created during the period of his artistic maturity, seems to be so free of that ambivalence toward them that some more recent critics claim to have detected in his prose fiction.

Ultimately, it should perhaps be also noted that an a priori belief that successful authors usually have difficulties in perceiving and expressing truthfully things that fall across the biological boundary of their own sex tends to diminish the all-important role of talent and intellectual perceptiveness in the complex process of literary creation, since such views tend to misrepresent artistic endeavor by viewing it, not as an essentially acquired, humanist function, but as an inherited, biological one. In addition, one should also not forget that after an author's ink has dried on the page, characters in a well-written play (be they feminine or masculine) do acquire a semblance of their own tridimensional stage lives where we see them either as live, plausible personalities, or as papier-mâché marionettes, largely according to how successfully their exposure to our scrutiny can capture our interest in their existence and predicaments within the given circumstances of the play. And the centuries of the public's emphatic response to the joys and sufferings of the fictitious characters of both sexes in drama provide sufficient proof that in the audience's perception as well that same biological barrier is not a particularly significant limiting factor for the ability to enjoy all of great art. So if Flaubert could confidently say "Madame Bovary, c'est moi!" and have his readers agree with that so overwhelmingly that now this *bon mot* has an almost proverbial ring, then Chekhov too could have confidently assumed that the portraits of Ranevskaya, the Prozorov sisters, and Sonya entitled him as much to say "Les femmes dans mes drames, ce sont moi!" and with that all of us together, his viewers, readers, and critics alike, should be able to agree as enthusiastically.

NOTES

1. Sophie Lafitte, *Tchékhov: 1860—1904* (Paris: Galimard, 1963), p. 198.

2. Ilya Erenburg, "On Re-reading Chekhov," *Chekhov, Stendhal and Other Essays,* ed. and trans. A. Bostock and Y. Kapp (Leningrad: Iskusstvo, 1962), p. 51.

3. Beverly Hahn, *Chekhov: A Study of the Major Stories and Plays* (Cambridge: Cambridge Univ. Press, 1977), p. 218.

4. Virginia Llewellyn Smith, *Anton Chekhov and the Lady with the Dog* (London: Oxford Univ. Press, 1973), p. 134.

5. Ibid., Preface, p. xv.

6. Maurice Valency, *The Breaking String: The Plays of Anton Chekhov* (New York: Oxford Univ. Press, 1966), p. 110.

7. Smith, p. 71.

8. Ibid., p. 81.

9. Ibid., p. 78.

10. Eugene K. Bristow, ed., *Anton Chekhov's Plays* (New York: Norton, 1977), p. 206.

11. Ibid., p. 123.

12. Ibid., p. 141.

13. Ibid., p. 49.

14. Ibid., p. 19.

15. Ibid., p. 20.

16. Ibid., p. 1.

17. Ibid., p. 35.

18. Smith, p. 21.

19. Hahn, p. 280.

20. Bristow, p. 149.

21. Hahn, p. 281.

22. Bristow, p. 79.

23. Hahn, p. 290.

24. Ibid., p. 308.

25. Bristow, p. 157.

26. Ibid., p. 194.

27. Ibid., p. 153.

28. Smith, p. 30.

29. Valency, p. 156.

VERSHININ

BY MAURICE VALENCY

The Three Sisters may well be considered Chekhov's masterpiece in the drama, but it would be extravagant to pretend that its meaning is, or ever has been, clear, or that anyone has ever been entirely sure of the manner of its production. The great plays, it is true, generally elude comprehension, and their mystery may be accepted as a measure of their magnitude. *The Three Sisters* surely ranks high enough in the scale of greatness to justify its share of obscurity; nonetheless, the play presents an unusual challenge to the director, the more so as on the surface it appears deceptively translucent, not to say transparent.

Chekhov had the theme in mind as early as the spring of 1899, perhaps earlier. Shortly after the opening of *Uncle Vanya* in October of that year he wrote his friend Vishnevskiy, who was eventually to play the part of the schoolmaster Kulygin, that he was having a hard time with the play they had previously discussed in Moscow: "The play we were talking about does not exist, and I very much doubt that it will be ready soon. Twice I began it, and twice I had to give it up—each time I got something other than I intended."

Later that fall he wrote Nemirovich that he could expect nothing from him that year. But the Moscow Art management was insistent, and in December, Chekhov wrote that he would do his best to give them a play for the coming season, only, "What if the play simply won't write itself?" And he added that he would discuss the whole thing with them at Easter.

The following year, in the first days of April, Stanislavskiy came to Sevastopol with his company and a carload of scenery, and a few days later Chekhov arrived by steamer from Yalta. He was far from well, but the enthusiastic reception of *Uncle Vanya*, and the conviviality of his friends, did wonders for his health, and when Stanislavskiy departed the

Crimea he took with him a firm assurance that Chekhov would have a new play for him that fall.

Chekhov sat down to work at it seriously toward the beginning of August 1900, after spending a delightful month with Ol'ga Knipper in Yalta. For the first time in his life, he felt, he was really in love. His mood was joyous. The new play was to be a bright comedy. Some days later, on August 5, he wrote Vishnevskiy that he had already finished a good bit of the play, but that as yet he had no idea of its worth: "Quite possibly what I am writing is not a play at all, but some sort of Crimean hash. The title is, as you know, *The Three Sisters*. For you I am writing the part of the second master of a grammar school, the husband of one of the sisters. You will wear the customary uniform with an order around your neck."

But the play proved to be stubborn, and in the course of the next weeks he wrote to his sister, and also to Maksim Gor'kiy, of the difficulty he was having in putting this "very crowded" piece together. On August 14, 1900, he wrote to Ol'ga: "I am actually writing a play now—well, not actually a play, perhaps, but a sort of hash. A great many characters—most likely I shall soon get in a muddle with it, and give the whole thing up." Some days later he apparently felt better about it—the beginning was turning out "fairly well, pretty smooth, I daresay." But before long he was again in the dumps: "It has all gone cheap in my eyes," he wrote Ol'ga, ". . . and now I don't know what to do." He continued working, nevertheless, though now in a deeply depressed and doubtful mood, until the early part of September when, for a time, he was too ill to work at all.

On October 23 he appeared in Moscow in high spirits. His comedy was finished, and he settled in comfortably at the Hotel Dresden to make a clean copy of the script. He was still of two minds about entrusting its production to Stanislavskiy. A month before he had written to Ol'ga: "Four important female parts, four young women of the upper class: with all due respect for his gifts and his understanding, I cannot leave that to Alekseyev. I must have at least a peep at the rehearsals."[1]

The formal reading took place soon after his arrival. The entire company was present, down to the ushers and cleaners. The result was disastrous. According to Ol'ga Knipper, and also Stanislavskiy, the actors listened to the new comedy in dismay. Nobody laughed. Some of the listeners were actually seen to wipe away a tear. During the reading Chekhov was several times heard to mutter, "But what I wrote was a vaudeville!" At the end there was a silence, then a heated discussion. There were objections. It was not really a play. There were no proper acting parts. One actor was heard protesting in a loud voice that while he did not agree with Chekhov in principle. . . . Chekhov left the theater without a word. Stanislavskiy hurried after him: "I found him in his hotel room, not only upset and hurt, but actually furious, which he seldom was. . . . It turned out that he had thought to write a gay comedy, but his listeners took it for a drama, and wept."

Ultimately, in the printed volume of his plays, Chekhov subtitled *The Three Sisters, Drama in Four Acts*, the first and only time he dignified one of his plays with so serious a title. He had been doubtful of the outcome of his idea from the first. Now he was convinced that he was on the wrong track and that drastic revisions were indicated if the play was to work properly. He rewrote the first two acts at once, in Moscow, and gave them to Stanislavskiy, who put them in rehearsal without delay. On November 13, before leaving Moscow, he wrote to Vera Komissarzhevskaya that his new play was now ready but that it would definitely not suit her. It had turned, he wrote, into a long, gloomy, and clumsy drama: "Its mood is dreary, as dreary can be. If I sent it to you for the Aleksandrinskiy your actors would have none of it. All the same I shall send it to you. Read it and let me know if it might be a good idea to take it on tour for the summer." [2]

Early in December, Chekhov left for Nice, taking the last two acts with him. The changes he had made in Act IV, he wrote Ol'ga, were drastic, but he was barely retouching the third act. The completed script was in Stanislavskiy's hands by the end of the year. By this time the rehearsals were well under way, with Ol'ga in the part of Masha, and Kachalov playing Vershinin. Chekhov was in Nice, at the Pension Russe, cruelly bored. There was a constant flow of letters to and from Moscow— questions, suggestions, revisions—but, though he begged Ol'ga repeatedly for news, he was quite out of touch with the play's progress. What scraps of information came to him did not at all please him. Stanislavskiy, with his customary preference for realism, was interrupting the flow of the dialogue with offstage noises. He was having Tuzenbakh's dead body carried across the stage. Chekhov objected strenuously. Alekseyev was ruining the play: "If the play is a failure, I shall go to Monte Carlo and lose till I can't see straight." On January 28 his sister Masha reported that she had attended the first dress rehearsal: "I sat in the theatre and wept, in the third act especially. They staged and acted it splendidly."

The Three Sisters opened in Moscow on January 31, 1901, while Chekhov was in Italy. In Rome he received a cable from Nemirovich reporting a successful opening, and some time later a letter from Ol'ga reached him in Yalta congratulating him warmly on his success. But the truth was that The Three Sisters had a disappointing première. The audience received it warmly, but the press was distinctly unfavorable. The critics did not know what to make of the play; they criticized the production, and for a time its fate was uncertain. The following season Chekhov came to Moscow and saw it performed. Much to Stanislavskiy's chagrin, he undertook to restage the third act himself. This time the reviews were good, and in January 1902 the Society of Dramatic Authors awarded The Three Sisters the Griboyedov prize. Before long the play was established as a masterpiece of the Russian theater.

The reason for this confusion is not far to seek. With The Three Sisters Chekhov in some sense initiated a genre in the drama, and one can readily sympathize with the dismay of the company of actors that first heard it read. Plays with stock characters and a strong, clear anecdote are easiest to play. The Three Sisters is relatively plotless. It interweaves four narrative themes so as to form a texture, but it has none of the usual amenities of the pièce bien faite. The action is molded into something like unity by means of the theme of waste and the enclosing symbol of the unattainable city. What is achieved in this manner hardly leaps to the eye. The Three Sisters is, at bottom, a novel.

For the rest, the portraiture is executed with the broad, epigrammatic strokes of the impressionist, so that much is left to the imagination. In a novel such techniques may be considered advantageous, since when the degree of control is minimal, the reader is at liberty to exercise his wits, with a consequent intensification of the work's vitality. On the stage the problem becomes embarrassing. A production necessarily involves an interpretation and is, in some measure, exclusive. The actor who plays Vershinin, for example, will be convincing only insofar as he realizes the character he is meant to portray, and the manner in which the other characters react to his portrayal will, to a great extent, determine the mood and meaning of the play. In *The Three Sisters*, Andrey, Solenyy, Chebutykin, and Tuzenbakh are relatively clear characters, and none of the young ladies offers any unusual difficulty of interpretation. But the play provides little guidance for the interpretation of Vershinin.

In such circumstances Stanislavskiy was accustomed to ask his actors to rummage their souls. But it is a rare actor who can manage to locate a Vershinin in his soul. Normally what the actor finds there is some equivalent aspect of himself or, more likely, some reflection of the director's self, depending on whose is the more dominant personality; and there is no reason to assume that either version will represent to the audience the universal Vershinin, much less the particular Vershinin who took shape in the author's mind when he composed his play. In consequence, Vershinin is normally played as a stereotype, and the actor is usually offered a choice of several. Those who consider, as did Stanislavskiy, that Chekhov was at bottom a tragic writer, tend to make Vershinin a pathetic figure, the manly, but submissive victim of his *moira*, perhaps, in some sense, the military counterpart of Trigorin. Those who insist that Chekhov's bent was predominantly ironic and satirical see Vershinin as a wistful comedian, like Gayev, a futile figure whose philosophical tirades are habitually received with impatient snickers, or with boredom. Finally, those of a Marxist turn of mind are likely to dignify Vershinin as a precursor of the Russian Revolution, a prophet of the future who is sick with the illness of the times, and is thus unable to lift a finger to bring about the wonders he foresees. To this list of possibilities there must certainly be added the posture of the cautious professional who moves warily through his lines without committing himself in any way, careful to offend no one with a definite intonation or gesture.

The responsibility for this confusion must be laid, once again, at Chekhov's door. Unwilling, apparently, to engage himself completely with regard to *The Three Sisters*, a play that had already caused him much trouble, he left his actors, in the words of Vladimir Yermilov, to "cudgel their brains over the question: is it a comedy or a tragedy? not knowing whether to laugh or to cry. . . ." This critic continues:

> Chekhov worked out an aesthetic principle according to which the tragic and the comic are divided by no wall, but merely represent the two sides of one and the same phenomenon of life, which has its tragic and its comic

sides. Any phenomenon, from Chekhov's point of view, can be regarded simultaneously in a tragic and a comic aspect.[3]

This approach to Chekhov's work has, of course, much to recommend it, and it has found ready acceptance in many quarters. But on reflection it appears that not every phenomenon can be regarded simultaneously in a tragic and a comic aspect, not even in the theater, and certainly not from Chekhov's viewpoint. The Chekhovian effect is neither comic nor tragic, nor is it a blend of the two, a sort of French dressing that flavors the events of the play with a mixture of contraries. It elicits an altogether new response, vibratory, and in the highest degree ambiguous, that defies comparison even with its closest relative in the theater, the effect Pirandello called humoristic, his special version of the Italian *grottesco*.

Chekhov himself spoke of trying for an "acid effect," but he never alluded to his plays his plays as a blend or an alternation of comic and tragic. He spoke of *The Seagull* and *The Cherry Orchard* forthrightly as comedies, and he protested repeatedly that he had never any intention of producing an effect of pathos.[4] Toward the end of his life he tended to emphasize, as did Pirandello in his time, the didactic tendency that he had formerly denied. Thus in 1902, while staying at Savva Morozov's villa, he told the young student Tikhonov:

You say my plays have made you cry, yes, and not just you have told me that. That is not why I wrote them. It was Alekseev who made such cry-babies out of them. What I intended was very different. What I wanted was to say honestly to people—"Have a look at yourselves, and see how bad your lives are and how boring." The main thing is for people to realize this, for when they do they will most certainly create for themselves another and better life. I shall not live to see it; but I know that some day it will be quite different, quite unlike what we have now. And so long as this life does not exist, I shall go on telling people, "Please see how badly you live, and how dreary you are."—What is there to cry about in that?

This sort of conversation readily brings Vershinin to mind, and also the respected madman Ivan Dmitrich Gromov of "Ward No. 6." But these sentiments do not altogether describe that Chekhov of whom Gor'kiy wrote: "Chekhov walks the earth like a doctor in the hospital; there are many patients there, but no medicines; besides, the doctor is not sure that medicines are of any use." The idea that experience involves a continual choice between the tragic and the comic, so that in the theater the audience must be kept informed by evident signs whether it is to laugh or to cry, is possibly a vestige of the assumptions underlying the classic *séparation des genres*, but it has the advantage of convenience, and probably justifies itself in practice. In real life, under dramatic conditions, and especially in the presence of others, people are apt to behave as actors do on the stage, and it is among the advantages of the theater that it provides models for acceptable behavior at the more demanding moments of one's life. It was precisely this sort of self-dramatization that interested Chekhov. It is certain that he derived much amusement from the postures his characters affect in the situations in which he placed them. Unquestionably, he was alive also to the pathos inherent in these caricatures, for they seldom lose touch with humanity. *Ivanov* is the outstanding example of the equivocal nature of his irony, but there is no lack of instances in *The Seagull, Uncle Vanya, The Three Sisters*, and *The Cherry Orchard*. It was his specialty as an artist.

Chekhov admired Zola, and no doubt thought of himself as a naturalist. But he was no mere observer of "life as it is." His plays seem to involve a minimum of contrivance, but the truth is, he arranged his effects carefully, and when he wished his intention to be clear, there is seldom any doubt as to what it was. In *The Three Sisters*, Natasha is obviously meant to arouse not only distaste and indignation but also a measure of awe and respect. Like Aksin'ya, her counterpart in the story, "In the Ravine," which was also written in 1899, one feels "a great power in her." In contrast, Andrey, whom Natasha marries on her way to the summit, is meant, no doubt, to be played as a weakling, one of nature's *ratés*, a clear example of social waste. He is accordingly calculated to arouse both scorn and pity, but he is not at all pitiful in the manner of Vanya, much less in the manner of Astrov, who are also examples of the waste of what are now called human resources. These, along with characters like Solenyy and Tuzenbakh, are straightforward characterizations that need cause the actor no sleepless nights.

Similar things may be said of Chekhov's plotting. The appalling neglect of old Firs in *The Cherry Orchard* is intended, clearly, to elicit the necessary pang at the end of the play; but, unlike Natasha's shameless treatment of the old nurse Anfisa in *The Three Sisters*, it represents, not the brutality of the upstart, but the shiftlessness of well-meaning people of the upper class, whose habitual kindliness does not prevent them from being at the same time inexcusably self-centered. All this, while delicately nuanced, is clear enough to puzzle no one.

It is otherwise with Vershinin.

It may be that *The Seagull* and *The Cherry Orchard* were meant to elicit neither tears nor laughter, nor a blend of the two, but a quite special emotional response, akin to what was called by the Renaissance critics "admiration." Chekhov's plays are by no means clinical demonstrations. They make an occasional statement, but a great deal more is implied than is said, and the implications are not often clear. In *The Three Sisters*, the characters—with the exception of the energetic Natasha—are strangely passive. It is as if they were suffering—as their author often suffered—from a mortal languor, and their well-bred inability to assert themselves brings them so close to the abstract as to make their roles difficult to play. The strange predicament of General Prozorov's children, the touching compliance of Kulygin with his wife's unfaithfulness, the senseless death of Tuzenbakh, which no one bothers to prevent, have all the kind of absurdity that recalls the postures of old daguerreotypes, true to life, no doubt, but nevertheless so quaint and so mysterious as to be hardly believable.

"Portraits and only portraits," Griboyedov wrote to his friend Katenin, seventy-five years before the date of *The Three Sisters*, "form the substance of both comedy and tragedy. These portraits, however, include certain traits common to many, and some of which belong generally to the human race." [5]

This tendency to subordinate plot to portraiture seems entirely characteristic of Russian drama. Necessarily, much of what was done along these lines in the theater came under the influence of such potent characters as Chatskiy, Onegin, Arbenin, Khlestakov, and, most of all, perhaps, Polevoy's Hamlet. A consequence was the development of a succession of magnificent character actors; another was the corresponding tendency to people the Russian drama with interchangeable parts.

In *Ivanov*, Chekhov drew a full-length portrait of the "superfluous man." But it is permissible to treat Ivanov ironically, and in that light, his self-revelations become comic. In January 1889 Chekhov wrote to Suvorin:

I have been cherishing the bold dream of summing up all that has been written hitherto about whining, miserable people, and of saying the last word on the subject with my Ivanov. It seemed to me that all Russian novelists and dramatists have been drawn to depict despondent men, but that they all write instinctively, without any definite image in mind and without any views on the subject. [6]

Chekhov had definite views on the subject of Ivanov, and he set them forth with some clarity, so that Ivanov is hardly debatable; but after *Ivanov*, Chekhov wisely refrained from clarifying his major characters to any such extent. He was certainly capable, if he wished, of penetrating his creatures to the bottom of their souls; but it was characteristic of his diffidence as an artist that, in general, he scrupled to give his characters away. In his view the revelation of truth was something to be engaged in with the utmost tact. His characters, consequently—even those who are tolerably well defined—tend to preserve their mystery, so that while we are dimly aware throughout of the discerning eye of the observer, his creatures maintain their autonomy and live in our minds with the vitality, not of characters, but of people.

Similar things may be said of Pirandello, particularly in his role as a short-story writer, and from both these masters, so much alike in so many ways, we receive, without realizing it, a wealth of information that seems to be the fruit of our own insight rather than that of the author. In the case of Vershinin, by the time he leaves the play to rejoin his battery we feel that we know him very well indeed; as well, certainly, as the other characters know him—and, at the same time, that we know him not at all, no better than anyone else we know.

"Every play," Galsworthy wrote in a noteworthy passage, "must be shaped so as to have a spire of meaning. Every grouping of life and character has its inherent moral, and the business of the playwright is to pose the group so as to bring that moral poignantly to the light of day." [7] It is easy to see how this may work in a play like *Strife* or *Justice*, but the tableaux that Chekhov arranged in his major plays do not so readily yield up their moral essence. The cosy family group, for example, at the end of *Uncle Vanya*, or the family group at the end of *The Three Sisters*, each set off by its pleasant musical accompaniment, are scenes vibrant with irony, but in each case the moral escapes us. Chekhov was hardly a moralist. It may seem that all his plays, in some measure touch the question of waste, which Bradley thought was of the essence of the tragic mood, but that is about all one can say with confidence of the message of *The Three Sisters*. Our lives, it is intimated, are a lost opportunity; but it is never quite clear in Chekhov's plays what the opportunity was, or what, in the circumstances, might have been done to make the most of it.

In "A Dreary Story" the eminent professor of medicine Nikolay Stepanovich, after a lifetime of service to science, has reason to complain that, having lived out his years without the benefit of a "general idea," he has, in the end, degenerated into complete impotence, a cipher among the living. "A Dreary Story" was written in 1889 in Yalta and most likely reflects the author's depression of the preceding year, but it is altogether possible that in spite of, or perhaps because of, his amorous involvement with Ol'ga Knipper, he was in a similar frame of mind ten years later when he sat down to rewrite *The Three Sisters* in accordance with ideas that were not quite his own.

Chekhov wrote to Suvorin on May 30, 1888: "It seems to me that writers of fiction are not required to solve such problems as God, pessimism, and so on. The business of a writer of fiction is only to describe the characters who talked or thought about God or pessimism, how they did it and in what circumstances. The artist is not supposed to be the judge of his characters or of what they say, but only an impartial observer." Chekhov had expressed himself to the same effect many times in other letters, but as an observer he was seldom impartial. He was often accused of aimlessness, and he defended his lack of tendentiousness, but his writings imply constant judgment, and quite unobtrusively he makes his readers aware of an ideal against which each character and each action may be measured. The result is the gallery of magnificent cartoons that enlivens his theater, cartoons that are never cruel in the style of Daumier or Gavarni, comic portraits, no doubt, but always warm and tender, portraits that say: "*mon semblable, mon frère*," without a trace of bitterness.

In an often-cited letter to Suvorin, dated October 27, 1888, he wrote:

. . . the artist observes, conjectures, composes—these activities in themselves presuppose a problem; if, from the first, the artist did not set himself a problem there would not be anything to conjecture, or anything to select. . . ."

He continued, in the same vein:

> You are right in insisting that the artist must have a conscious relation to his
> work, but you confuse two ideas: to solve a problem, and to pose a problem
> correctly. . . . . The court is required to state a problem correctly, but the
> members of the jury must solve it, each according to his views. [8]

Such an approach, obviously, poses problems of its own. In the case of
The Three Sisters the problem is very beautifully posed, but we have no
clue as to its nature. What we are aware of in this play is not so much
the problem that is posed as the enclosing symbol that poses it.

The symbol is, of course, the vision of Moscow, the Chekhovian pro-
totype of Ionesco's radiant city, or, on quite another plane, the London
of Restoration comedy. In the short story "On Official Business," which
Chekhov published in 1899, about the time when he had *The Three
Sisters* in hand, the examining magistrate Lyzhin, consigned to a boring
job in the provinces, reflects: "To live, one must live in Moscow. Here
nothing is of any consequence; one grows easily resigned to one's insignificant role and looks forward to one thing only in life, to get away from
here, quickly, quickly. . . ." It is in the vicinity of Syrnya, hundreds of
miles from Moscow, that he comes upon von Taunitz's beautiful daughters, and he feels sorry "for those girls who were living their lives and
would end them in this wilderness." The irony, here again, is clear, and
would be clearer still to those who knew the Moscow of the day; nevertheless, life in Moscow would certainly be a more interesting experience
than life in Syrnya, or even in Yalta where Chekhov was condemned to
spend his winters.

In *The Three Sisters*, however, the dream of Moscow reduces everything to triviality. It inhibits all purposeful action, so that the consequence is a progressive devaluation of present reality in favor of a vision
of the unattainable paradise. Thus it is with the three sisters, but Moscow
means little to Vershinin. Its equivalent in his mind is the utopia of the
future that makes everything in the unhappy present unimportant and
therefore endurable. In these terms, the problem is posed in a manner
that may not readily recall the final tableau of *Uncle Vanya;* but the
dreams of Vershinin, and Irina's longings, are clearly of the same texture
as Sonya's dream of heaven with its attendant angels and its promise of
peace and rest.

But the examining magistrate Lyzhin, in "On Official Business," experiences in the middle of the night an unexpected flash of insight that affords us a glimpse into another compartment of Chekhov's mind. To Lyzhin it occurs suddenly that all the seemingly unrelated events he has experienced in his wilderness and all the disparate characters he has met are "parts of a single organism, marvelous and rational." Nothing is accidental. All is related. "Everything is filled with a universal idea, everything has one soul, one aim, and to understand this it is not enough to think, perhaps one must have also, it would seem, a special gift of insight into life which is not vouchsafed to all." This idea, perhaps symbolist in its origin, appears to have attracted Chekhov long before the date of *The Three Sisters*. In one way or another it turns up in his stories from the time, at least, of "An Attack of Nerves," which he wrote in 1888; and its negative aspect is emphatically developed in "A Dreary Story," in which the unhappy Nikolay Stepanovich is unable to think of his life as "part of that universal whole" but only as "an accidental fragment." It would appear that in these years Chekhov had periodic intuitions of the existence of something in the nature of a world soul, an ethical substance, possibly Hegelian in character. It was a concept that sorted badly with his generally skeptical and scientific materialism, but it served to rationalize the idealistic strain that was at the core of his feeling of kinship with humanity, and the real concern for the sufferings of others that eventually sent him across Russia to the prison island of Sakhalin.

This deep-seated ambiguity in his nature is perceptible in much of his work, perhaps in all. He was said to be a cold man, a man, as he himself wrote Suvorin, "without passion." "You look on everyday life with complete indifference," Ol'ga Knipper wrote him in a letter toward the end of his life. "It is not because you are cold or indifferent by nature, but because there is something in you that does not let you consider the things of this life as of any consequence." As a man, according to all indications, he preserved his detachment—perhaps out of some primitive instinct of self-preservation—but he could not help identifying his personal discomfort with the discomforts of others. It is doubtless this equivocal mood that, as an artist, he transmitted to his work, and that gives it its curious vibrance, its irony, and also its warmth and sincere compassion.

The Chekhovian mood is hardly unique among men of great talent, particularly among those writers whose sense of the comic transcended comedy. In the extremely scholarly essay on humor he published in 1908, Pirandello cites Giordano Bruno as a precursor in the humoristic style, and he adopts Bruno's *"In tristitia hilaris, in hilaritate tristis"* as the basis of his own idea that *l'umorismo* consists in the sense of the contrary. In the preface to *Erma Bifronte*, a collection of stories he published in 1906, Pirandello described his inner vision in terms that quite aptly recall the Chekhovian effect:

> I see a sort of labyrinth in which the soul moves through all sorts of diverse, opposed, and intricate paths without finding any way out. And in this labyrinth I see a herm with a laughing face and another face that weeps: it laughs indeed with one face at the tears of the other.[9]

Schiller recalled that Goethe once spoke to him of *Faust* as "that very serious jest." *The Three Sisters*, whatever its original conception may have been, became, in the course of time, something also of that nature, but its quality is unique among the great comedies. It does not belong to what Flaubert called *"le grotesque triste."* That mood is properly applicable to such stories as Chekhov's "Carelessness," and also to "The Duel" and "Ward No. 6," and perhaps one may wish to characterize *Uncle Vanya* and *The Cherry Orchard* in this fashion. Chekhov's early comedies end with a suicide, and both *Uncle Vanya* and *The Cherry Orchard* end in heartbreak. It is understandable that not everyone can see the joke in them. Chekhov wrote to Ol'ga in April 1904, alluding presumably to *The Cherry Orchard:*

> Why is it that on the posters and in the newspaper advertisements my play is so persistently called a drama? Nemirovich and Stanislavskiy see something absolutely different in my play from what I have written, and I would be ready to bet anything that neither of them has ever read my play through attentively. Forgive me, but I assure you it is so.

The Three Sisters was properly called a drama, but it had been conceived as a vaudeville, and it ends ambiguously. It is certainly far from tragic. The final speech is not a *threnos*, a lamentation. It is an impassioned plea for life, for enlightenment, by no means coherent, in which we hear once again the leitmotif of so much of Chekhov's work, the question "Why?"

This question no man can answer. As for the question of Vershinin, this must be resolved, if it can be resolved, mainly with reference to the persona with which Chekhov represented himself to himself, a figure that is occasionally visible but by no means easy to define. In this regard his letters to his wife, his sister, and his friends provide very contrary indications. It is to his plays and his stories that one must go for something reasonably trustworthy; unhappily, there too one looks in vain for a consistent image. In a sense, all Chekhov's works involve a question posed by one to whom life evidently seemed to be a practical joke in questionable taste. "On my way here," says Ivanov in his fourth and final act, "I laughed at myself, and it seemed to me that the birds and the flowers were laughing at me also."

There was, however, another element in Chekhov's nature, perhaps more deeply based, that is particularly visible in such a story as "Ward No. 6." In that story Ragin and Gromov may well be thought to illustrate the twin aspects of Chekhov's character in somewhat the same way that Chebutykin and Vershinin seem to define them in *The Three Sisters*. In the squalid madhouse that is their common ground, neither Andrey Yefimych nor Ivan Dmitrich doubts for a moment that the future of mankind will be glorious, and neither has the faintest idea of how this is to come about. What they know is that the stolid warder keeps order by pounding everyone indiscriminately with his fists. In *The Three Sisters* the situation is less poignant. For Chebutykin nothing is real and nothing matters. Vershinin is in closer touch with reality, but he withdraws readily into the sustaining dream of the earthly paradise in which he will one day participate by proxy. Both seem to be, though at different stages of life, under the influence of an opiate without which, perhaps, they could not bear to live. In both cases the essential ingredient of nepenthe is love.

The Three Sisters ends with a question. It suggests no answer. It leaves one only with a mood. It is a mood, in some ways reminiscent of Maeterlinck, that very effectively reflects the ambiguity that lies at the heart of all Chekhov's work, the doubt at the bottom of his soul, out of which he created stories and plays and characters—Ragin and Gromov, Lyzhin, Chebutykin, Trofimov, Trigorin and Konstantin, Nikolay Stepanovich, and Vershinin—these characters who live with his life and speak to us with his words. One thing is clear. Vershinin must be played with dignity for, without doubt, he meant much to the author. If he provokes a smile, it must be a smile of sympathy, of friendship. For the rest, it is perhaps not necessary to understand him any further than he was meant to be understood. He speaks more cogently to the feeling than to the understanding.

"To understand?" Jouvet is made to ask in Giraudoux's *L'Impromptu de Paris.* "The word understand does not exist in the theatre. Do you understand the word understand, you, Renoir?"

"The good thing is," Renoir answers, "that the real public does not understand. It feels. It can therefore be shown everything without compromise and without reticence. Those who insist on understanding in the theatre are those who do not understand the theatre." [10]

NOTES

1. The letters to Vishnevskiy are published in *Polnoye sobraniye sochineniy A. P. Chekhova,* 20 vols. (Moscow, 1944–51), XVIII, and translated in *A. P. Chekhov, Letters on the Short Story, the Drama, and Other Literary Topics,* ed. L. S. Friedland (New York: Minton, Balch, 1924), pp. 155 f. The letters to Ol'ga Knipper are translated in Constance Garnett, *The Letters of Anton Pavlovitch Tchehov to Olga Leonardovna Knipper* (New York: George H. Doran, 1924), pp. 40, 41, 42 f., 45, 49, 53, 68, 72.

2. Letter of November 13, 1900. Translated in Chekhov, *Letters,* ed. Friedland, p. 156. For the nature and extent of Chekhov's revisions see A. R. Vladimirskaya, "Dve rannie redaktsii p'esy *Tri Sestry,*" in *Literaturnoye Nasledstvo,* 68 (Moscow: 1960), pp. 1 ff.

3. Vladimir Yermilov, *Anton Pavlovich Chekhov,* trans. Ivy Litvinov (Moscow: Foreign Languages Publishing House, n.d.), p. 90.

4. See, for example, letters to Suvorin, October 21, 1895, and to Ol'ga Knipper, April 10, 1904. Translated in the two collections cited in notes 1 and 2, above.

5. Aleksandr Griboyedov, letter to P. A. Katenin, February 14, 1825. In *Polnoye sobraniye sochineniy A. S. Griboyedova,* ed. Piksanov, 3 vols. (Petersburg: 1911–17), III. Translated in A. Griboyedov, *Works* (Moscow, 1953), letter 39, p. 527.

6. Letter to Suvorin, January 7, 1889. Translated in Chekhov, *Letters,* ed. Friedland, p. 143.

7. John Galsworthy, "Some Platitudes Concerning Drama" (1909), in John Galsworthy, *The Inn of Tranquillity* (New York: Scribners, 1919), p. 189.

8. Letter to Suvorin, October, 27, 1888. Translated in Chekhov, *Letters,* ed. Friedland, pp. 59 f.

9. Luigi Pirandello, *Erma bifronte* (Milano, Treves, 1906), Preface.

10. Jean Giraudoux, *L'Impromptu de Paris* (Paris, Grasset, 1937), pp. 43 f.

CHEKHOV'S MAJOR PLAYS:
A DOCTOR IN THE HOUSE

BY LOUIS PEDROTTI

Medicine gets in his way. If he weren't a doctor, he would write even better.

Tolstoy to Gor'kiy, about Chekhov [1]

Anton Chekhov belongs to the considerable list of writers who, so to speak, have "black-bagged" their way through literature. In this respect he occupies an important position in the illustrious company of artists of the word whose professional medical training and experience find reflection in their works: Rabelais, John Keats, Oliver Goldsmith, Tobias Smollett, A. Conan Doyle, W. Somerset Maugham, Louis-Ferdinand Céline, Gertrude Stein, William Carlos Williams, Arthur Schnitzler, Walker Percy, Richard Selzer, and Lewis Thomas, among others.

In 1899, when Chekhov had already moved to his "warm Siberia" in Yalta on the advice of his own doctors, Doctor Grigoriy Rossolimo, who had studied medicine at the University of Moscow along with Chekhov from 1879 to 1884, asked Chekhov for an autobiographical sketch for an anniversary album honoring the class of 1884. At this time Rossolimo was himself professor of medicine at the University of Moscow and a leading neuropathologist in Russia's second capital. What Chekhov sent him may serve to illustrate, both in content and in style, the concerns of this essay.

I, A. P. Chekhov, was born January 17, 1860, in Taganrog. I first studied at the Greek school run by the Church of Tsar Konstantin and later at the Taganrog High School. In 1879 I enrolled in the Department of Medicine at the University of Moscow. At that time I had little understanding, generally speaking, about the departments there, and I don't remember for what reasons I chose the Department of Medicine, but I have not regretted the choice. Even during my first year of studies I began to publish in the weekly magazines and newspapers, and already in the beginning of the eighties these literary activities took on a steady, professional nature. I received the Pushkin Prize in 1888. In 1890 I traveled to the island of Sakhalin in order to write a book about our penal colony. Not counting court reports, book reviews, newspaper articles, notes, everything that I wrote from day to day for the newspapers and that would now be hard to locate and collect, during the 20 years of my literary activity I have written and published more than 300 printed folios of novellas and short stories. I have also written plays.

I do not doubt that my medical studies had a strong influence on my literary activity. They significantly broadened the field of my observations and enriched me with knowledge whose true value for me as a writer can only be understood by someone who is himself a doctor. They also served as a guiding influence, and more than likely because of my familiarity with medicine I was able to avoid making many mistakes. My acquaintanceship with the natural sciences and with the scientific method has always kept me on my guard, and I have tried, whenever possible, to take scientific data into consideration, and when it has not been possible, I have preferred not to write at all. By the way, I want to say that the conditions of artistic creativity do not always allow a full agreement with scientific data. Death from poisoning cannot be represented on stage the way it actually occurs. But agreement with scientific data should be felt even in these conditions, that is to say that it is necessary that the reader or spectator should realize that these are only conventions and that he is dealing with a knowledgeable author. I do not belong to those fiction writers who react negatively to science, nor should I want to belong to those who would use reason alone to solve all problems.

As for my medical practice, when I was still a student I worked at the Voskresensk *Zemstvo* Hospital (near New Jerusalem) under the well-known *zemstvo* Doctor P. A. Arkhangel'skiy. Later I served for a short time as a doctor in the Zvenigorod Hospital. During the cholera years ('92, '93) I was in charge of the Melikhovo section of the Serpukhov District.[2]

Over and over again in his letters may be found reference to the debt that Chekhov the writer owes to Chekhov the physician. "As a man of medicine I feel that I have accurately described mental suffering," he wrote, in reference to his story called "An Attack of Nerves" ("Pripadok"), "in accordance with all the rules of the science of psychiatry."[3] Soon after the completion of his medical studies at the university, Chekhov admitted how much "fictional material" was available from his present experience as a country doctor in the village of Zvenigorod.[4] Later he confided to Aleksandr Suvorin, his publisher, that his medical knowledge provided him with insight into a woman's world during the period of her pregnancy, when he was writing his story called "The Nameday Party" ("Imeniny"). "You know," he wrote, "it's great to be a doctor and understand what you're writing about. The ladies are saying that the childbirth is described *correctly*."[5] At times Chekhov criticized other writers for showing a lack of understanding of medical matters in their works. After reading Émile Zola's *Dr. Pascal*, Chekhov lamented the author's ineptness in depicting the life of a doctor.[6] And to a friend of his, a woman writer who was excessively squeamish about treating the subject of venereal disease in her writings, Chekhov gave the following appraisal:

> But the women in your story treat syphilis like a scarecrow. There's no need to do this. Syphilis isn't a vice. It's not a product of an evil will, but a disease, and those who are sick with syphilis also have need of tender, loving care. It's a bad thing if a wife runs away from her sick husband on the excuse that the disease is infectious or nasty. However, *she* may react to syphilis as she wishes, but an author must be humane to the tips of his fingers.[7]

More than once Tolstoy expressed his dislike for Chekhov's plays. The sage of Yasnaya Polyana, a far more subjective writer than Chekhov, missed the point of the younger man's artistic approach when he accused him of lacking direction and moral instruction in his plays. He once told Chekhov himself what he thought about his stagecraft: "You know, I can't stand Shakespeare, but your plays are even worse. At least Shakespeare grabs his reader by the collar and leads him toward a certain goal, without letting him turn aside. But where do you go with your heroes? From the sofa where they are lying to the [outhouse]—and back?"[8] For his part, Chekhov, whose mature writing eschewed the subjective approach and all suggestion of homiletic style, at times lost patience with Tolstoy's cranky carping at his medical mentality. "Here's Tolstoy calling us scoundrels," he wrote Suvorin in 1892, during the great cholera epidemic, "and I'm absolutely convinced that without us doctors the country would be in a real mess."[9] And the good doctor did not hesitate to point out Tolstoy's weak medical background in his writings. Although he admired parts of *The Kreutzer Sonata*, Chekhov was frustrated by Tolstoy's obstinacy in the face of medical facts. Especially irritating for him was the "boldness with which Tolstoy handles something that he doesn't care to understand. For instance, his opinions about syphilis, foundling homes, about women's disgust with copulation, etc., not only can be disputed, but they openly expose him as an ignorant man who in the course of his long life hasn't bothered to read two or three books written by specialists."[10] And in 1891, when he was battling sieges of insomnia by rereading *War and Peace*, Chekhov expressed his impatience with Tolstoy's hostile attitude toward the facts of medical science in his novel:

> If I had been at Prince Andrey's bedside, I'd have cured him. It's odd to read that the wound of a prince, a rich man who was attended day and night by a doctor and who enjoyed the care of Natasha and Sonya, was giving off a putrid smell. What a lousy thing medicine was in those days! When he was writing his fat novel, Tolstoy must have become involuntarily saturated with hatred for medicine.[11]

Doctor Chekhov firmly believed that there was a great affinity between bodily and mental ailments, that one should not try, as he put it, "to separate the soul from the body" in making a diagnosis.[12] So interested was he in the workings of the mind upon the body that at one time he even regretted that he had not devoted his life to psychiatry. "If I hadn't become a writer," he confessed, "I'd probably have turned out to be a psychiatrist, but of necessity a second-rate one, and I preferred to be a first-rate psychiatrist."[13] In fact, in giving his advice to another lady writer, he put in a plug, not only for the medical profession as a whole, but for psychiatry in particular. This piece of advice gives evidence of Chekhov's interest in psychiatry and his debt to it in producing his literary works. "Study medicine, my dear," he said, "if you want to be a real writer. Especially psychiatry. It has helped me a great deal and has kept me from making mistakes."[14]

In evaluating the psychological influences upon Chekhov's writing made by his medical studies, it should be remembered not only that Chekhov was a doctor but that he was a patient as well, right from the beginning of his mature literary career. In the year that he completed his medical studies in Moscow he suffered his first hemorrhaging from the lungs. As one present-day physician states the case, "in 1884 he had his first hemoptysis. In retrospect, we know it was tuberculosis, but a single hemoptysis does not make a diagnosis, and Chekhov was quite willing to assume a posture of anosognosia."[15] We have before us the ironic anomaly of a physician choosing to ignore, at least in public, the nature of his own disease right up until the time his doctor insisted that he move from his beloved Moscow (and the Moscow Art Theater) to the warmer climate of the Crimea. Even as late as 1897 he could joke with Suvorin about the serious bleeding from his mouth that occurred while the two friends were having dinner in a Moscow restaurant. Here the now frightened doctor grimly diagnoses himself as patient. "In order to allay the patient's fears," Chekhov told Suvorin, "we say when he is coughing that it's a gastric cough, and when he is bleeding, we say it's hemorrhoids. But there's no such thing as a gastric cough, and the bleeding is certainly from the lungs. I have blood coming from the right lung, just as my brother had and another relative of mine had who also died of consumption."[16] Chekhov was, indeed, a patient most of his life, but he chose to concentrate on the less serious ailments and ignore, until too late, the one that would eventually carry him off in his forty-fifth year. So it is that he would complain constantly about diarrhea, hemorrhoids, constipation, varicose veins, heart palpitations, migraine headaches—but seldom even a hint about the condition of his lungs. Chekhov once told his school friend and fellow doctor, Grigoriy Rossalimo, that he could understand his patients' mental condition because of his own physical and mental sufferings. "For example, I suffer from intestinal catarrh," Chekhov confided, omitting to say anything about his tuberculosis, "and I fully understand what someone suffering from this malady experiences, what mental pains he endures, and this a doctor rarely understands."[17] Indeed, there are critics who believe that Chekhov may have been able to identify all too closely with his patients and to have been prompted by too nervous a reaction toward human suffering to be a truly successful doctor.[18] It is true that, as Chekhov's brother Mikhail relates, the young doctor, fresh out of medical school, met with defeat by his feelings of delicacy on one of his first cases in Zvenigorod. Chekhov was faced with a five-year-old boy who was suffering from paraphemosis. The constriction around the head of the poor boy's penis was so great that a serious swelling of the organ had resulted, and the possibility of gangrene setting in became apparent. It was in this dreadful condition that the parents brought the screaming child to the town hospital. Mikhail Chekhov continues:

> And so, my brother Anton, practically from the first day, had to perform an operation. But the child was yelling so loudly and jerking his legs so franti-

cally, that Anton Pavlovich couldn't bring himself to undertake the business at hand. The peasant woman who had brought the boy was sobbing violently, while two assistants, Neapolitanskiy and I were standing around meddling and waiting for the outcome of such an interesting operation—and all this embarrassed my brother still more." [19]

The business ended with Doctor Chekhov's turning the operation over to another district doctor, who performed the operation in short order.

Among Dr. Chekhov's first patients were the wife and daughters of a Moscow artist, A. S. Yanov, a friend of Chekhov's brother Nikolay, also an artist. When Mrs. Yanova and one of the girls died from typhoid fever, Chekhov was thrown into despair, according to his brother Mikhail: "While she was dying in agony, the daughter grabbed Anton Pavlovich by the hand, and it was thus that she gave up her spirit, squeezing it firmly in her own hand. Feeling utterly powerless and guilty, and for a long time aware of the dead girl's cold handclasp on his own hand, Anton Pavlovich there and then decided to give up medicine altogether, and once and for all he gave himself over to literature." [20] It is apparent that Mikhail Chekhov somewhat melodramatically overstated his brother's sensibilities as a young doctor, since, of course, he continued to practice medicine for many years to come. But even in 1889, when his brother Nikolay was dying from tuberculosis, there is evidence of Chekhov's exquisite sensitivity to the sufferings of others. Fully aware of the finality of his brother's condition and of his own helplessness to reverse the dying process, he is reported to have voiced his despair: "There are moments when I sincerely regret that I'm a physician and not an ignoramus." [21]

No, Chekhov did not desert his "wife" (medicine) for his "mistress" (literature), either in practice or in artistic method. But his acuteness to the physical (and mental) plight of his fellow patients finds abundant expression throughout his literature. Doctor Astrov in *Uncle Vanya*, one of Chekhov's most optimistic physician characters, certainly echoes his creator's anguish over the difficulty in keeping feelings of humanity out of medical treatment. In his monologue from the beginning of Act I, Doctor Astrov repeats Dr. Chekhov's own dreadful experience with typhus in his early years as a country doctor:

ASTROV: . . . The third week of Lent I went to Malitskoye because of the epidemic there. . . . Typhus. . . . People lying in the huts in rows. . . . Filth, stench, smoke, calves together with the patients on the floor. . . . Little pigs, too. . . . I was on the go all day long, didn't even sit down, didn't get a bite to eat, and when I got home I didn't get any rest. They brought me in a switchman from the railroad. I laid him on the table to operate on him, and he ups and dies on me under chloroform. And just when I didn't need it, my feelings woke up in me, and my conscience began to hurt, just as if I had deliberately murdered him. . . .[22]

And Chekhov's own "ignoramus-instead-of-physician" wish comes into full bloom in the character of Doctor Chebutykin, in *The Three Sisters*, the most existential of the doctor characters in his plays. He reads only newspapers and seems content to pull out news items from them from time to time. His terrifying confession in Act III, during the great fire in town, is reminiscent of Gogol"s madman, Poprishchin—"Why am I a titular councillor, and why should I be a titular councillor? Maybe I'm some sort of count or general and only seem to be titular councillor? Maybe I don't know myself who I am."[23]—But Dr. Chebutykin's soul-baring is also the ultimate product of a once sensitive doctor's despair over some of the anomalies of his profession:

CHEBUTYKIN *morosely:* . . . They think I'm a doctor and can cure all kinds of diseases, but I know absolutely nothing. I've forgotten everything I did know. I don't remember anything, not a single thing. . . . Last Wednesday I was treating a woman at Zasyp. She died, and it's my fault that she died. Yes . . . I used to know a thing or two some twenty-five years back, but now I don't remember anything. Not a thing. Maybe I'm not even a man, but I only pretend to have arms and legs and a head. Maybe I don't even exist at all, and I only think that I walk around, that I eat, that I sleep. *Weeps.* Oh, how great it would be not to exist! *Stops weeping. Morosely.* Who the hell cares! The other day there was a conversation at the club—about Shakespeare, Voltaire. I've never read them, never a word of them, but I made out that I had read them. And so did everyone else. How vulgar! [*poshlost'*] How despicable! And I remembered that woman whom I murdered on Wednesday. . . . And everything came back to me, and inside I felt all bent up, nasty, vile. . . . So I went and got drunk. (574)

Chekhov's interest in medical psychology is well known, and a modern American doctor-critic has paid him tribute for this aspect of his writing: "It was half a century before the term 'psychosomatic medicine' came into vogue, but we can credit Chekhov with having such an idea in embryo and for having derived it himself."[24] And Tolstoy was not the only critic to comment on (in his case, complain of) his compatriot's cool, medical attitude toward his literary subjects. Once again, a present-day American physician presents a positive evaluation of the literary approach taken by his earlier Russian colleague: "Chekhov's success as a writer stemmed from his ability to adopt a detached clinical attitude, to observe people's conduct, their mixed motives, their compromises with reality—much as a sensible doctor looks at a patient."[25] Still another doctor, French this time, finds Chekhov's literary talent in this very detachment, the emphasis upon the concrete, upon observation and experience, on the scientific method, with no attempt to teach or to render "service."[26] Chekhov admitted as much in his self-diagnosis in regard to his early play *Ivanov*: "I'm telling you honestly and sincerely that these people were born inside my head, not out of seafoam, not from preconceived ideas, not from 'intellectualizing,' and not accidentally. They are the result of observing and studying life."[27] Certainly his medical training had prepared him to observe and to diagnose—but first of all, to observe. As a practicing physician, Chekhov was exposed to all types of the human condition—"richmen, poormen, the exploiters and the exploited," as a Soviet critic puts it—"peasants, workers, landowners, factory workers. He gathered abundant material for his creative work during his visits to his patients in their home environment. And Chekhov the doctor constantly observed much human grief and suffering, wrongs and injustice, and he presented them in his literary works."[28]

Chekhov himself confessed his detachment toward his literary subjects, his neutrality in the face of their problems, his belief that a writer should let the reader or spectator come to his own conclusions from the evidence supplied: "In *Anna Karenina* and in *Onegin*," he wrote to Suvorin, "not a single question is resolved, but you are completely satisfied, simply because all the questions in them are correctly posed. The court is obliged to pose the questions correctly and let the jurors decide each according to his own tastes."[29] And to his brother Aleksandr he gave his advice about presenting the emotional conditions of his fictional characters. "God save you from generalizations," he cautioned the budding writer. "It's best to avoid giving descriptions of the mental state of your heroes. You should try to make this clear from their actions."[30]

So it is that Chekhov in his plays (as in his stories, for that matter), presents us, the audience, with the evidence of the ailments and allows us, the audience, to arrive at our own diagnosis from the symptoms given. Thus, the characters in his major plays may be seen as patients, each suffering more or less, each in his own way, from the maladies inherent in the process of living. The spectator in Chekhov's theater is made, then, to partake of the physician's method, and his understanding and enjoyment of the dramatic action will depend upon how sensitive and *observing* he is of, not only what the characters say about themselves and others, but also of how they say it and what they do (including the attention given by the playwright to some of the discomforting pauses in the stage directions). Thus, we are made to share in the creative process, as well as in the very viewpoint, training, and experience of the playwright himself. What we are faced with in a performance of *The Seagull*, *Uncle Vanya*, *The Three Sisters*, or *The Cherry Orchard* is not only a doctor's treatment of his patients, performed before our eyes; we are also drawn into the diagnostic process. We are asked to observe the effect of words and actions on these "patients," and we are called upon to come to an appraisal of the evidence as given us in the brief time span of four acts, as well as the unspoken, unseen, unobserved (and, of course, unwritten) prologue and epilogue. Chekhov has given us in each case a more or less static initial point into which an intruding force is brought in from the outside. Nina and Konstantin's own little world of creativity is "invaded" by the grand world of the arts represented by Arkadina and Trigorin. The given "norm" of Uncle Vanya and Sonya's "service" is upset by Professor Serebryakov and Yelena. The life of the Prozorova sisters is assaulted by Vershinin and his officers. And in a variation on the scheme, the cherry orchard, representing Ranevskaya and Gayev, is threatened by Lopakhin. Each character responds to the given "intrusion" in his own way, and the spectator has the task (and, perhaps, the satisfaction) of making his own prognosis of the patients onstage. How successful he is depends on his acuteness of observation of words and actions, in interpolating where Chekhov merely suggests, and in making a whole out of the bits and pieces of each soul as Chekhov reveals it to the audience.

When Doctor Chebutykin in *The Three Sisters* diagnoses himself in Act III and discovers that he is suffering from the "disease" of commonplace vulgarity (*poshlost'*), the audience is made to face up to and recognize one of the abiding human ailments, an affliction endemic in the human genus. An adequate translation of the Russian word still awaits its Noah Webster. One critic has tabbed *poshlost'* as "that peculiarly Russian term and the vice it denotes—a trivial, dreary and common vulgarity and pettiness of spirit—a mood that Gogol evoked so memorably in his *Inspector-General* and *Dead Souls*." [31] Vladimir Nabokov, also running to Gogol' for help, has tried his hand at rendering the concept into English. Spelling it phonetically (*poshlust*), he has offered "cheap, sham, common, smutty, pink-and-blue, high falutin' and in bad taste" as possible entries. "*Poshlust*," he continues, "is not only the obviously trashy but also the falsely important, the falsely beautiful, the falsely clever, the falsely attractive." And then he proceeds to what may be, in the long run, the only realistic way to approach a definition of *poshlost'* in English: by citing examples from the world of advertising and from literature. [32] Indeed, *poshlost'* merits a Greek or Latin designation of its own, to accord it a proper place among other maladies in the physician's handbook, such as delirium, paranoia, acedia, aphasia, neurasthenia, hypochondriasis, and melancholia—all of which may be found in Doctor Chekhov's literary "case histories."

"His enemy was *poshlost'*," Maksim Gor'kiy once said about Chekhov. "All his life he fought against it, he made fun of it, and he portrayed it with his dispassionate, sharp pen, knowing how to find the fungus of *poshlost'* even where, at first glance, it seemed that everything was arranged very nicely, suitably and even brilliantly." [33]

Chekhov's last four plays are, accordingly, peopled with patients, and except for *The Cherry Orchard*, there are also doctors there to help the audience with the diagnoses. Doctor Dorn, the gentle physician of *The Seagull*, quietly dispenses his valerian drops as a mild sedative to his "nervous" patients at Sorin's country estate. Doctor Chekhov, too, made use of the drug derived from the roots of *Valeriana officinalis* to calm down the nerves of his own patients, including his publisher, Aleksandr Suvorin. [34] Even at the very conclusion of the play it is Doctor Dorn, the sedating physician, who tries to allay the fears of the others by explaining away Konstantin's offstage gunshot as the explosion of a bottle of ether in his black bag. [35] Through the observations made by this fifty-five-year-old doctor who, in his own words, was the only decent obstetrician in the whole province ten or fifteen years back, we in the audience are provided with the symptoms of those around him. In the remarkably revealing ending to Act I, we learn from Doctor Dorn's remarks something about Konstantin Treplev: "Hey, how nervous you are. Tears in your eyes . . ." (441). We learn something about Doctor Dorn and his attitude toward the medical profession. Like Doctor Chekhov himself, he had expected the soul-satisfying reward of artistic creation from medicine, instead of the drudgery and the frustrations of daily ministrations to the ailing: "You know, I've lived a varied and tasteful life, and I'm satisfied. But if I'd ever had the chance to experience the elevation of the spirit that artists have when they're in the midst of the creative process, I think I'd have turned my back on my material shell and everything peculiar to this shell, and I'd have soared off this earth into the skies above" (441).[36] And perhaps we learn most of all about Masha in this scene—about the comic role that her *poshlost'* has forced her to play in this comedy in four acts. Masha enters the play in high *poshlost'* with her melodramatic remark that she is wearing black in professional mourning for her life. And at the end of Act I she continues to play the hammy, pseudotragic role, through which Doctor Dorn cuts with his cry of "That's disgusting!" as he grabs her snuffbox and throws it into the bushes (442). Doctor Dorn has given us the cue: we may pick it up and follow the comic diagnosis to the end of the act:

MASHA: Wait a minute.
DORN: Why?
MASHA: I want to tell you again. I feel like talking. . . . *Excitedly.* I don't love my father . . . , but I feel drawn to you. Somehow I feel with all my heart that we are close to each other. . . . So help me. Help me, or else I'll do something silly, I'll make my life a farce, I'll spoil it. . . . I can't go on. . . .
DORN: What can I do? How can I be of help?
MASHA: I'm suffering. No one, no one knows my sufferings! *Lays her head on his chest quietly.* I love Konstantin.
DORN: How nervous you all are! How nervous you all are! And how much love. . . . Oh, enchanted lake! *Tenderly.* But what in the world can I do, my child? What can I do? What? (442)

What, indeed, except observe (for us) and dispense his tranquilizing valerian drops? And when it comes to choosing between the exuberant and faultlessly groomed Irina Arkadina and the sloppy and depressed Masha, Doctor Dorn does not hesitate to hand the golden apple to the mature actress (who claims she could play a girl of fifteen) rather than to the young girl (who feels herself to be a thousand years old). We should, of course, expect such a reaction from a man of science, whose creator back in his own medical school days took his brother Aleksandr to task for running a filthy household: "By the way, speaking of esthetics. Excuse me, my dear fellow, but don't be a parent in words only. Teach by example. Clean underwear mixed up with dirty underwear, scraps of food left on the table, foul rags, your spouse with her boobs hanging out and with a ribbon as dirty as Kontorskaya Street around her neck—all this will ruin your little girl even in her earliest years."[37]

At the very beginning of Act I of *Uncle Vanya* the audience sees another of Chekhov's theatrical physicians, Doctor Astrov, who has been called "Chekhov's fullest study of a country doctor."[38]

This vodka-tippling doctor has become worn out by the hard lot of his country practice, with its long hours and dreary surroundings:

> ASTROV: Yes. . . . In ten years I've become a different person. And what's the reason? I've overworked myself, Nanny. On my feet from morning to night, not a moment's peace, and you lie under your blanket at night, afraid that you'll be dragged out to some patient. All the time that we've known each other I haven't had a single free day. How can you avoid aging? And the life here is by itself boring and stupid and dirty. . . . This life drags you down. . . .(483)

Doctor Astrov takes refuge from the hard life of a country doctor in a search for beauty, and the specific path he has chosen is the reforestation of the land. Once again, through a doctor's observations, we in the audience are presented with other "patients" in the play. And, if we take the malady of *poshlost'* for our analysis, we are introduced at the beginning of Act I to the principal case history, Professor Serebryakov. His only words upon arriving in grand style back in the country from his "important" work in the city are pompous and meaningless: "Beautiful, beautiful. . . . Marvelous scenery." And then: "My friends, be so kind as to send me my tea in my study! I still have a thing or two to finish off today." And then he sweeps off to his own quarters, leaving Voynitskiy and the others to comment on his creature comforts. Doctor Astrov observes for us: "Looks like he takes good care of himself" (485).

At the beginning of Act II, we spectators, urged by Chekhov to assume the role of fellow diagnosticians, are allowed to listen to the *poshlost'*-

ridden complaints of Professor Serebryakov. His whining demands set the tone for all his future actions, and by the time the curtain comes down on Act II we are at least partially prepared to expect the professor's petulant, willful denial of Sonya and Yelena's request to bring music into his shabby world of selfish vulgarity by playing the piano. And when in Act III Serebryakov cavalierly drops his bombshell announcement of his decision to sell the estate, which Voynitskiy and Sonya have been selflessly maintaining for him over the years, we are given the reaction of the fallout from the explosion upon the other characters.[39] Doctor Astrov's diagnosis in Act IV that the professor and his wife have infected everyone on the estate with their idleness, that they have spread destruction wherever they have gone, even his own operatically orchestrated "Finita la commedia!" (528)—all these indignant appraisals are powerless against the staunch bulwarks erected by *poshlost'*. The professor pompously echoes Voynitskiy and Sonya's earlier call for work, and the departing petty tyrant preaches his banal homily to those he leaves behind, much in the infuriating tradition of Foma Fomich Opiskin in Dostoyevskiy's *The Village of Stepanchikovo and Its Inhabitants*: "Permit an old man to include but one observation in my farewell wishes: ladies and gentlemen, you must get down to business! You must work!" (529). As the curtain slowly descends on the last act, the audience is made to feel the triviality, the dreary commonplaceness, the *poshlost'* of the scene, as the leaden dullness of this sterile country existence repeats itself as it began—with Voynitskiy and Sonya "whistling in the dark" in the midst of their betrayed illusions.

In *The Three Sisters*, Doctor Chekhov presents us at once with the dream of the Prozorova sisters of returning to Moscow. More to the point, we learn through practical considerations that their Moscow dream is based on unreality—that Masha, for instance, would hardly be prepared to leave her husband, that the other two girls would only be trying to live in the unsubstantial past, on nostalgia. They do not see the charms of country living (as Chekhov himself knew and prized them). But their common malady is presented through the compensating and redeeming filter of Chekhov's firm belief in civilization, in culture, in poetry, even (Masha's frequent evocations of Pushkin). Natasha Prozorova, the "fourth sister," is, however, the most seriously afflicted patient in Chekhov's *poshlost'* ward—although others, like Masha's husband,

Kulygin, may be found there, as well—the pious, Latin-spouting author of the history of the little town's high school. Natasha's appearance in Act I already labels her in the cultured sisters' book as a girl of bad taste, with her ill-matched sash. Little by little, her disease spreads over the house as she moves in and takes over the sisters' property. Her *poshlost'* infects everything in the house to the point that, by the end of the play, she has introduced another whole character into the family—her lover Protopopov—unseen throughout, but potently virulent all the same. In Natasha, Chekhov has produced a case history of *poshlost'* triumphant. In her last appearance onstage, she is in full control of the sisters' patrimony, as she declares her intention of having the fir trees (and the maple tree, too) chopped down. And all that Doctor Chebutykin, Chekhov's last physician character, can do is help the curtain descend for the final time with newspaper in hand and his nihilistic comment on everything that has happened: "It makes no difference! It makes no difference!" (601).

Since in *The Cherry Orchard* Chekhov has not given us a doctor in the house as a guide for diagnosing the patients onstage, we in the audience are left to our own resourcefulness and to our own powers of observation. Right from the moment that Ranevskaya and her brother, Gayev, arrive back in their country nursery in Act I, we are made aware of their afflictions. More than that, we can readily render our prognosis for the health of the play's namesake. Chekhov has tampered with dramatic form to such an extent that he has effectively removed the element of dramatic suspense surrounding the question of "saving" the cherry orchard. We can be sure that neither Ranevskaya nor Gayev, grown-up children trying to return to their innocence, are going to be able to do anything practicable to keep the estate in the family. And although Chekhov produced his extreme case histories of *poshlost'* with Natasha Prozorova and Protopopov, the malady is not absent from the characters of his last play. Rather, the virulent strain found in *The Three Sisters* has become more benign under Doctor Chekhov's playful diagnosis, so that almost all the characters can be seen as suffering from mild doses. Thus, almost no one is immune from the author's gentle mockery in this comedy of high irony. Chekhov's subtlety, however, should not make us unwary. What kind of woman is Ranevskaya if she can abandon a twelve-year-old daughter and her beloved cherry trees for an unreliable lover in Paris?

She is the type who gives gold coins to beggars, simply because she has no silver money at hand. Surely the *poshlost'*-rash is discernible to us in her suspiciously tearful farewell oration to her nursery in Act IV: "I'll just sit here for another minute. It's as if I had never noticed what the walls and ceilings in this house were like, and now I'm looking at them so greedily, with such tender love" (660). And the same with her brother, Gayev. How seriously should we receive the news of his job at the bank—"Now I'm a financier" (655)? Is he really capable of handling other people's money—this shallow (but lovable) man who in moments of stress pops candy into his mouth and nervously calls out billiards shots? The banality of his departure words embarrasses even Anya and Varya: "My friends, my dear, good friends! Upon leaving this house forever, am I capable of remaining silent? Am I capable of refraining from expressing upon leaving the feelings that now fill my whole being?" (659). Are not people like these (including even Trofimov, the eternal student, and Sharlotta Ivanovna, the pickle-munching trickster) victims of a virus that knows no cure?

One French physician has said that "medicine helped Chekhov realize his literary work. It developed in him the observation, the acuteness, the critical spirit and the good sense that are qualities common to the doctor and the writer."[40] A Russian psychiatrist paid tribute to Doctor Chekhov in the year of his death: "He gave us a series of types of sick people . . . , he indicated to the public those social ailments that we psychiatrists treat, and in this sense we may boldly consider the late writer our colleague in the matter of revealing those ulcers the battle against which our calling and our mission are arrayed."[41]

Tolstoy believed that the study of medicine hampers the fictional writer, that it interferes with the act of creating. Other critics (and here, most likely, the numerical preponderance lies) would disagree, as does a contemporary American reviewer:

Medical school gives a writer something that is unavailable in other academic disciplines: a direct experience of human suffering and a professional familiarity with the defective organization of the mind and the body. The medical student sees at first hand the pathology of human beings and learns that the "normal" is not easy to come by. He also learns to observe his patients with scientific detachment, a method the writer can adapt to his material.[42]

And this is what Chekhov calls upon his audience to do—to join with him, a doctor, in observing the actions and listening to the words (and the pauses) of his "patients" onstage. By suggesting that we partake of the method of his creative process, Chekhov the playwright not only appeals to us as fellow "patients"; in a sense, we spectators are also invited to be "doctors in the house."

NOTES

1. M. Gor'kiy, "Lev Tolstoy," *Literaturnyye portrety* (Moskva: Goslitizdat, 1959), p. 143.

2. Letter to G. I. Rossolimo, October 11, 1899, in A. P. Chekhov, *Sobraniye sochineniy v dvenadtsati tomakh* (Moskva: Khudozhestvennaya Literatura, 1964), XII, 323–24.

3. Letter to A. N. Pleshcheyev, November 13, 1888, in A. P. Chekhov, *Polnoye sobranie sochineniy i pisem v tridtsati tomakh* (Moskva: Nauka, 1976), III, 68.

4. Letter to N. A. Leykin, middle of July, 1884, in A. P. Chekhov, *Polnoye sobranie sochineniy*, I, 120.

5. Letter to A. S. Suvorin, November 15, 1888, in A. P. Chekhov, *Polnoye sobranie sochineniy*, III, 70.

6. A. I. Kuprin, "Pamyati Chekhova," *Chekhov v vospominaniyakh sovremennikov* (Moskva: Khudozhestvennaya Literatura, 1952), p. 425.

7. Letter to E. M. Shavrova-Yust, February 28, 1895, in A. P. Chekhov, *Polnoye sobranie sochineniy*, VI, 30.

8. S. D. Balukhatyy, *Chekhov dramaturg* (Leningrad: Khudozhestvennaya Literatura, 1936), p. 171.

9. Letter to Suvorin, October 27, 1892, in A. P. Chekhov, *Sobranie sochineniy*, V, 126.

10. Letter to A. N. Pleshcheyev, February 15, 1890, in A. P. Chekhov, *Sobraniye sochineniy*, IV, 18.

11. Letter to Suvorin, October 25, 1891, in A. P. Chekhov, *Sobraniye sochineniy*, IV, 291.

12. Letter to Suvorin, May 7, 1889, in A. P. Chekhov, *Sobraniye sochineniy*, III, 208.

13. Ieronim I. Yasinskiy, *Roman moey zhizni* (Moskva: Gosizdat, 1926), p. 268.

14. T. L. Shchepkina-Kupernik, "O Chekhove," *Chekhov v vospominaniyakh*, p. 276.

15. William B. Ober, M. D., "Chekhov Among the Doctors: The Doctor's Dilemma," *Boswell's Clap and Other Essays* (Carbondale and Edwardsville: Southern Illinois Univ. Press, 1979), p. 194.

16. M. P. Chekhov, *Vokrug Chekhova* (Moskva: Moskovskiy Rabochiy, 1960), p. 272.

17. G. I. Rossalimo, "Vospominaniya o Chekhove," *Chekhov v vospominaniyakh*, p. 504.

18. Boris Zaytsev, *Chekhov* (New York: Chekhov Publishing House, 1954), pp. 52–53.

19. M. P. Chekhov, p. 134.

20. M. P. Chekhov, p. 137.

21. Yevgeniy Z. Balabanovich, *Iz zhizni A. P. Chekhova* (Moskva: Moskovskiy Rabochiy, 1967), p. 159.

22. All citations from Chekhov's plays are from A. P. Chekhov, *Sobraniye sochineniy*, X.

23. "Zapiski sumasshedshego," N. V. Gogol', *Sobraniye sochineniy v shesti tomakh* (Moskva: Goslitizdat, 1959), III, 185.

24. Ober, p. 199.

25. Ober, p. 197.

26. Dr. Pierre Debray, "Le docteur Tchékhov," *Médecin de France*, Paris, No. 81 (1957), p. 15.

27. Letter to Suvorin, December 30, 1888, in A. P. Chekhov, *Polnoye sobraniye sochineniy*, III, 115–16.

28. V. V. Khizhnyakov, *Anton Pavlovich Chekhov kak vrach* (Moskva: Medgiz, 1947), p. 37.

29. Letter to Suvorin, October 27, 1888, in A. P. Chekhov, *Polnoye sobraniye sochineniy*, III, 46.

30. Letter to Aleksandr Chekhov, May 10, 1886, in A. P. Chekhov, *Polnoye sobraniye sochineniy*, I, 242.

31. William E. Harkins, trans. and ed., Alexander Pushkin, *Three Comic Poems* (Ann Arbor: Ardis, 1977), p. 43.

32. Vladimir Nabokov, *Nikolai Gogol* (Norfolk: New Directions, 1944), pp. 64–70.

33. M. Gor'kiy, "A. P. Chekhov," *Chekhov v vospominaniyakh*, p. 397.

34. See his letter to Suvorin, October 27, 1892, in which he prescribes valerian drops but warns that doctors should not lie to their patients about serious maladies, such as cancer and tuberculosis. A. P. Chekhov, *Polnoye sobraniye sochineniy*, V, 125–26.

35. As if to highlight Doctor Dorn's light and gentle nature, his role is assigned to that of a tenor voice in Thomas Pasatieri's opera based on Chekhov's play. See Kenwood Elmslie, *The Seagull* (Melville, New York: Belwin-Mills, 1974).

36. See Margaret Croyden, " 'People Just Eat Their Dinner': The Absurdity of Chekhov's Doctors," *Texas Quarterly*, 11, No. 3 (1968), p. 133.

37. Letter to Aleksandr Chekhov, between October 15 and 28, 1883. A. P. Chekhov, *Polnoye sobraniye sochineniy*, I, 89.

38. W. H. Bruford, *Chekhov and His Russia* (London: Kegan Paul, Trench, Trubner and Company, 1947), p. 158.

39. See J. L. Styan, *Chekhov in Performance* (Cambridge: Cambridge Univ. Press, 1971), pp. 128–31.

40. Henri-Bernard Duclos, docteur en Médecine, *Antoine Tchékhov. Le médecin et l'écrivain* (Paris: Bernard Grasset Edit., 1929), p. 82.

41. Dr. M. P. Nikitin, "Chekhov, kak izobrazitel' bol'noy dushi," *Vestnik Psikhologii, Kriminal'noy Antropologii i Gipnotizma*, S.-Petersburg, No. 1 (1905), p. 13.

42. Ted Morgan, "Is There a Doctor in the House?" *Saturday Review*, August 1979, p. 53.

TWO CHEKHOVS: MAYAKOVSKIY ON CHEKHOV'S "FUTURISM"

BY NILS ÅKE NILSSON

In the June 1914 issue of the journal *New Life* (*Novaya zhizn'*), Vladimir Mayakovskiy published an article entitled "Two Chekhovs" ("Dva Chekhova"). The editors accompanied it with a note that pointed out that they did not share all his views. A similar note was added to a previous article by Mayakovskiy, written for the May issue of the same journal. That time the reservation was even a bit stronger—"we are far from agreeing" (*my daleko ne soglasny*)—and for an obvious reason. Mayakovskiy wrote on contemporary artistic life in Petersburg and Moscow. This was a field that he knew from personal experience: he had recently, after two years of rather casual studies, been expelled from the respectable Moscow Institute for the Study of Painting, Sculpture, and Architecture. His criticism was summed up in a statement that artists and art institutions in Russia "did not express the spirit of contemporaneity" (*sovremennost' ne vyrazhayut*).

But what could a former art student, a twenty-year-old futurist poet who had just published his first poems, have to say about Chekhov? Was he going to declare the Chekhov's stories and plays did not correspond to the spirit of modernism? This would have been logical: in a recent manifesto, the futurists had thrown previous Russian literature overboard, the symbolist poets as well as the realist novelists. The manifesto did not mention Chekhov in particular, it is true, but Dostoyevskiy and Tolstoy were there, representing a realist tradition in which critics included Chekhov as well.

The title of Mayakovskiy's article suggested, however, that he did not dismiss Chekhov altogether. There were "two Chekhovs." One was the narrator of funny or lyrical stories from "twilight Russia." This Chekhov was of little interest to the futurists. But behind the popular image was another Chekhov who so far had not been fully recognized for his merit: the writer, the artist, or, as Mayakovskiy calls him, one of the "kings of the Word." This was a Chekhov whom the futurists could accept and even hail as a precursor, a writer who belonged not only to the past but also to the future.

The question now was what the advocates of "transrational language" (*zaumnyy yazyk*) and "the word as such" (*slovo kak takovoye*) could find of interest in Chekhov's language and style. The futurists were, for instance, interested in a new poetic language, including unexpected word formations and newly coined words (as *leuna* instead of *luna*, moon). It is difficult to find any examples of such verbal experiments in Chekhov's stories and plays. This is true. But if the futurists had known his letters, especially those directed to his brother Aleksandr, to his wife Ol'ga Knipper, and to his intimate friends, they would have been surprised. These letters are usually written in a personal jargon, full of puns and humorous word formations that, no doubt, have something in common with the futurist attempts to renew the poetic language. [1]

In his earlier poetry, Mayakovskiy often uses, for instance, the augmentative suffix, *-ishche*, to increase both the acoustic and semantic effect of a word. Of a neutral cliché *ad goroda*, "the hell of the city," he makes a more expressive *adishche goroda*; he multiplies the euphonic effect of a simple *shum*, "noise" or "sound," by creating a *shumishchi*. In "A Cloud in Trousers," he addresses God and intensifies an ironic "mighty god," *vsesil'nyy bog*, to a *vsesil'nyy bozhishche.*

Chekhov's letters to his wife Ol'ga Knipper are full of similar expressive word formations. *Zhara*, heat, becomes *zharishcha*; *kholod*, cold becomes *kholodishcha*; *skuka*, boredom becomes *skuchishcha*, formations that are not uncommon in colloquial language. *Zharishcha*, for instance, is used by Astrov in the last act of *Uncle Vanya*. A *spasibo*, "thank you," raised to a humorous *spasibishche* sounds more uncommon. And *aktrisishcha* from *aktrisa*, "actress," *dramishcha* from *drama*, or *p'esishcha* from *p'esa*, "play," seem to indicate a special theater jargon.

In an often-quoted poem ("At night the manor—Genghis Khan! . . ."), Khlebnikov makes verbs of names like Genghis Khan, Zarathustra, and Mozart to indicate some kind of action connected with these names, and puts these verbs in the imperative mood (which in Russian simply means to change the last hard consonant into a soft one)—in English translation, "At night the manor—Genghis Khan! . : . The nightly luster—Zarathustra! But the blue sky beyond—Mozart!" [2] In Chekhov's letters—and occasionally in his plays—there are several examples of such expressive verbs. In *Ivanov* occurs, for instance, *nagavrilitsya*. Lebedev calls for his servant whose name is Gavrila, and Shabel'sky comments, *Ty i tak nagavrililsya*, "you have called enough for this Gavrila." An additional effect stems from the fact that the verb is formed with another verb, *nagovorit'sya*, "to talk to your heart's content," "to talk enough," used as a model. Other examples of similar verbs are *nalisabonit'sya*, formed from Lisbon together with *nalizat'sya*, "to get drunk," used as a model, and *proermitazhit'*, from the name of the restaurant Ermitazh, which gives an approximative meaning of "to spend a night of eating and drinking at the Ermitazh restaurant."

Most of the neologisms in Mayakovskiy follow, as has been pointed out, the rules of the Russian grammar,[3] but they have nevertheless a function of *parole in libertà* in a context of regular words. The novelty sometimes resides in giving the root a suffix that it usually does not take, or in making a quite new verb from a noun or a personal name that otherwise does not form a verb. Chekhov's word formations are of a similar type. It seems likely that many of them were not created by Chekhov himself but were characteristic of a colloquial jargon among writers and journalists of that time—a jargon that certainly was familiar to Mayakovskiy as well. Some of Chekhov's expressive word formations appear not only in his letters but also in the earlier stories and plays. We know that these stories were usually printed in small occasional journals that addressed a large reading audience and for that reason used a more colloquial style than the serious literary magazine. In Chekhov's later stories—and this is a notable fact—these expressive word formations are much more scarce.

Although Mayakovskiy could not recognize in Chekhov a precursor of futurist neologisms (since he did not know his letters), he could point out something else that Chekhov had in common with the futurists: he had the same feeling of a need for new and fresh words. A whole vocabulary of "poetic" and "honorable" words called for rejuvenation: " 'Love,' 'friendship,' 'truth,' 'decency' dangled worn out on their hangers." Chekhov understood it and introduced into the literature "coarse names for coarse objects." By this, Mayakovskiy apparently had in mind his use of colloquial language and the concrete description of everyday reality (*byt*). As an example of how the style of prose had changed, he compares a line by Turgenev with some lines by Chekhov. It is, of course, easy enough to find in those two writers lines that clash against each other stylistically (it is not difficult either to single out lyrical passages in Chekhov which bring to mind Turgenev). As for the "coarseness" of language, it has, to be sure, many different shades. To the futurists it implied, above all, provocation, *épatage*, and blasphemy in a way that was alien to Chekhov's style.

Besides, with the coinage of individual new words, some of the *zaumniki* (transrationalists) tried to write whole poems (usually very short ones) in this transrational language. The best-known example is a five-line poem by Kruchenykh, which begins "Dyr bul shchyl." None of the words or syllables of this poem has any obvious relation to the Russian language that could give them or the poem as a whole any common meaning. One could consequently argue that the "meaning" of the poem is its "meaninglessness," understood as a challenge to ordinary communicative poetry, or that its meaning is its character of a provocative sound gesture; with its tone of primitiveness and archaism (from a Russian phonematic and poetic point of view), the sound structure seems to oppose the euphonic cadences of romantic or symbolist poetry. But the poem illustrates another tenet of futurist poetics as well. To the futurists, the transrational language was actually not "a language beyond comprehension" but rather a sign system that should be comprehended with faculties other than reason. For the futurists, such a faculty was intuition, that "divine intuition," as Marinetti called it in one of the manifestos of Italian futurism. With the development of an increasing sensibility in modern society, the communion established between two persons could be so perfect that one word or one sign would tell everything. Such poems as "Dyr bul shchyl" would consequently be easily understood by the man of the future; so the futurists believed.

Chekhov's play *Three Sisters* contains what could be called a parallel to Kruchenych's poem, namely Vershinin's and Masha's "duet" in the third act: *Tram-tam-tam . . . Tam-tam . . . Tra-ta-ta.* These are not, it is true, an unfamiliar or provoking combination of phonemes but well-known onomatopoetic signals. But they could be given different meanings, and for that reason Vershinin and Masha can exchange them freely in the presence of other people. They are the only ones who understand what they actually mean. This is an example of a perfect communion where one partner intuitively comprehends any arbitrary signals by the other one.[4]

This is, to be sure, an extreme example, but it is not difficult to find others of a similar type. Let us remember Gayev's billiard terms in *The Cherry Orchard*. He constantly mixes his talk with expressions like "carom to the right into the corner pocket"; "I cut into the side pocket"; and so on. Compared with Vershinin's and Masha's "duet," there is a difference here. The meaning of the signals was understood only by the lovers themselves. Gayev's terms have a clear meaning that, as it seems, is open to every one. Even if they do not know exactly what the terms refer to in the game, they understand that Gayev is an enthusiastic billiard player. To Lyubov' Andreyevna, they also recall days of the past; her first reply is directed to Gayev: "How was it? Let me remember. . . . Yellow into the corner! Duplicate in the middle!" But the terms have another and more important function as well. Gayev usually utters them in moments of confusion or when he does not know otherwise what to say or how to end a sentence. The terms serve, in other words, as a cover for feelings he is unable to express, as a system of signals that appeals to the intuition of the listeners.

Another such type of signal is what has sometimes been called "unmotivated replies" in Chekhov's plays, that is, short, sudden replies that do not seem to be immediately motivated by the context. One could say that they represent realism of a kind: such sudden shifts of thought may happen in an ordinary conversation. On the other hand, Chekhov accepted, as we know, the convention that "if a gun hangs on the wall in the first act it should fire in the last." An audience accustomed to such a convention expects that even such seemingly "unmotivated" replies should refer to some logical structure—open or hidden in the subtext— in the play.

In the last act of *Uncle Vanya*, to take a well-known example, Doctor Astrov, before leaving the house, looks at a map of Africa hanging on the wall and says: "In that Africa it must be awfully hot right now." If we apply the principle of the gun to this map, we expect that it hangs there for a reason and that it has, together with Astrov's reply, a specific meaning in the play. But it is not obvious what the map and the reply actually refer to, and several different interpretations have been suggested. Such replies may, in other words, cause stage directors certain difficulties. If the actor does not know what the words mean and does not find the right way to pronounce them, they will simply come out flat or bizarre. It happens for that reason in performances in the West that such replies are either completely or (as in the case of Gayev's billiard terms) partly left out.

In the Astrov example we have moved one step further on the semantic scale. The *Tra-ta-ta* signals could be directly compared with Kruchenykh's "Dyr bul shchyl," although they still have a semantic reference, being a kind of common humming that is mostly used to express a happy mood. Gayev's terms have a specific meaning: when used in a conversation that does not touch upon billiards, however, they suggest a different function and meaning. Astrov's reply, finally, is a quite ordinary statement. Since it is uttered in a situation in which it does not seem to fit—this is, as we see, a condition that applies to all the examples—its semantic content is challenged, and we consequently look for another meaning.

From an avant-garde point of view, such passages in Chekhov could exemplify a kind of *parole in libertà*, or a "liberation of the word." In his article, Mayakovskiy uses this latter expression. This is, in his opinion, exactly what makes Chekhov a precursor of the futurists. His stories demonstrate in a special way their slogan of "the word as such," since "you cannot find a single light-hearted story which is motivated only by a 'necessary idea.' " All works by Chekhov, Mayakovskiy maintains—and one may assume that this was one point where the editors of the journal did not agree with him—are "solutions of exclusively verbal tasks."

Mayakovskiy quotes Astrov's reply as an example. He characterizes Chekhov's plays as "bloodless" in the sense that life is only vaguely glimpsed through "the stained glasses of the words." Chekhov does not need a suicide to get things moving on the stage, Mayakovskiy says, since he is able to suggest by means of simple "gray words," as those in Astrov's reply, the highest dramatic intensity.

The reason that Mayakovskiy singles out precisely Astrov's reply as an example apparently stems from Stanislavskiy's interpretation of the doctor in the Moscow Art Theater performance of *The Three Sisters*. Instead of letting the scene with the map pass by unnoticed, Stanislavskiy put a special emphasis on Astrov's way of pronouncing his words and gave them a definite emotional content. This was obviously noticed by audience and critics. Ol'ga Knipper later remembered this scene as a typical example of the famous Chekhovian "subtext": "How much bitterness and experience of life he put into this phrase. And how he pronounced these words with a sort of bravura, challenging almost."[5]

Mayakovskiy goes even so far as to say that if somebody were to read Chekhov's stories so much that the book would fall into pieces, this would not really matter. One can read every line as an individual story. This recalls some essential tenets of futurist poetics: the fragmentation of the text, the autonomy of each of its parts. And the imaginists later declared that every stanza in a poem should have an individual quality of its own. It should consequently be possible to read an imaginist poem backward, or to shuffle around the order of the stanzas.

It is surprising that Mayakovskiy does not touch upon another well-known feature of Chekhov's style that also can be linked to futurist poetics: the semiotization of intonation. This feature is, to be sure, best illustrated in his plays which have an abundance of stage directions indicating how the replies should be spoken. In *The Cherry Orchard*, for instance, one can find no less than about 175 such directions. After having read this play, Meyerkhol'd said: "The producer must first of all understand it with his hearing."[6]

In futurist poetry, sound structure was certainly more important than intonation. Since this poetry was often recited, however, and perhaps to some extent written with a public performance in mind, intonation was, no doubt, important too. We would perhaps better understand a poem like "Dyr bul shchyl" if we had known how it was read in public, and one may be equally curious about what intonation Vasilisk Gnedov put into his famous one-letter poems. Apart from such examples of transrational poetry, Mayakovskiy handled intonation masterfully in his long poem, as we know, an art that he developed further in his later agitational poetry (see his essay "How to Make Verses").

Already in the first article he ever wrote, Mayakovskiy pointed out the significance of intonation—in the theater. The article, entitled "Theatre, Cinema, and Futurism" (1913), discussed the theater of the future precisely in terms of intonation. Until the appearance of futurism, the theater was not an independent art, Mayakovskiy declared. The "word" was used simply as a means of communicating certain moralist or political ideas. In the past there had been attempts to liberate the theater: by Shakespeare, for instance, or at the Oberammergau theater; but these attempts were only vague presages of a new theater of the future. Here, "the very intonation of words which have no definite meaning, as well as the invented but free rhythmical movements of the human body, will express the greatest inner experiences."

At the end of his article on Chekhov, Mayakovskiy brings up one more point that further highlights Chekhov as a harbinger of modern literature. Slogans like "dynamism," "movement," and "rhythm" were magical words to the futurists. The new rhythm—of the big cities, of the airplanes and automobiles—should influence art, not only by offering new themes and metaphors, but also by changing the forms of art. For prose, such a demand implied shortness, concentration, "phrases of just a few words, instead of periods with dozens of sentences." In all of Chekhov's short stories, Mayakovskiy said, the claim of the future can be heard: "Economy!"

A new prose rhythm: this involved problems of syntax, new ways of combining words and sentences. Beside the traditional vocabulary, the established syntax was, as we know, a main target of the futurists and the avant-gardists in general. "The man who has witnessed an explosion does not stop to connect his sentences grammatically," the Italian futurists declared, looking for a *rapidità economica*, an expressive, telegraphic style. [7] In his article on Chekhov, Mayakovskiy's slogan, "Economy," apparently has this Italian origin, and the call for an abolition of syntax was taken up by the Russian futurists in their slogan: "the more disorder we bring to the composition of sentences, the better." [8] Somewhat later, the Russian imaginists proposed a radical way of creating such a new syntax: the verb, being the "conductor of the sentence" that brings order and logic to it, must be abolished in order to let the nouns demonstrate their metaphorical possibilities.

What then could be called "syntax" in a dramatic work? First of all, apparently, syntax stands for the way the replies are connected to each other. A "scene" in which two or more persons take part could be compared with a sentence. When a person leaves the stage or a new person enters it, this corresponds to a period and to where a new "sentence" begins. To "dramatic syntax" belongs, further, the way in which these "sentences" are combined into a paragraph (which equals an act).

In older plays, it was easy to distinguish the "sentences," since every scene constituted an individual unit within an act (and was marked as such in the printed text). In nineteenth-century drama, this system was gradually dropped. But usually the playwright still organized the act as a series of distinct scenes that developed along a logical line in order to expose step by step the plot and the characteristics of the dramatis personae. And the individual scenes were also arranged with the same rational principle in mind. Ibsen was one of the first to drop the division into scenes, while Strindberg still stuck to it in his naturalistic plays (for instance, *The Father*). Strindberg nevertheless argued that his dialogues were spontaneous and realistic, whereas Ibsen's were much more thoroughly calculated and always predictable. He compared them very aptly to a card game for two persons in which the one player must always answer in the same suit as his opponent. In other words, every reply follows logically from the preceding one.

Chekhov's plays introduced here a new dramatic syntax, a new rhythm onstage. He found new ways of combining replies and connecting scenes. This became evident from the first reactions of the audience and the critics: they found his plays "plotless" and "formless." Against the background of the contemporary play (especially the tradition of the so-called well-made play) to which the audience was accustomed, such a reaction was understandable. The first thing critics observed in Chekhov as a playwright was consequently his challenge to the established principles of composition, to the traditional "dramatic syntax."

Today's audience, brought up with the modern drama, including Chekhov, no longer senses any "formlessness" in Chekhov's plays. Critical examinations have furthermore revealed that they certainly possess dramatic structures in the traditional sense of the word; but such analyses have also demonstrated how these structures follow, challenge, or break with the conventional patterns of their time. There seems to be general agreement that in the last play, *The Cherry Orchard*, this new technique reached its climax. It is also here that we most clearly recognize Chekhov's new syntax. In a formalist approach to the play, S. D. Balukhatyy emphasized that its originality consisted in the fact that it had no dramatic plot, no dramatic moments, no love themes, the fate of the characters their actions and behavior being motivated entirely by common everyday situations. An examination of the themes through the acts gives the further result that the movement "is accomplished according to the principle of unorganized articulation, of a kind of disintegration of composition in which the devices of interruption, severance, and recurrence of themes clearly stand out."[9] In such a characterization we feel how close Chekhov, operating in his medium, comes to the futurists' call that only by breaking up traditional syntax is it possible to create a new *poetic* language. In the drama, the traditional dramatic syntax must be challenged—by pauses, "unmotivated" replies, constant changes in the tonality and rhythm of the play, and the use of various nonverbal sign systems interrupting the text. Only this way could a modern *dramatic* language be created.

Mayakovskiy's article on Chekhov has always struck me as probably the most underrated of everything written on Chekhov. It is, no doubt, easy enough to follow the editors and say that one cannot go along with all his exaggerations and overstatements. But the article nevertheless contains some very accurate and suggestive observations. It was probably the first to place Chekhov as a precursor of modern literature by pointing to something very essential: his way of challenging the poetic language of his time over the full linguistic range, from phonetics and vocabulary to syntax. Mayakovskiy could have granted him the same title of honor he gave to Pushkin: "the happy host on the great wedding-day of the words."

NOTES

1. N. Å. Nilsson, "Leksika i stilistika pisem Chekhova," in *Scandoslavica*, 14 (Copenhagen: Munksgaard, 1968), pp. 33 f.

2. V. Khlebnikov, *Snake Train: Poetry and Prose*, ed. Gary Kern (Ann Arbor: Ardis, 1976), p. 69.

3. G. Vinkokur, *Mayakovskiy—novator jazyka* (Moskva: Sovetskij pisatel', 1943), p. 53.

4. J. Meyer, "Chekhov's Word," in J. van der Eng, Jan M. Meyer, H. Schmidt, *On the Theory of Descriptive Poetics: Anton P. Chekhov as Story-teller and Playwright* (Lisse: The Peter de Ridder Press, 1978), p. 133.

5. K. Stanislavskiy, *O Stanislavskom* (Moskva: Vseross. teatral'noe obshchestvo, 1948), p. 266.

6. V. Markov, *Russian Futurism: A History* (Berkeley and Los Angeles: Univ. of California Press, 1968), p. 128.

7. Rosa Trillo Clough, *Futurism: The Story of a Modern Art Movement: A New Appraisal* (New York: Philosophical Library, 1961), p. 48.

8. S. D. Balukhatyy, *"The Cherry Orchard: A Formalist Approach,"* in R. L. Jackson, *Chekhov: A Collection of Critical Essays* (Englewood Cliffs, N.J.: Prentice-Hall, 1967), p. 139.

9. N. Å. Nilsson, *The Russian Imaginists* (Stockholm: Almqvist and Wiksell, 1970), pp. 74 f.

INDEX